My Work
in Films

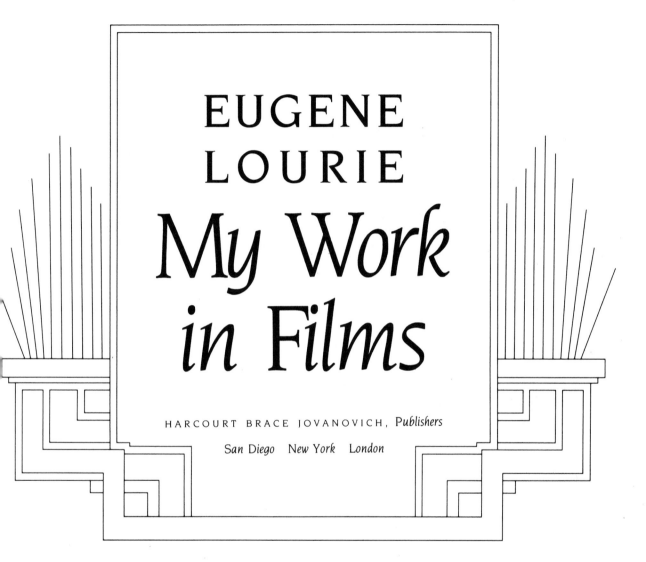

EUGENE LOURIE

My Work in Films

HARCOURT BRACE JOVANOVICH, Publishers

San Diego   New York   London

HBJ

Requests for permission to make copies of any part of the
work should be mailed to: Permissions, Harcourt Brace
Jovanovich, Publishers, Orlando, FL 32887.

Grand Illusion *and* The Rules of the Game, *courtesy of Janus Films, Inc.,*
distributors for the U.S. and Canada.
Werther, *courtesy of Harold Nebenzal.*
The Human Beast, *credit Paris Film Productions.*
This Land Is Mine, *courtesy of RKO General Pictures.*
Sahara, *courtesy of Columbia Pictures.*
From the motion picture The Imposter *(Univ. 1944), courtesy of Universal*
Pictures.
The Long Night, *courtesy of Video-Cinema Films, Inc.*
The Southerner, *credit United Artists.*
The River, *credit Taurus Films and the estate of Marcus Lipsky.*
The Adventures of Captain Fabian, *courtesy of National Telefilms*
Associates, Inc.
A Crack in the World *copyright © MCMLXIV Paramount Pictures*
Corporation and Security Pictures International.
Limelight, *credit RBC Films.*
Gorgo, *courtesy of Frank King, King International Corp.*

Beast from 20,000 Fathoms, Battle of the Bulge, *and* An Enemy of the People, *courtesy Warner Bros. Inc.*

Krakatoa, East of Java, *photos courtesy of ABC International, Inc.*

Flight from Ashiya, *courtesy Metro-Goldwyn-Mayer/United Artists.*

Royal Hunt of the Sun, *courtesy CBS Theatrical Films.*

Photographs from La Cinémathèque Française appear on pages 24, 35, 41 (Top, bottom) 53, 58 (Bottom), 68 (Bottom), 183.

Photographs by Sam Levin appear on pages 14, 17, 27, 49 (Top, bottom), 58 (Top, center), 59, 60 (Center), 68 (Top).

Photograph by Alex Karle appears on page 133.

Photograph by David Peskin appears on page 172.

Photograph by Bob Milnes appears on page 269 (Right).

Library of Congress Cataloging in Publication Data
Lourie, Eugene.
My work in films.
Includes index.
1. Lourie, Eugene.   2. Moving-picture art directors—
France—Biography.   I. Title.
PN1998.A3L75   1984   791.43'025'0924 {B}   84-9130
ISBN 0-15-164019-X
ISBN 0-15-662342-0 (A Harvest/HBJ book : pbk.)

Designed by Joy Chu
Printed in the United States of America
· First edition
A B C D E

This book is dedicated

to all the construction craftsmen in motion pictures,

with whom I was privileged to work

in many countries; they skillfully helped me

convert fantasies into realities.

CONTENTS

ACKNOWLEDGMENTS

This book began as an oral history project for the Directors Guild of America, which has an active program taping, transcribing, and editing the reminiscences of film and broadcast pioneers willing to share their experiences with later generations of fellow craftspeople.

The guild commissioned Ann Lewis Hamilton to conduct the interviews. It became clear, however, after the first few sessions that taping was not my métier. Thus we decided to screen the relevant films and have me write my recollections subsequently. Ann and I then discussed and expanded my first draft, and she adapted the results into chapters that became the basis for the present work. I am very grateful to her for motivating me throughout this long project as well as for rendering my Russian and French constructions into idiomatic English.

David Shepard of the Directors Guild encouraged me by reading and commenting on each draft, by obtaining and screening each of the films to refresh ancient recollections, and by bringing the book to the attention of its publisher. Audio Brandon Films, David Bradley, CBS Films, Bernard Eisenschitz, Films Incorporated, Kenneth McEldowney, National Telefilm Associates, Pacific Theaters, Paramount Pictures, UCLA Film Archives, United Artists, Universal Pictures, and Warner Bros. lent prints for screening.

My good friend and one-time assistant Max Douy cheerfully searched out many important photographs in his personal collection, in the collections of still photographers such as Sam Levine, and in the archives of the Cinémathèque Française in Paris. And Donald Knox and Naomi Grady of Harcourt Brace Jovanovich ably edited the manuscript in preparation for its publication.

My Work
in Films

INTRODUCTION

It *is* usual to begin a memoir with some autobiographical information. This is very difficult in my case since it is hard to explain the complexity of everyday life, as seen by a young boy born in czarist Russia during the turbulent early years of this century. Life in the Russian city of Kharkov was full of turmoil for my family and me: war, revolution, exile, and eventual escape to Turkey, then France. These events, at least for me, seemed to take place at blinding speed. So instead of the usual biographical details, I will mention a few episodes of my youth when motion pictures played a part.

My first encounter with the infant art form came in 1911 when I was seven. A cinema theater, the first of its kind, opened in Kharkov. The theater was called the Illusion. Once the admission price was paid, we were ushered into a waiting room, where the sounds of a piano could be heard coming from behind a velvet-curtained doorway. After the previous audience had left, the curtain opened, and we were admitted into the inner sanctum. The pianist,

began to play a heroic overture by von Suppé. Soon there appeared, projected
onto the blinking screen, a man watering a garden, followed by scenes of firemen rushing through streets. Then I was amazed to see a well-known opera
singer performing what titles flashed onto the screen said were selections from
Carmen. No sound came from her moving mouth. The piano furnished the only
sound. The singer's opulent bust heaved, and the rose in her hair swayed back
and forth to the music. Each session was forty minutes long. For the first time,
I was watching moving photographs. The experience was unforgettable.

Some years later a high school friend of mine had to look for a job, and
soon I learned he was working in the cinema theater as a projectionist. I think
he discovered then, before the motion picture theoreticians did later on, that
by changing the speed as he cranked the projector handle, he could change the
speed of the movements on the screen as well. He cranked comedies faster, and
the syncopated movements of Max Linder became much more exaggerated.
Dramas became ponderously serious when my friend cranked more slowly.

Nothing deterred us from our weekly viewings: not the violent happenings during the revolution in 1917, not even gunfire in the streets of Kharkov.
We loyally followed the serial *The Perils of Pauline* with Pearl White and the
exploits of Eddie Polo in *The King of the Circus* as if nothing else were happening in the world.

A number of years later in Yalta, I was standing with about fifty other
people in front of the gates of the Khanjonkin studios in the hilly outskirts of
the city. After a long period of inactivity during war and revolution, the studio
had finally resumed shooting pictures in 1919. On this day, they had needed
extras and bit players for a one-picture deal, an anticommunist film portraying
the White Russian point of view.

Our names were taken down and we were led inside. A bored assistant
director explained to us that we would participate in the making of a big movie
called *Black Crows.* Together with some other young men, I was to portray a
red guard, drunk with power. Our task was to invade the property of a country
landlord, break his furniture, kill everyone in sight, and burn down the place.
We were given arm bands, caps with red stars, and a disparate collection of

rifles and revolvers. Other extras were dressed in sailor uniforms and decorated with machine gun ammunition belts.

The director, Volkov, a gray-haired man with a superiority complex, looked us over with a certain amount of contempt. He then explained to us in a patronizing tone that we should act realistically and not look at the camera or laugh.

Another man, with his cap turned backward and wearing an incredible sports outfit, looked at the sky through a dark glass.

"We have to shoot fast," he said, "or wait another hour for a break in the clouds."

Shooting began.

We started the scene by destroying the iron gates—which were made out of plywood—and running down the alley toward the camera, brandishing our guns wildly and shouting insults.

"Cut. How was it?" Volkov asked, arranging his hair with a white-gloved hand.

"Good," the cameraman answered, "except at the end when these guys ran into the camera and toppled it over."

We waited for a break in the clouds before we could start the next scene. The set had been erected on an open platform in the garden, and the only light came from the sun. The set represented a drawing room, which had been overstuffed with furniture and props, all done in realistic bad taste.

Once more the cameraman looked at the sky and again announced it was time to shoot. The camera was placed inside the drawing room. For this scene, we had to break through the front door and smash everything in sight.

"Be savage. Be beastly. Be realistic," the suave Volkov admonished.

We followed his instructions. To the letter. We began breaking everything breakable.

"Hit the chandelier, smash it!" the bloodthirsty assistant shouted.

Crystals rained down under the blows of the gun butts. An inventive extra enthusiastically bayoneted the sofa cushions, releasing thick clouds of flying feathers.

For me, the scene had a comic effect. I began laughing. I started tearing down pictures from the walls and smashing flower vases, laughing uncontrollably. I couldn't stop my near hysteria.

"Stop laughing, you idiot," the angry assistant shouted at me. But I couldn't stop.

"Cut," Volkov ordered.

The assistant jumped, ready to hit me, but Volkov stopped him and said reflectively, "It was very good, very realistic, this savage laughter of a man drunk with power. Very good."

There were no retakes. There was no more furniture left to break. Then the sun hid behind the clouds. Our day of filming was over.

The following year in 1920, when I was seventeen years old, I found myself in Istanbul. My first night in this foreign city was spent in a cinema theater, the Russo-American, where the friendly manager allowed Russian refugees to pass the night sleeping in the first row on hard benches without armrests, where it was easier to stretch out. Later on I got a job at the same theater arranging its publicity campaign. New posters had to be drawn and painted for the biweekly changes of program, and production photographs had to be pinned on large panels placed in the lobby for "coming attractions."

To minimize my expenses (I was trying to earn money for my fare to Paris), I chose to sleep in the theater. The only cool and clean surface available was on top of the grand piano.

Usually I prepared my posters in a small second-floor office in the back of the auditorium next to the restrooms. The only window in the office was open to the auditorium, so by the changes in tunes from the indefatigable piano player, and by the noisy reactions of the Turkish audience, I knew at each moment what film was being shown on the screen. When I heard gay polkas, I rushed down to join the audience to view again and again a comedy by Harold Lloyd and Clara Bow or the cross-eyed Ben Turpin or the gray-eyed cowboy, William S. Hart. I often painted posters of all of these performers.

Then fortune changed. I lost my job to a clever competitor, who persuaded my employer that he could paint posters faster, better, and for less money than I could. This entrepreneur also knew Turkish lettering and could complete his posters without the help of a Turkish painter. The posters had to be lettered in English, French, Russian, and Turkish.

Soon, though, I found a similar job in a summer theater Kadakoi, close to Scutari, the vacation suburb of Istanbul, on the Asiatic side of the Bosporus. There I continued my accustomed nighttime arrangement of sleeping at the place where I worked; but at that summer theater, called Moda Park, the orchestra used an upright piano. So I selected another spot, sleeping on top of the bar between the lemonade fountain and the ice cream dispenser. In my spare time I composed imaginary scripts of gag comedies for Charlie Chaplin and Harold Lloyd. It was in this theater that I saw D. W. Griffith's *Intolerance,* a big picture made in bad taste—especially in the excessive spectacle of its Babylonian sequence.

In 1921 I finally made it to Paris, where one of my first jobs was as a scenery painter at Albatross studios. The first day in the studio, a small, gray-bearded man in a white smock, Loshakov, the art director, led me outside to the back lot. There they were building an imposing Gothic cathedral set for a film directed by Ivan Mosjouchine called *Le Brasier ardent* or *The Fiery Furnace.* The set consisted of eight huge columns of the sort that are typical in Gothic churches. The columns were some forty feet high. The art director asked me if I were subject to vertigo.

"Not that I know of," was my answer.

"Then you can climb up there," he said, as he showed me the back of the columns. "If you use the criss-cross of the two-by-fours here it will not be hard," he continued. "At the top, step around the face of the column and sit down on the boatswain's chair; paint the divisions and lines between the individual stones, leaving thirty centimeters between each line. Use this small brush for the lines and the large one for coloring the stones. That way you'll be able to shade each stone differently. Make sure one stone is either darker or lighter than the one next to it."

It had been simple for Loshakov to say, and the wood supports were relatively simple for me to climb; but to make the final step over the void of forty feet from the back of the column to the boatswain's chair dangling in front was something different. I asked myself at this point if I were not in fact actually subject to vertigo. But the only answer I could come up with was *"Noblesse oblige."*

I did it. I took this difficult step, and for many days, swinging lazily above the roofs of the Montreuil suburb of Paris, I painted the stone divisions on the columns and enjoyed the fresh air and independence of my lofty place of work.

Soon Loshakov offered me a permanent position with the studio where I could eventually become his assistant. But my primary objective in coming to Paris had been to study painting at an art school. I had taken the studio job as temporary summer work. A permanent position in the unpredictable milieu of this motion picture studio—spending long days, sometimes nights, building sets—was not in my program. I told all of this to the disbelieving Loshakov.

Some years later I assisted my teachers at the Jakovlev Academy in Paris in painting murals and stage scenery for theaters. Eventually I had an offer to design costumes for a film, a historical superproduction, *Le Joueur d'échecs* (or *The Chessplayer*); then the costumes for another big picture, *Cagliostro*. Finally I succumbed, and instead of quietly painting canvases on my easel, I joined this crazy profession—working and worrying day and night, dealing with ideas, and fighting with practical problems and budgets. I became a film production designer.

Now as I write down my recollections of the films I worked on, I want to convey the feelings I had, the feelings an art director or production designer has, while tackling those day-to-day problems that occur during the preparation and shooting of films. I also want to describe my work since I am frequently asked, "What exactly does an art director do?" (It is amazing to me how even some professional cinema technicians are not aware of an art director's or production designer's function.)

Is he the person who chooses locations where the film will be shot? Does he supervise the choosing and placing of the furniture, the set dressing, the colors used in the sets? Does he design and coordinate the construction of new sets when they are needed? Does he supervise the making of hundreds of action sketches, the storyboards that illustrate the continuity of the shooting script? Is he the artist who does the pretty paintings that show what the sets will look like? Or is he the mysterious advisor with whom the director confers during the preparation of the film and often during the actual shooting?

The simplest answer to the question is—all of the above, and very often more, much more.

Films need production designers. In films depicting historical events or taking place in fantastic surroundings, the need for such a designer is obvious. But even the most realistic or contemporary film needs to be placed in its own specific visual surroundings. The room where a gruesome killing takes place, for example, will undoubtedly be different from a room where a happy family gathers for a reunion. It is the art director who knows how to show that special difference.

My own contention is that there cannot be a neutral, indifferent background for any occasion. The setting must be a vital part of the action. Placing actors in a particular atmosphere influences and explains the motivations for the action. The setting also is one of the principal elements for creating the mood and style of a picture.

By the very nature of his work, the art director is the director's and cinematographer's closest collaborator. Together they read the script and make basic decisions, such as whether the film should be shot on location or on a stage. This collaboration continues through the entire production: gathering research and designing the sets; building, decorating, and lighting them; and finally, shooting the film.

Often after a production is finished, I am not able to tell what guided me to choose one solution in preference to another. Such artistic decisions result not from step-by-step logical reasoning but from intuition. Can a painter explain why he chooses a particular blue from among the numerous hues on his palette? Sometimes there are many possible solutions; but for the designer himself, there is only one right decision—the one he makes. How he arrives at it can seldom be explained, even in retrospect.

For me, every film is as different as the design problems I face, which vary with the subject of the film or the personality of a particular director or producer. This infinite variety of problems has been one of the most exciting aspects of my profession.

I consider myself extremely lucky to have worked during one of the most inspiring periods of the cinema, when filmmakers strongly believed in sets that were conceived and built for specific films. Moreover, in my particular case, I made many films for independent producers, where I had to work without the help of a well-established studio art department. As a result I had a deep, personal involvement in the making of many of the films I worked on, and had to invent many effects—special or purely visual—and work out the devices of how to achieve them. In many instances I had to use not just my brains but also my own hands to construct what I wanted.

These films left me with a sense of fulfillment, a special satisfaction that I did not experience in "normal" studio productions, when I had only to preside, like a supervisor, over a brain trust of painters and technicians.

In the recollections that follow, I have treated each film as a separate tale. I hope that these tales will be as diverting to read as they were for me to write.

And I beg your indulgence for the French accent.

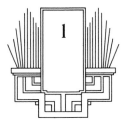

GRAND ILLUSION

In 1933 I was working in Paris as an art director for Albatross Pictures, originally a Russian company. The head of it was Alexander Kamenka. We became friends, and he often asked my advice on his future productions. One day he told me about a projected film version of *The Lower Depths,* the famous stage play by Maxim Gorky. Kamenka showed me a list of prospective directors, one of whom was Jean Renoir. At this time Renoir had a reputation as an avant-garde director, who had a strong following among young moviegoers. I didn't know him personally, but once while scouting stages at the Billancourt studios, I had walked onto a set where Renoir was directing *Madame Bovary.* His quiet authority and his approach to working with actors strongly impressed me. By all means, I told Kamenka, Renoir should direct the picture.

"Don't you think that Tourjansky would be more suitable and better understand the Russian atmosphere of the play?" Kamenka objected.

I said that Tourjansky's fidelity to making things Russian could be a danger. Renoir, in my opinion, could bring a more unexpected and fresh approach and be more in tune with a modern French audience. A few weeks later Kamenka introduced me to Jean Renoir, who had agreed to direct *The Lower Depths*.

From the very first meeting there was mutual understanding, and we discovered we had similar ideas on how to approach the film. I remember telling Jean that I didn't consider *The Lower Depths* to be a particularly Russian play—the struggle of destitute people being a universal theme, understandable everywhere. Such a struggle could take place in any large city in the world, be it Berlin, Moscow, or Paris. In my mind I began visualizing the terrifying images of Gustave Doré, the French artist who had made a book of etchings of London in the mid-nineteenth century.

In designing *The Lower Depths*, I proposed to Renoir that we omit all ethnically Russian details: the obvious samovars, icons, Russian boots, and Russian beards. Renoir smiled happily and told me that our views coincided and that his intention was to rewrite the script in collaboration with Charles Spaak, with the same idea of universality in mind. From that day there started a most gratifying and fruitful collaboration that continued for many years.

During the last days of shooting *The Lower Depths*, my friend Charles Spaak called me. I already knew that he and Jean had been working for some time on a script about a group of First World War French prisoners of war. These men of different characters and class backgrounds are brought together by their imprisonment and grow close to each other in spite of their differences. Their escape from prison would form the dramatic plot of the picture. This project had been presented and rejected by many French production companies. Now Charles was calling to tell me that a young new producer was interested in the project, and Renoir wanted to work with me again if I were free.

I made sure I had no other commitments. Soon Jean called me to meet the producer, Frank Rollmer, and his production manager, Raymond Blondy. A few days later we were driving through the snowy Alsace region to scout locations.

We were quite a large party driving out of Strasbourg that early morning in November 1936: Jean Renoir; his assistants, Jacques Becker and Carl Koch;

During a break while shooting THE LOWER DEPTHS in 1936: Jean Re-noir (third from left); Alexander Kamenka (fifth from left); Jean Gabin (center, without a jacket); Jacques Becker (fourth from right, with arm through Gabin's); Eugene Lourie (far right).

Frank Rollmer and associate producer, Monsieur Albert; Charles Spaak; Raymond Blondy; Christian Matras, the cameraman; and myself. The primary objective of our trip was to find exteriors for two prison camps, the inaccessible castle in the mountains, and some other locations, all presumably in Germany. Alsace was the logical location for these scenes, as it had been under German rule for some fifty years and its architecture reflected this German influence.

The first successful find was a castle on the mountain, Haut Koenigsburg. It had been built by Kaiser Wilhelm in the severe style of the German Gothic period. The castle fortress was situated on the top of granite rock, surrounded by a dark pine forest. It looked formidably grim and foreboding on this cold gray day.

The visit took some hours, and our unanimous decision if authorization could be obtained was to use it for exteriors. Shooting interiors in the castle was out of the question. The configuration, the size of the rooms, everything was all wrong. Moreover, Renoir preferred shooting under the controlled conditions of a stage. He was convinced, as was I, that studio sets could be more dramatically expressive and fit the story better than some actual locations. The technical ease of shooting on stage was also an irresistible advantage. The short winter day was coming to an end as we returned at dusk to our base, the hotel in Strasbourg.

Jean decided that scouting in such a large group was too time consuming since he was eager to expedite the casting and the rewrite of the script. We would all return to Paris. Later when shooting authorization was secured, I would have to return for a more thorough survey of the area and then, along with Becker, find the other locations.

The basic plot of *Grand Illusion* concerns a group of French prisoners of war and their indomitable urge to escape. After many fruitless attempts, they finally succeed, their escape made possible by the sacrifice of de Boïldieu, an aristocratic career officer. The story is also about the cruel futility of war.

Charles Spaak and Renoir had at first hoped that many producers would rush to do this "escape and adventure" project. However, war pictures without war scenes, without heroics and flag waving, were not to the taste of producers.

Renoir and Spaak's first draft seemed more bitter and harsh to me than the final draft. As they rewrote it, influenced partly by now knowing who would play the parts, the script became more human, richer in detail and meaningful facts. I think it also lost the skeptical, disillusioned outlook on life that came from Spaak's influence and acquired a more humanistic understanding from the wise and benevolent Renoir.

When the producers announced that they could get Erich von Stroheim for the part of the German general, we were elated. The influence of Stroheim's films was growing. His sense of bitter realism and his dramatic, romanticized vision of the world helped reshape the conception of film stories from this time on. The acid etching of Stroheim's acting was greatly admired by Renoir and by all of us. Including Stroheim in the film also altered the script. In the first

draft his part was small, just an episode involving the German airfield commander. This part grew and grew and became one of the pivotal parts of the
picture, greatly enriching it. The idea that people belonging to the same class
could relate to each other with better understanding than members of the same
nation became an important theme.

Stroheim's personality also influenced my conception of the settings where
he was supposed to reside—his room in the mountain castle, for example. When
his participation in our film was confirmed, I went to meet him. In the new
script, which Jean was now elaborating, Stroheim was first seen as the airfield
commander, who greets the two French officers when they are taken prisoner
after their observation plane is forced to land behind German lines. Later in the
script he is seen after he has been severely wounded. In his own words, he has
"multiple spine fractures repaired with silver plates, a silver kneecap, and a
rigid chin support," all of these details Stroheim's own invention of genius.
Now he is reduced to serving in the castle as a prison camp commander, the
post of a simple policeman.

I felt that the character Stroheim portrayed would choose to live in the
least confining room in the castle, probably the chapel. I told Stroheim that I
planned on placing his field bed under a large crucifix, which would dominate
the Gothic emptiness of the chapel. Stroheim was elated with this conception.
I also asked him what props he thought would be appropriate for his living
quarters.

"Wonderful question," he said, "let me think about it. Give me time.
Please come back tomorrow. Come for a drink and I will have a list ready."

And what a list it was. Three typewritten pages: six pairs of white gloves,
a collection of riding crops, five photographs in silver frames of heavy-set blonde
Wagnerian singers, the book *Casanova's Memoirs,* and more. This meticulous
list was characteristic of Stroheim's way of enriching characters with a profusion
of sharply observed details of their dress and surroundings. He had an acute
facility for observation.

I gave this list to my usual collaborator, Maurice Barnathan. His title was
regisseur d'extérieurs, in France a post that combined set decorating, prop gathering, and location managing.

"Stroheim was first seen as the airfield commander, who greets the two French officers when they are taken prisoner."

"I told Stroheim that I planned on placing his field bed under a large crucifix, which would dominate the chapel."

Von Raffenstein (Stroheim) and de Boïeldieu (Fresnay) in the chapel-living quarters at the Haut Koenigsburg castle.

I liked my idea for the huge crucifix that would dominate Stroheim's bedroom. It had the visual impact I search for in designing sets, for which I try to find a dominant visual idea, almost like a dominant musical theme. I also knew of Stroheim's penchant for theatrical expression in sets, which I was to learn more about later on in my career.

After *Grand Illusion,* I worked with Stroheim in two more films: *Alibi,* by Pierre Chenal, and an unfortunate project, *The Prisoner of the Sky,* directed by René Sti. Unlike Renoir, Sti was so intimidated by Stroheim's personality that he avoided shooting Stroheim's scenes. I remember building a large circus set requiring 300 extras, along with tigers, horses, and elephants. Stroheim was playing the ringmaster and was dressed for his role in shiny boots and a red frock coat; but he spent the day in his dressing room, nursing a bottle of Scotch along with his daily check for $1,000, delivered by a diligent producer. Instead of directing the important scene with Stroheim, René Sti passed the day staging an insignificant scene, played by a secondary part, a clown. Appalled by this mess, the producers canceled the next day's shooting, and I remained on the empty sets, which occupied three stages of the Paramount studios in Joinville. It was the end of *The Prisoner of the Sky.*

I found Stroheim fascinating and very friendly. I used to visit him in Fontainebleau, where he lived in a hotel, preparing the screenplay for his projected production of *The Iron Crown,* an ambitious film about the fall of the Austrian empire. Stroheim asked me to design this film. I still remember some sequences Stroheim described to me. They were sharply interesting and visually surprising.

In the film one Viennese bakery has the exclusive privilege of baking pastries for the emperor. Early each morning the imperial coach, resplendent with golden insignias and drawn by a four-horse team, comes to the bakery to take delivery of four pastries for the breakfast of His Imperial Highness. The son of the baker, one of the main characters of the film, is an anarchist who contemplates poisoning the emperor with one of his father's pastries. The son's bride also plays an important part in the story. She accidentally falls in the street and is run over by the imperial coach. Next time we see her she is a legless torso in the Prater (a popular amusement park in Vienna), where she is featured as

Dita Parlo as the German widow with Gabin and Dalio.

"In looking for a logical place where the prisoners would stage a musical spectacle, I thought of the empty stables."

the enigmatic "Legless Lady," telling fortunes for the crowds. Many other sequences based on surprising turns of events, characteristic of Stroheim's imagination, were told to me. The film, alas, was never made.

To return to *Grand Illusion,* in addition to Stroheim's casting as von Rauffenstein, the other casting that made a drastic change in the script was that of Dita Parlo as the German farm widow.

In the first draft there was a short but strong, almost bitter, scene showing the chance encounter of the sex-starved prisoners and a German woman. Now that scene evolved into a meaningful sequence expressing human compassion. It also recalled one of the main themes of *Grand Illusion,* that human love transcends the boundaries of national frontiers and patriotism.

For me, this changed sequence meant that instead of finding a barn and a cowshed on location, I would only have to find the exterior of the farm buildings. I would then design the interior on a stage in Paris with the location shot in Alsace. It also gave me the chance to design an interior set that could reflect a certain way of life, a simple nobility of character.

Meanwhile we got the authorization to film in Haut Koenigsburg. I left with Maurice Barnathan to thoroughly survey the castle there, take many still pictures, and get certain measurements. Barnathan also had to secure living accommodations for the cast and crew in neighboring villages. We took a drive on a winding mountain road looking for appropriate, isolated farmhouses. We selected one situated on the top of a hill bordering a country road and overlooking the valley. It was perfect. In the dark barn we saw round ripening Muenster cheeses on straw-covered shelves. We bought two of them and put them in the trunk of Maurice's car. When days later we opened the trunk in Paris, we were overwhelmed by the strongest smell cheese can produce. These were definitely ripe—and delicious to taste.

We stopped in many small villages to buy typical props. I found antique porcelain stove tiles at a village stovemaker. They became useful for the farm set as well as for the set of the prisoners' room. We finished our trip in Colmar where I had to meet Becker and our cameraman, Matras. We also visited the military barracks that we intended to use as the first prisoners' camp.

Earlier we had decided that the interiors of the prisoners' quarters would have to be built on a sound stage. The action, however, was so integrated with many scenes happening in the yard outside the prisoners' room that I decided to build the part of the yard next to their room and corridor on the stage. To place the prisoners' window at the correct height so it would be the same distance from the floor as in military barracks, I decided to build the floor of the barracks' interior four feet above the stage floor. The space between the barracks' floor and the stage floor could be used for the scenes where the men descend to dig the escape tunnel; it could also enable Renoir to use dolly shots of the narrow yard from the prisoners' window to the guard's room opposite.

In looking for a logical place where the prisoners would stage a musical spectacle, I thought of the empty stables. They were not only a logical choice but added visual interest as well.

A benevolent French colonel was attached to our scouting party. From him I borrowed a saddle rack and a bridle hook, used to hang saddles and harnesses. These were typical props in stables, fixed on posts separating the individual stalls.

Since we had decided not to shoot any practical interiors where scenes are played in the Colmar barracks, we didn't have to provide for complicated lighting equipment or cumbersome materials and numerous electricians.

As we planned the picture we realized we would need more space than was available at the Tobis studios, our headquarters. Tobis studios in Epinay sur Seine, the northwestern suburb of Paris, had only one large sound stage and one small one. And since Tobis was now a rental studio, each producer had to organize his own construction crew and electricians. And there was no commissary either. Usually we all had lunch in a small restaurant on the tree-lined plaza, across from the studio gates.

However, many important films had been shot there, among them Jacques Feyder's *Carnival in Flanders* and René Clair's *Sous les toits de Paris*, *The Million*, *A nous la liberté*, and others. These films required many sets, so set construction had to continue day and night because overnight changes of sets were often needed. For that, Tobis studios was perfect: their two stages had four large barn-type doors that opened onto a large cement platform. Sets were often pre-built on this platform, and the large doors allowed for quick removal of old

Left: *A preliminary sketch for the French military cantina at the airfield.*

Right: *Sketch of the corridor at the prison. "I imagined how ominous the sound of running German boots would be on these flagstone floors."*

GRAND ILLUSION: Lourie and the Tobis studios' construction crew, photographed in Epinay in 1936.

sets and rapid set-up of new ones. Often the exterior sets were built on the outdoor platform, as was the Flemish town in *Carnival in Flanders* and the huge Paris rooftops miniature for René Clair's picture.

But even with its outdoor platform, the Tobis studio was not sufficient for the needs of our production. We were able to rent additional stages not far from Tobis at the Éclair studios in the same small suburb of Epinay. We had also shot *The Lower Depths* at Éclair. On these stages I planned to build two important large sets: the stables at the barracks and the German widow's farm complex. Shooting at Éclair would give us time to have the castle set back at Tobis when it was needed.

In the first draft of the script, the German officers' cantina was placed in an abandoned chateau, the French cantina in a temporary prefab building erected on the airfield. The producer, or rather his father, who supplied the financing, objected to the use of a "chateau" as the setting for a German cantina. In his opinion it would be too costly. In studying the research, I noticed that the Germans often used a prefab building almost identical to the French one. Using this similarity, staging both cantinas in the same prefab, could make an interesting statement on the sameness of military establishments. Jean adopted this solution.

In designing the castle sets, I tried to visually express the severity and grimness of the inaccessible stone fortress. I wanted to make evident von Rauffenstein's words, *"Nobody* escapes from here. *Nobody."*

My dominant impression of this place was stone—stone walls and stone floors built on top of granite rock. I imagined how ominous the sound of running German boots would be on these flagstone floors.

In 1936 sound engineers were the capricious masters of the stage set. The stage walls at Tobis were covered with dirty brown felt, loose lengths hanging down here and there. They were called sound "baffles." If we had to build stone floors, we had to build them in cellotex, a soundproof material. The actual sound of steps would have to be dubbed in later. I spoke to Renoir and asked if we could possibly break this tradition and use natural-sounding pavement.

"The idea is excellent but you will have to speak to de Bretagne." De Bretagne, our adventurous sound engineer, agreed. From that time on we used real paving stones. They were cast in reinforced cement slabs, heavy to handle but almost indestructible. Twenty years later I saw the same stones still in use at Tobis.

While I was busy designing and constructing the sets, the company moved to Alsace. I joined them some days later, arriving in Colmar late in the afternoon. At the hotel where Renoir and some actors and technicians were staying, I was told I could find them in a restaurant in the old district of the town, celebrating the launching of the film. When I reached the restaurant, I was ushered into a private dining room. A strange scene was taking place within. Dinner was obviously over. Stroheim, erect, dignified, a glass of champagne in his hand, was proposing a toast. Suddenly, rigid as a ramrod, he fell backward, knocking over a large bamboo screen, which had been standing behind him. Stroheim landed flat on his back on top of the screen. When it was time to leave, his friend just rolled him up in the screen and carried him back to the hotel like a carpet. The next day Stroheim remembered none of this.

In Colmar Renoir and I had to devise one sequence in the barracks yard. It was the scene where our group of prisoners prepare their costumes for their musical spectacle. They are in a second-story room, overlooking the yard where young German recruits are exercising (the prison camp is supposedly located in military barracks still occupied by the German army). To show the yard, however, we didn't want to use rear projection. At this time—even more than today—rear projection gave a blinking and unsteady image. It was all right for a view from a moving car or railroad train but not for a steady view from a barracks window. One solution to this problem was to build the entire set for the room on a platform in the middle of the actual barracks grounds, with a window view of the exercises. But building a complete set on location would mean difficult shooting and problems of lighting and sound, so we discarded this idea. Instead we decided to build only the window wall on a platform at the barracks location, from which we could make the point-of-view shot through the second-floor window. The total scene, with the actors, would be shot on a four-wall set on stage. It was so satisfactory that I later used the same technique in Renoir's *The Human Beast.*

I was with the company when we moved to the Haut Koenigsburg location. The first days of shooting were difficult. We started in dry cold weather and shot many scenes. Then snow began to fall and continued for many days. Jean was obliged to reshoot all the previous work in the snow. It was done with infinite patience and good humor. The sequence was almost finished when the sun appeared and the snow melted. Jean called me for consultation, and we urgently organized parties to scout all the neighboring towns for rough salt, naphthalene, white bedsheets, anything white to cover the ground in Haut Koenigsburg.

I had to leave Jean and the company in Alsace to proceed to Paris to finish the sets.

When the company arrived in Paris, our first day of interior shooting took place on the set of the French cantina at the airfield. The set was a typical prefab wooden military structure. Girlie photos from the Folies Bergères and Casino de Paris were pinned on the walls. The old phonograph on the bar loudly played the popular song "Frou-Frou." The primitive bar was decorated with cartoons, samples of military jokes: "Alcohol drives you crazy! Alcohol kills you! Our colonel drinks it!" The scene was short. The company moved to the adjoining set, the office of the commanding officer for the brief introductory scene between Maréchal (Jean Gabin) and de Boïeldieu (Pierre Fresnay), which sharply delineated the differences between the two—their characters, backgrounds, and social class.

Then back to the cantina set, now changed and redecorated as the German cantina. A portrait of the kaiser is on the wall instead of the girlie photos. The phonograph plays a waltz by Strauss. Stroheim appears, erect in his flier's uniform. The first days of studio shooting were also the opening scenes of *Grand Illusion*.

Next we moved to the large stage and the complex interior-exterior set of the first prison camp. Here we came to the meaty part of the script involving the largest part of the cast. Rehearsing with actors, Renoir would sit with them around the table on the set, running over their dialogue. This was done without any acting, without any expression. In fact, for the first reading, Renoir asked his actors to read as if they were reading the phone directory. The next readings were more like friendly conversations, and little by little, the relation-

Gaston Modot (pouring wine), Gabin (to his left),
Marcel Dalio (standing), Julien Carrette (sitting,
second from right), Pierre Fresnay (far right).

ships between characters developed, their personalities sharpened, and the scene took shape. New dialogue was sketched in and logical stage movements were suggested by Renoir. Usually Christian Matras, the lighting cameraman (or director of photography), and Claude Renoir, Jean's nephew and the camera operator, were present at rehearsals and with Jean they decided on the mechanics of shooting the sequence: a dolly shot here, a change of camera angle there, or how to cut the scene. Usually actors were followed by the camera in a continuous, flowing movement. Sometimes close-ups were used to accentuate certain parts of a scene.

At such times the stage became the domain of the technicians, each one knowing his special job. These were lively occasions, and the actors who were the subjects of the close-ups, were personally involved in the creative process, or so they felt, and the sequences came out enriched by this collaboration. Renoir, always attentive, had the gift of calling on the best abilities of each of us. Using and praising the contribution of each member of the team, whether the work of a grip or the ingenious lighting of Matras, he made us feel the importance of our efforts, which became organic parts of the action. We all felt, and were, real collaborators on Renoir's films.

After shooting the first prisoners' camp on the large Tobis stage, we moved to the smaller stage for many sets, including the office where packages were delivered, the underground passage where Carette is almost asphyxiated, and the solitary cell where Gabin goes into his frightening rage.

The company then deployed to the Éclair studio where the stable set had been completed. (Many books about Renoir's films give incorrect information about where *Grand Illusion* was shot. It was at the Tobis and Éclair studios, and not at Billancourt.)

The gloomy emptiness of the stables looked appropriate for the tense sequence of the prisoners' musical extravaganza. Long rows of posts with saddle holders punctuating the deep narrow set separated the individual stalls. But the saddle holders were empty and there were no horses because they were all at the Front. To contrast with this gloomy emptiness, gaudy paper decorations were hung everywhere and a naively painted Eiffel Tower was used to decorate the proscenium arch.

Despite the zesty buffoonery of the comedian Carette, you could feel the prisoners' inner tension. And surely enough, it suddenly exploded in exuberant enthusiasm at the news that the fort of Douaumont at Verdun had been retaken by the French army.

While the company was shooting this scene at the Éclair studio, I was finishing the castle sets at Tobis. The two principal sets for the castle sequence were Stroheim's chapel bedroom and his adjoining office and anterooms and the set of prisoners' rooms with a corridor and partial view of the Russian prisoners' rooms. Also on this stage were numerous sets that had to be inserted in sequences shot on location at Haut Koenigsburg. The work was a jigsaw puzzle. I had to view the moviola continuously to match scenes on location with what was needed to complete these scenes.

The basic visual idea of Stroheim's room was, as I mentioned before, the dominance of the crucifix and vertical structure of the chapel. The original idea as shown to Stroheim was drawn on a paper napkin in a café. My problem as production designer was to turn a simple geometric statement into a convincingly realistic set without losing its simplicity.

The walls, arches, and floors had to be of a stone texture, but I wanted to find an antique wood-carved church partition to add detail. I visited some important antique dealers who specialized in dismantling old churches and selling them stone by stone to museums or to American millionaires. You can probably find an authentic twelfth-century chapel next to an oil rig in Oklahoma, just as you can see London Bridge in Arizona.

At one of these dealers I had the good luck to find an entire wood-paneled chapel wall, complete, with carved partition grills and impressive crucifix.

Furnishing the set of Stroheim's room showed Renoir's creative capacity to develop a meaningful sequence from a fortuitous detail. When we were first scouting the Haut Koenigsburg location, I noticed a small pot of geraniums on the windowsill of the janitor's lodging. I was impressed by this little speck of color amidst the gray stone surroundings. I asked Jean if he would not object to my placing a geranium in Stroheim's room. "By all means, put it there. I could use it," he said. This little flower became a highly poetic symbol. Stro-

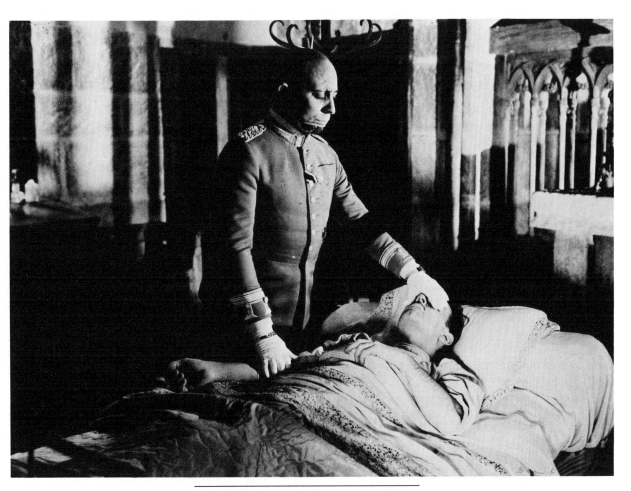

"I had the good luck to find an entire wood-paneled chapel wall, complete with carved partition grills and impressive crucifix."

heim's cutting the geranium captured the emotional moment of the scene showing the death of Boïeldieu.

In the same set I discovered that we can often create illusions by the simplest means. The scene was the Fresnay-Stroheim conversation in front of the window. The backing for the window was a photographic blow-up of the castle walls at Haut Koenigsburg. On this still you could see a gallery running along the top of the crenellated wall. While rehearsing the scene, Renoir mentioned that the castle walls looked quite real from the blow-up, but the illusion would be perfect if we could see a sentinel moving on the gallery. I hastily cut out the silhouette of a German soldier from a cardboard box. Hiding myself below the ridge of the photographic wall of the backing, I moved the silhouette by hand. The results were amazingly realistic.

In World War I prisoners of war of higher rank had the privilege of receiving packages and buying many commodities, using camp officials as intermediaries. In this film Boïeldieu enjoyed a comfortable armchair, wore an extraordinary warm checkered shawl, and had photographs of his racehorses beside his bed. One of the prisoner's had a thick book by the Greek poet Pindar, and another had a cage with a chipmunk. Rosenthal decorated his room with reproductions of paintings.

An amusing sequence occurred when the Russian prisoners received a box of presents from their czarina. Hungry from the meager German rations and expecting food and vodka and all the other marvelous goodies they could eat, they eagerly opened the box only to find that it contained books. Enraged, they set fire to their present. This episode was derived from a story I heard about an incident in the Russo-Japanese War of 1904. Russian soldiers fought under terrible conditions. There was only one rifle for every four soldiers. They would run barefooted with wooden dummy rifles, waiting for soldiers with real rifles to be killed so they could possess themselves of rifles that would shoot. Often they didn't have any ammunition. Their uniforms were tattered and the soles of their boots were made of cardboard. Finally boxes arrived, presents from the czar. When they opened the boxes, they found thousands of icons. The war with Japan had been lost, and this episode was never mentioned in the czarist newspapers.

After escaping from the castle, Gabin and Dalio try to reach the Swiss border. Hiding in ravines, they sleep in the daytime and walk at night, trying to avoid people. After spraining his ankle, Dalio is almost incapable of moving. They see a cowshed, seemingly empty, close to an isolated farmhouse. They enter, hoping to find a temporary hiding place. The exteriors for this episode were shot in Alsace; on stage we continued with the interior of the shed and the unexpected encounter with the German woman, Dita Parlo.

The German farm widow takes the prisoners into her house, gives them food, and cares for Dalio's leg. The two men find refuge there for several days with the woman and her daughter. Together they celebrate Christmas and prepare, as a surprise for the daughter, a Christmas tree and a manger scene. I had to improvise the making of the crèche with materials the prisoners could have found on the farm. A visit to the vegetable market gave me the white turnip from which I carved the child Jesus; and a leek with a beardlike root. It became Joseph. Twigs and straw were used for the manger itself.

For the farmhouse set I used the same method we used for the Colmar barracks yard. To avoid process shots I brought one wall of the farmhouse set with its window and curtains to the location. This wall was used in the scene where Dalio opens the window (in an over-the-shoulder shot) and sees a pensive Gabin leaning against the fence and behind him, a wide vista of the distant hills. It was the scene before the separation and departure of Gabin and Dalio.

The last scenes of the picture, the crossing in the snow at the Swiss border, were to be shot after the end of our studio schedule. However, Gabin, due to a previous engagement, was unable to go to the snow location. The problem was how to shoot close-ups of Gabin and Dalio on stage, before the master scene in the snowy landscape was shot and even before we knew exactly where we would shoot the scene. I proposed the following solution: I would build on stage a hole in the ground covered with deep snow—a truckload of Epsom salts would suffice. A cut pine placed across the hole would provide refuge where the prisoners could hide. Their last conversation would be filmed before they braved the run to freedom down the snowy hill. I reasoned that on any snowed-in location, it would be easy to cut a pine tree and duplicate the set-up with doubles, shooting them from behind. It was done so, successfully.

Once more a picture was finished and a group of technicians and actors who had become inseparable friends had to say farewell to each other.

Grand Illusion was my second film with Jean Renoir. In this film I had the chance to fully understand and appreciate the meaning of collaboration between a film director and his crew. Often Renoir compared the functions of a film director with those of a chef in a restaurant. A chef can create great meals, but they are also the result of his collaboration with his helpers, the meat chefs, the wine stewards, the saucemakers, and the rest. Renoir knew how important his collaborators were to his work, and being a truly great director, he did not deny their influence but tried to assimilate it to reinforce his own point of view. The feeling of being an intimate collaborator with Jean made my work with him exhilarating. He sometimes called me his "accomplice." I consider Renoir's accomplice to be a title of nobility in the film world. After *Grand Illusion* was finished, it was hard for me to adjust. This feeling of letdown was new to me then, but later occurred after almost every film I completed. After a period of intense activity, of continuous absorbing concern with delivering a set on schedule, after sleepless nights worrying over creative decisions, all of it would suddenly come to a stop. The end of an affair, as it were. Happily, this spell of blues would dissipate when a new project appeared to dominate my thoughts.

WERTHER

Some films are artistically more interesting than others, and you feel more affection for their memory. One of my favorite films was *Werther*, made in France in 1938. From the very beginning of this project there was exciting anticipation: the subject of the story based on Goethe's novel; the prospect of creating a vision of intimate life in a small eighteenth-century German town; the warm personality of Max Ophuls, the director; our close understanding of visual approach in filmmaking and the similarity of our tastes; all of this promised a very satisfying collaboration.

I had met Ophuls some time earlier when he asked me to design *Yoshiwara*, a Japanese romantic saga starring Sessue Hayakawa. At this time I was busy with Jean Renoir's *Grand Illusion* and had to decline Ophuls's offer. However, in 1938, when the project of *Werther* appeared, I eagerly accepted it.

To prepare myself for the film, I first reacquainted myself with Goethe's novel, as well as with some German romantic illustrations and genre paintings of the period. These showed a particular way of life, *Gemütlichkeit*—"an intimate warmth"—that would be interesting and challenging to recreate. I would also have to try to capture and convey the subtle poetry, the elusive nuances of Goethe's romantic novel.

All elements of this project presaged a happy, satisfying work. My first preproduction meetings with Ophuls confirmed these expectations.

We assumed that the action of *Werther* took place in a small town in southern Germany, possibly in Bavaria or in a charming town in the Black Forest region. Alsace, in France, was the closest geographically and visually to these towns; so our scouting trip took us to this region, with its enchanting towns surrounded by gardens and vineyards, which had retained the intimate atmosphere and architecture of the eighteenth century.

I felt, as did Ophuls, that visual atmosphere can help a director and actors express the style and essence of a film. A memorable scene where the visual element creates the reigning mood is the love scene under the huge blossoming apple tree in Erich von Stroheim's *Wedding March*. The falling blossoms, like snowflakes, somehow express even more than the actors' emotions, the poignancy of the scene.

In starting a film, the production designer has many options of how to create the desired environment. The reasons for designing one way or another are often impossible to explain. Designing addresses senses, not reason; it has to be judged on an emotional level and thus is almost impossible to express in words. The emotional impact of visual images can be compared with listening to music or seeing a painting; no reasoning can explain your reaction.

The title of Goethe's novel is *The Sorrows of Young Werther*. Written in 1774, it heralded the birth of the romantic novel, describing the passion and turmoil of human destinies.

The young Werther of the novel, a sensitive musician and poet, comes to live in a small German town where he will serve a probationary term, first as a librarian, then as a justice in the local courthouse. He meets and befriends a fellow courthouse member, Albert. Soon Albert has to leave town to take his final examinations before becoming a full-fledged judge. Horseback travel was not safe then, and Albert asks to borrow Werther's pistols for the trip.

Left: *"We assumed that the action of* WERTHER *took place in a small town in southern Germany, possibly in Bavaria."*

"The emotional impact of visual images can be compared with listening to music or seeing a painting."

Meanwhile a chance meeting with a beautiful young girl, Charlotte, changes Werther's life. Their mutual attraction leads to weekly meetings and long walks in the countryside. Unaware of what is happening, they fall deeply in love. But Charlotte's shyness and discretion prevent her from revealing to Werther that she is betrothed to Albert. Finally, however, she tells him.

Albert returns. He assumes his functions as judge and presses Charlotte not to postpone their marriage. She gives in to him and they marry. From this moment on, life is tragically changed for Werther and Charlotte.

You must remember that this was the sensibility of the time, when the world was "suffering" from love. Love was a disease, a kind of passionate insomnia that filled its victims with torment.

In a desperate mood Werther begins to drink, spending long evenings in local dives of the sedate German town. He neglects the social obligations demanded by the strict provincial society, and his position in the courthouse is jeopardized. The head magistrate of the court forces Werther to explain his actions, and Werther confesses that the cause of his behavior is hopeless love of a married woman. Knowing of Albert's friendship with Werther, the magistrate tells Albert of Werther's plight. Charlotte overhears the conversation and realizes the tragic impasse in her life.

Finally Werther decides to leave town. For the trip he will need his pistols; he sends his servant to Albert to fetch them back. He leaves at nightfall, in a driving rain.

At daybreak he stops his horse, dismounts, and slowly walks to the edge of a forest. We hear a shot. The frightened horse runs away. Thus ends this romantic film.

The plot is deceptively simple, and the novel is short. However, the suspense holds us by delicate nuances and subtle emotional detail.

In our scouting we had to find towns and gardens that captured the pastoral charm of the novel. Each small town or borough of Alsace presented endless possible sites for our film, making the final choice difficult.

For the scene of the village festivities, I drew inspiration from a charming eighteenth-century painting where a dance platform was erected around a tree in a garden. Wooden steps ascended to the dance floor and the platform was

"Love was a disease, a kind of passionate insomnia that filled its victims with torment." Charlotte (Annie Vernay) at the piano.

large enough to accommodate numerous dancers as well as an orchestra. With this painting in mind, I chose a flowering glade and built a ten-foot-high platform around an old oak tree.

There are common problems a designer faces when shooting an historical film in an old town that has been adapted for modern life. While many houses retain the original architecture of the period, almost all of them are spoiled by the multitude of electric and telephone wires. (We were fortunate in 1938 not to have the problem of TV antennas.) We only had the problem of choosing the location for one of the primary exterior sets, that of the village square with the inn entrance and the stagecoach terminal. We found the most appropriate town square with a quaint public fountain and an ideal inn entrance in the little town of Ammerschwihr. But the exterior of the "inn" was actually the local post office and the terminal point of hundreds of telephone lines. A typical designer's trick would have been to camouflage the wires by hanging an ornate sign—but this would not work in our case. I decided to ask the local mayor for permission to temporarily plant a pine tree against the building to conceal the wire terminal. Not only did I get permission, but the benevolent town council also provided us with a magnificent pine tree, some forty feet high, cut down by the town services from the local forest and planted exactly where we wanted it, hiding the offending wires and adding extra charm to this quaint square. The city fathers were happy and honored that Goethe's *Werther* would be filmed in *their* town.

I was assisted on this film by Max Douy, who had previously been my assistant. Now back from one of his repeated calls to military service, he joined me as co-art director. I remember spending many happy hours with him in the Alsace countryside, choosing or refining numerous shooting locations. Each location was cataloged after being carefully evaluated during daylight for the most favorable time for lighting. Ophuls and our cameraman had to give the final okay. Often we decided to complement these sites with pictorial details, adding a roadside crucifix here, a rustic bench on a forest lane there, and many other characteristic or interesting foreground pieces.

We had to prepare a selection of prefabricated pieces for instant camouflage of unwanted details in the town, such as a too-modern sign or an electric fixture. I remember preparing a collection of wrought-iron signboards, so handy to use and so characteristic of shop fronts in old German towns.

Our work was divided between Alsace and Paris, where we were preparing the interior sets on the stages of the Rue François-Premier studios. I went back to Alsace to assist Ophuls with the exterior shooting. For Ophuls, the visual aspects of the film were as important as the dramatic content. In my opinion that approach was the correct one for filmmaking, and so our collaboration was harmonious and complete. He was very careful to inspect every visual detail, be it costumes or a piece of the set dressing.

The glade we chose for the dancing scene was filled with wild flowers. However, when it came time to shoot, it was later in the season and the flowers were gone. Max Douy and I spent considerable time trying to find artificial flowers in the neighboring towns.

This preoccupation with flowers reminds me of a meeting I had with Ophuls years later in Nice. He was preparing some scenes for *Lola Montez* and I was working with Sacha Guitry on battle scenes for his *Napoleon.* We met by accident on a hilly road close to the village of Cagnes. Ophuls told me that for his next scene where the carriage of Lola Montez passed down the road, he had asked his prop men to cover the entire hillside with live red carnations. He described with enthusiasm the would-be effect of Lola's glorious ride against the red background of carnation-covered hills.

Several days later on the same road I saw the poor prop men painstakingly planting carnations in the reluctant ground. They had purchased all the available flowers from Nice's flower markets. I must confess that the result of their efforts seen in the finished film did not achieve the flamboyant look that Ophuls had described.

The shooting of *Werther*'s exteriors progressed successfully. The photography was done by Stelly, a young cameraman replacing Eugene Schufftan, who would join the film for the studio sequences. The summer Alsace sequences were gloriously lit and each composition recalled the delicate landscapes of eighteenth-century paintings. These images beautifully expressed the meaning of the story. The sentimental walks of Werther and Charlotte needed no dialogue to convey.

Finally location shooting ended. Some days earlier I had left for Paris where Max was busy preparing the sets. The first set on our schedule was the monumental hall and stairway of the baroque courthouse. Heavy wood-carved balusters accented the curving handrail; a double door led to a hall of records where the deeds were stored, shelves and shelves of heavy bound volumes.

Eugene Schufftan was still busy and the first set had to be photographed by Stelly. In spite of the fact that his exteriors were visually outstanding, the young cameraman worried over the lighting of the interior set. "Gene, how can I light this set? There aren't any windows. I have no justifiable source of light!"

"But Stelly," I said, "the set is L-shaped. You can imagine high windows on the camera side of the set and light accordingly." But Stelly couldn't understand my suggestion and shooting was postponed until Schufftan became available.

Was it the whimsical Schufftan's intention to astound us by his brilliant lighting? He used the strongest lights I have ever seen assembled on a motion picture stage, putting a row of arc lights projected through silhouettes of window frames and creating the effect of glorious sunlight. The cheerful lighting influenced the actors and the crew and shooting proceeded quickly.

The studios we were working in were situated in the very center of Paris, not far from the Champs Élysées, and were formerly the plush showrooms of an antique dealer. Through the connections of the studio manager, we had access to many pieces of rarely found, Biedermeier furniture in the German provincial style. This furniture had the elegant simplicity of the late nineteenth century and was usually made of light-colored fruit woods, perfectly suited to our restful whitewashed interiors and white curtains. I wanted to give the feeling of light and clarity, so akin to Charlotte's personality.

But to pinpoint the somber despair of Werther, we built the taverns to reflect a dark sinister emptiness. Then Ophuls added a sequence that took place in a brothel. The mood of the sequence was to be a feeling of turmoil. I remember designing a highly expressionistic set, but as the sequence had not been preplanned by the production office, we did not have the money to build it. I told Ophuls I could transform another of our sets.

The set of the inn where Werther resided was an interior-exterior set of the inn's backyard with stairs that led to a balcony-corridor and doors that opened to the guests' rooms. This set was built on the studio back lot and was exposed to a light continual breeze. I transformed the set, hanging black gauze separations between individual sections of the divided space. The gauze panels sometimes overlapped, forming uneven semitransparent curtains that moved freely in the breeze, creating strange shapes of dark moving transparencies. The results successfully captured the tortured mood of Werther that Ophuls sought. It proved to me once again that often the need to improvise quickly forces creativity more successfully than long sittings at the drawing board.

Lourie's sketch of Charlotte's bedroom.

Left: *Corridor outside Werther's room.*

Right: *Werther's room in the hostelry.*

Lourie's sketch of the brothel for a scene that was eventually cut.

The magistrate's office as it appears in the film.

A preliminary sketch of the magistrate's office.

The film expressed the pastoral atmosphere of Goethe's novel.

I am not sure that Frenchmen living in the sinister apprehension of the years of 1938–1939 welcomed this filmed version of a sentimental eighteenth-century novel, but in itself the film was one of the most delicate that Max Ophuls ever created.

Annie Vernay, the young heroine of the film, was disarmingly vulnerable; Pierre-Richard Willm somberly romantic; and Jean Galland honorably portrayed the role of the unhappy husband.

I think the film visually fulfilled the artistic goals set up by Ophuls and expressed the pastoral atmosphere of Goethe's novel.

The collaboration with Ophuls brings to mind a seldom-explored facet of film designing: the close affinity of designing to musical expression. Working with him, I became especially conscious of this affinity.

When Ophuls broke down a script, he often annotated it by a series of musical symbols, marking the different moods and tempos of each scene. One scene might call for "allegro" or "allegro cantabile," another "andante," and so forth. And each change of mood would demand a different visual treatment of the given scene. Ophuls was especially sensitive to the visual moods of the setting, which he was convinced could enhance the emotional expression of the scene in much the same way as a musical score.

This conviction of the emotional potential of visual elements is shared by many filmmakers, and I had the unique chance to collaborate with many of them in my career.

THE HUMAN BEAST

It *was* one of the most unexpected films. Jean Gabin had
a contract with Paris Films Productions, the Hakim brothers' company, to appear in a film directed by Gremillon. Gabin also had script approval. The date
of production approached, while the script was still being written. Finally, three
weeks before shooting was scheduled to begin, the script was delivered and rejected by Gabin.

It happened, though, that an earlier, tentative project of Jean Renoir's had
been a film based on Émile Zola's novel *La Bête humaine* (*The Human Beast*).
Renoir had probably mentioned this project to Gabin. At any rate Gabin still
had a contract to appear in a film produced by Robert Hakim, who likewise
had a commitment to deliver a film with Jean Gabin, and Renoir had a general, vague idea that was agreeable to Gabin. *The Human Beast* became their
next project, and shooting was set to begin in three weeks.

Renoir called me; this was in June 1938. "Lourié, if you are free, I would be happy if you would join me on this project. It is rather urgent." I found a seemingly valid reason to bail out of a picture I had started to prepare, a musical with Pierre Fresnay, *The Three Waltzes*, and the next day I was at Hakim's office on the Champs Élysées.

Zola's novel was long, complicated, and meandering, with numerous subplots. Jean, however, in a few days distilled a short step-by-step outline for the film script. The Hakim brothers wanted to keep to the dates of Gabin's contract, and as time was short, guided by Jean's outline, we began scouting and preparing for the film at once.

Our production manager was the urbane Roland Tual. Claude Renoir, Jean's brother, was the first assistant, and Claude Renoir, Jean's nephew, his camera operator. We called them Claude Senior and Claude Junior. The lighting cameraman was Curt Courant; the second camera operator, Jacques Natteau. My usual assistant, Max Douy, was due back from his military service and would join us later.

The railroad station in Le Havre was the principal setting of our film. We had to obtain authorizations to use one or two platforms, the railroad yards, locomotive depots, and the areas around administration and service buildings for our shooting. We decided to converge on Le Havre without losing any more time in Paris.

With Claude Senior and Claude Junior, I drove to Le Havre, stopping on the way to scout for rural scenery along the small river and also to find a railroad-crossing keeper's house, where Gabin had to visit his godmother in the film. That night we were in Le Havre, dining in the old hotel facing the sea. Renoir was to arrive shortly afterward to write the script and spend some time with the cameraman and myself to discuss our idea for location shooting. One evening some days later, he alighted from the train, carrying a small package wrapped in newspaper. When the diligent porter asked for his luggage, he waved the package and said, "Here it is!"

We began preparing our sets. Under the high glass roof of the Victorian railroad station, we started to hang regular studio lighting platforms. We got authorization to use one, sometimes two, of the platforms and installed complete studio facilities there. We had to clear these platforms of our equipment

THE HUMAN BEAST: *Jean Renoir and the director of photography, Curt Courant, next to the window of the set overlooking the Le Havre railroad yard.*

"There is a strong, ever-present rhythm, like a heartbeat of the railroad, and the visual melancholic poetry of smoke, soot, and steam."

only for the arrival of the late afternoon express from Paris. However, from morning till 5 P.M., the platforms were our domain, filled with the grips' and electricians' paraphernalia.

The script was taking shape. It was a somber drama punctuated by the relentless rhythm of the railroad. Lantier (Gabin) is an engineer, whose life is dominated by his attachment to his engine, in which, with his stoker (played by Carette), he drives a daily train from Paris to Le Havre. Usually they spend the night in a dormitory for transient railroad workers and return the next day to Paris. On certain days, when the engine needs an overhaul, they have to lay off. The other protagonists are Roubaud (Fernand Ledoux), the stationmaster, and his wife, Séverine (Simone Simon), who has recently had a love affair. Discovering the affair, in a sudden crisis of jealousy, Roubaud kills the former lover and protector of his wife while the three of them are in the compartment of a night train from Paris to Le Havre. Lantier happens to be on the train; it is his day off, and he sees Roubaud and Séverine return from the compartment where the crime was committed. Having been strangely touched by the pleading eyes of Séverine, Lantier later keeps silent during the investigation of the crime, and does not tell the examining magistrate that he had seen Séverine and her husband in the train corridor. Thus begins the deepening attachment, and quasicomplicity, between Lantier and Séverine. Starting with the knifing in the train, the lives of the three protagonists move with mathematical precision to the inevitable tragedy.

This somber melodrama became, in my opinion, one of the most beautiful of Renoir's pictures, a human drama of three poor beings struggling in the cogwheels of their passion. In it there is a strong, ever-present rhythm, like a heartbeat of the railroad, and the visual melancholic poetry of smoke, soot, and steam.

At the time we shot the picture, this feeling of doom corresponded with the atmosphere in Europe. The air was charged with the tension of impending war. In Spain the civil war was at its full fury. Madrid was besieged by General Franco's forces, and the German Luftwaffe, helping Franco, bombed and obliterated the small Basque town of Guernica. In front of our hotel we often saw groups of stowaways being led from arriving steamers to police stations.

Idealistic young Americans, with no luggage and dressed casually as for a Sunday outing, were trying to sneak into Spain to join the Republican army in its fight against the Franco dictatorship. Usually they were repatriated on the next steamer back to the United States. Many, however, successfully passed through to Spain. And many ended their lives on Spanish battlefields.

Le Havre, one of the largest seaports in Europe, was the hub of shipments to Spain. The city was nervously aware of war rumors and full of secret agents working for or against Franco. It was a strange time.

Our closely knit group of technicians lived in the old hotel, done in pure *fin-de-siècle* decor. The grand circular stairway descended to a glass-roofed hall. Usually we dined in the popular La Grosse Tonne restaurant, so called because of two huge wooden barrels of cider that flanked the entrance. The apple cider was sweet and mild to taste, but potent, really treacherous. After two tankards you felt good, your head absolutely clear, but you couldn't walk straight. The wise ones remained seated and watched the adventurous ones who tried to exit without stumbling.

Preparations for the production went ahead speedily. Every day I spent some time with Jean, acquainting him with my scoutings and discussing with him the best way of realizing certain sequences.

Railroad people are a breed apart; their way of life is strongly influenced by the demands of tight schedules, arrivals, departures, loadings, and servicings. In Le Havre the stationmaster and service personnel were lodged in company buildings close to the railroad yards. Each day and night they could hear the heavy breathing of the passing locomotives.

We felt that this continual presence of the railroad in their private lives was a powerful and important element of the drama. I proposed to Jean that we locate Roubaud's lodging inside the railroad yard, tying it intimately to the surrounding steam and noise so that he would have an immediate close view of these activities.

As we had decided against using rear projection in our sets, I proposed to erect a high platform, the height of the second-floor apartment. This platform would be placed smack between a rail junction in the railroad yard, and on it I would build the interior window walls of Roubaud's apartment.

Here Jean would shoot the scenes played close to the window, such as Séverine's scene where she pets and strokes a kitten. This scene could be shot with the camera shooting down, encompassing the view of the railroad yard with its passing locomotives. However, the entire set of the Roubaud apartment would be built on the stage at the Billancourt studios in Paris. The set would be complete, including a repetition of the window built on the platform in Le Havre. As the view from the window (if you are shooting straight) would be *above* the railroad lines, you would normally see only the tops of some pylons and the silhouettes of neighboring buildings against the sky. Occasionally you could see puffs of smoke from the passing trains. So I had to back the windows on the stage with a photographic enlargement of the view, taken with a level camera from our platform in Le Havre.

We already had practical knowledge of this method of shooting scenes, partly done on location and partly on the stage, duplicating the same set. We had done scenes the same way in *Grand Illusion* using the view from the window of the barracks yard, and in the same film, the view from the farm's window, which we intercut with scenes shot inside the farm on the stage.

Throughout the picture, I tried to create the feeling of the ever-present life of the railroad. So when I had to design an apartment where the Roubauds stay while visiting Paris, I again proposed to connect the apartment visually with the railroad.

I traveled often to Paris to organize the studio work. During one of these trips I scouted buildings bordering the exit from the St. Lazare railroad station. The windows from the stairway of one of these buildings had a magnificent plunging view over numerous rail lines and traffic exiting the station. I chose to use this window for the Paris apartment. There Jean would shoot the view looking down on the busy railroad traffic. Again, we would build a complete, corresponding set on the stage.

The opening sequence of the film started with a close shot of the locomotive furnace being stoked by Carette. The camera then moved back to a comprehensive shot of the engineers' activity on the moving train. It was the start of an impressive sequence that set the tone for the entire picture and showed the trip from Paris to Le Havre seen from the engine's point of view. To do

The window wall of the "Roubauds' apartment," built on top of a platform erected in the Le Havre railroad yard.

Left: *Gabin in front of a forced perspective background.*

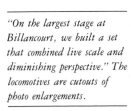

"On the largest stage at Billancourt, we built a set that combined live scale and diminishing perspective." The locomotives are cutouts of photo enlargements.

this opening shot we had to prepare a complicated dolly track leading from the very close shot of the furnace and backing up to focus on the coal heap in the tender. Due to the incessant movement of the engine, the camera had to be solidly anchored with security rails installed to prevent the grips and camera crew from sticking their heads above a certain height and being decapitated when the train passed below a bridge or through a tunnel.

The memorable continuous shot from the front of the moving engine, passing under tunnels, over bridges, fields, villages, and finally slowing down as it enters the depot of Le Havre, was done by Claude Junior, the cameraman, precariously tied down on the cowcatcher of the locomotive. He traveled in this fashion all the way from Evreux—halfway from Paris—to Le Havre. In spite of a protective mask and goggles, he finished the trip with swollen eyes and puffed cheeks, looking blacker than a chimney sweep.

Many scenes, particularly those inside the railroad stations, called for shooting in the semidarkness of twilight. The depots at Paris and Le Havre, typical old European railroad stations, were huge, high structures, not unlike cathedrals. Thus, with the slowing down of the locomotive entering the depot at the beginning of the picture, you were embraced by the specific atmosphere of the film, seeing the transition from the brightly lit exterior to the twilight of the glassed-in depot, hearing the hissing of released steam and footsteps resounding under the high glassed roof.

The brooding black and white photography of Curt Courant was especially effective for these scenes. I saw him carefully preparing shots, cutting out intricate gauze inserts for his lens filters, to darken the sky at one point, to darken everything at another, leaving only cutout holes for the lights from the parked locomotives in the distance. I don't see cameramen using this technique today. The last time was in 1943 when working with Rudy Maté on *Sahara.* Of course, such cutout mattes can only be used in static set-ups, not in moving or panning shots.

We now had to decide how to shoot the rainy night sequence when Lantier meets Séverine and they seek refuge in a toolshed in the railroad yard. To shoot this sequence at night, with rain, on location would be difficult, if not impossible. We could not create rain, and to light the depth of the yard that

Renoir wanted for this sequence was not possible. Jean turned to me for advice. I thought I could do it on stage.

On the largest stage at Billancourt, we built a set that combined live scale and diminishing perspective. The front part of the set was real: real ties and rails, adjoining brick walls, and a wooden toolshed. Toward the background, however, the rail lines started to run in diminishing perspective. The parked locomotives were the cutouts of photo enlargements, and farther back, the same photos were used but in smaller scale. The high pylons carrying railroad lights were miniaturized to scale, and some side buildings were also built in diminishing perspective.

The set looked real and very impressive. It fit with the other sequences shot in the actual railroad yard on location. The cutout locomotives emitted light steam; and under the somber lighting, the scene looked exactly as we imagined it.

At this point I moved to Paris to join Max Douy and prepare the stage sets, while Renoir and the shooting company remained in Le Havre to complete the numerous scenes.

In Paris we occupied all the stages at Billancourt. Apart from the forced-perspective railroad yard sequence, we built a very authentic-looking mock-up of two railroad cars: the long corridors, three compartments, interiors, and exteriors. The murder and the discovery of the crime were shot there. Here moving light effects successfully replaced the rear projection.

We also built a complete Roubauds' apartment with adjoining stairs and window wall, duplicating the one we had built on location in Le Havre. And we built the Paris apartment where the Roubauds stayed before their return trip to Le Havre when the killing took place. When Roubaud had to approach the window during a scene in the apartment, the shot was made on the stairway of the building overlooking the exit lines of the St. Lazare station. The remaining sequences in the apartment were shot on the stage set, where the window matched the one over the stairway.

On the set of the workers' washroom, I once more tried to include the visual presence of railroad life, placing in the background an open door leading toward the depot where steaming locomotives could be seen. I built this backing in the available narrow space between our set and the stage wall. I had to build it in forced perspective, again using the cutout photographic enlargements of locomotives, adding escaping steam and blinking lights to give some life to the background. Using forced perspective meant that I had to calculate the perspective for a predetermined camera position. The sequence was shot as calculated and the background worked fine. But Renoir, pleased with the effect of the background, decided to play another scene right in front of the open door, placing the camera much closer than the calculated angle and destroying, in my opinion, the methodically calculated perspective. I warned Renoir that it could appear all wrong. But Jean said, "*Mon vieux* [old pal], it looks all right to me. You would be amazed at how flexibly our perception adapts to false perspective!" I learned once more that the rules of perspective can often be broken.

Other sets of *The Human Beast* followed in quick succession.

We shot the waiting room of the inquiring magistrate, where the Roubauds sit anxiously waiting the inquiry, and the interior of the magistrate's office, where the falsely accused Chabuche makes his indignant outburst. On the same stage we also shot a romantic scene in the public garden in Paris, where Lantier meets Séverine and they sit on a park bench.

Finally on a large set we shot the wonderful scene of the railroad employees' ball. The cheerful vulgarity of the ballroom action is counterpointed by an underlying sense of doom and impending tragedy. My specific contribution here was the location where Séverine revealed her explanation of the fatal crime to Lantier. Instead of placing this scene in an adjacent room, I built a glass door that led from the ballroom to a garden terrace. The entire intimate scene takes place on this terrace against the background of waltzing couples, dimly seen through the glass of the French doors.

The last weeks of shooting *The Human Beast* took place in a turbulent political atmosphere. The French army mobilized and moved some units to the German border. Everyone was upset by war rumors. It was also the time when the English Prime Minister Neville Chamberlain traveled with his umbrella to meet Hitler in Berchtesgaden, as German troops were "peacefully" occupying Czech provinces.

Left: *The Parisian apartment where the Roubauds stay before returning to Le Havre. Simone Simon is seated on the couch.*

The backing, seen through the open doorway, has been built in the narrow space left between the set and stage wall.

"The cheerful vulgarity of the ballroom action is counterpointed by an underlying sense of doom and impending tragedy."

The shooting of the film was completed in September, and the editing went quickly. *La Bête humaine* opened in the Madeleine Theater in December 1938. The entire preparation, production, and shooting of the film took only two months.

I think *La Bête humaine* was a success, but as with almost every Renoir film, the recognition of its enormous qualities—its greatness—came later, very often years later. As with a really good novel or memorable painting, you can see Renoir's films again and again, each time finding something new and humanly satisfying.

THE RULES OF THE GAME

The years 1938 and 1939 in France were strange and disquieting. War seemed more and more inevitable. We lived in a trancelike nightmare that affected all our activities. Many film projects were abandoned; others were rushed through as if to race time before the impending disaster.

Soon after finishing *The Human Beast*, Jean Renoir told me that together with some friends he was forming his own production company. It was to be called N.E.F., Nouvelle Edition Française. Jean was writing the first film projected for production. Some tentative titles for it were *The Hunting Party*, *The Hunting Party in Sologne*, and *The Rules of the Game*. The story was influenced in part by Alfred de Musset's classical comedy, *Les Caprices de Marianne*. However, Jean's story was contemporary and would reflect modern morals in French society. The first draft of the script was a tangled mix of farcical comedy and somber tragedy.

An aviation ace, André Jurieu (Roland Toutain), lands in Paris after an astonishing solo flight across the Atlantic. He has accomplished this feat to prove his love for Christine (Nora Grégor), wife of the Marquis de la Chesnaye (Marcel Dalio). She is not at the airfield to meet him as he hoped, and he childishly airs his disappointment to a radio reporter.

In her bedroom Christine hears Jurieu's outburst on the radio, as does her husband, the marquis, who is appalled at this breach of Parisian society etiquette—sincerity is not in the "rules of the game." Driving back from the airfield, the desperate Jurieu tries without success to kill himself in a car accident. But later his close friend Octave (Jean Renoir) goes to see Christine and arranges an invitation for Jurieu to attend the hunt held at the marquis's property in Sologne.

Just before the hunt, while inspecting the hunting grounds, the marquis meets a poacher, Marceau (Julien Carette), and amused by his engaging personality, offers him a job in his household, despite opposition from his gamekeeper, Schumacher (Gaston Modot).

The guests arrive at the hunting castle and engage in the usual society pranks when they are installed in their respective bedrooms. Meanwhile the poacher, Marceau, begins to court Christine's chambermaid, the flirtatious Lisette (Paulette Dubost), Schumacher's wife.

The next day during the hunting party, Christine accidentally discovers that her close friend Geneviève is the marquis's mistress; he, however, is contemplating ending the affair. From all of these activities we now understand that the participants in this social game have problems of the heart to settle.

The final crisis in the film occurs during the fancy dress ball, which takes place the evening after the hunting party. Jealous of Christine's attention to de Saint Aubin, another guest at the ball, Jurieu exchanges blows with him and with the marquis. Meanwhile, armed with a revolver, a jealous Schumacher pursues Marceau through the frightened mass of people. The ball is now in complete pandemonium.

Disgusted with society, where sincerity is banned, Christine is ready to elope with Jurieu. By an accidental turn of events, Octave, Jurieu's friend, becomes the one with whom she chooses to make her escape.

In the end the berserk Schumacher shoots and kills Jurieu in the dark greenhouse, mistaking him for Marceau. And to save face and be true to the rules of the game, Christine walks back to the castle, hand in hand with her husband, the Marquis de la Chesnaye.

As was often the case in Renoir's films, the casting for *Rules of the Game* was surprising. Roland Toutain, who played Jurieu, was an actor who usually played in the French equivalent of "B" pictures. He was better known for his off-screen daredevil driving and spectacular accomplishments in sports. He also had a propensity for extravagant practical jokes. I had heard people speak of a party where, armed with scissors, he clipped off ties from the necks of party-goers. Toutain's boyish charm and spontaneous candor probably prompted Renoir to choose him for the role of the unhappy lover.

At the beginning of the project, Simone Simon's name was mentioned for Christine, but at this time Renoir made the acquaintance of Prince Stahremberg, an escapee from Austria where his party was in opposition to Hitler. His wife, the actress Nora Grégor, had a quality of noble sincerity and vulnerability. Her personality gave Jean an idea of how to develop the character of Christine.

For the part of Octave, the innocent confidant in the play, two names were originally mentioned: Pierre Renoir, Jean's brother and a very fine actor, and Louis Jouvet. Jean's decision to play the part himself came later, influenced, I think, by his successful performance as Cabuche in *The Human Beast.* Ledoux, who had so powerfully played the part of Roubaud, the stationmaster in *Human Beast*, was considered for the part of Schumacher, the jealous game-keeper. The role was eventually given to Gaston Modot, who created one of the most memorable performances in the film.

I seldom saw Jean during the hectic preparations for the film. He was working on the script, but mostly outside Paris. However, we had to hasten preparations if we wanted to shoot during the hunting season when the trees are usually bare.

I remember well our scouting trip to Sologne, the best-known hunting ground in France. The land reminded me of medieval tapestries, the so-called "verdure" kind where an entire tapestry is covered with thick foliage, with small animals and birds poking their heads through the greenery. In front of our car,

Above: *The kitchen in the basement of the hunting chateau. Eddy Debray, Paulette Dubost, Julien Carrette, Gaston Modot (left to right).*

Gaston Modot, as Schumacher, created one of the most memorable performances in this film of memorable performances.

Above: *Marcel Dalio, Mila Parely, Jean Renoir (left to right).*

Above: *"We now understand that the participants in this social game have problems of the heart to settle."*

Above: *The Marquis de la Chesnaye's study.*

Left: *Paulette Dubost and Nora Grégor.*

"We finally chose the seventeenth-century hunting chateau at La Ferté Saint-Aubin."

"I had to duplicate the terrace on the stage and provide for the entrances during the rain sequence."

The kitchen.

families of scurrying quail crossed the road. Sometimes the heavy flight of pheasants brushed against our car windows. It was a fantastic fairytale land of misty swamps and ponds. From time to time we saw isolated hunting manors, relics from the sixteenth and seventeenth centuries.

After visiting many castles for our location, we finally chose the seventeenth-century hunting chateau at La Ferté Saint-Aubin. It was a splendid example of a small castle and provided a spectacular setting for our film. Wide steps led to a terrace bordered by a stone balustrade. French doors opened to a central hall and to the side wings of the building. Nearby a small pond spanned by a high slender bridge led to an unkempt garden. The very isolation of the castle gave the right atmosphere for the film and a perfect layout for the action.

From the outset of our scouting we were determined to shoot the interior scenes on sound stages. Renoir, as usual, preferred the controlled conditions of a set to the hazardous accommodations of location shooting. I hoped, however, to shoot at least the connecting shots showing entrances and exits to and from the terrace on location. Unfortunately, it was impossible. In this particular case the entrance hall was partitioned into a series of small rooms decorated in the worst middle-class taste. It is amazing how succeeding generations of owners could change and spoil the noble interior architecture of these castles. It would be impossible to put a camera inside the entrance, since even a small portion of the interior in one frame would ruin the shot. Thus I had to duplicate the terrace on the stage set and provide for the entrances during the rain sequence.

Jean was in a hurry to start shooting. I left for Paris to design the sets while the final draft of the script was being completed.

Apart from the hunting scenes on the Sologne location, the film was played almost entirely in two basic settings at the studio. One was the Paris apartment of Marquis de la Chesnaye and the other was the interior of the castle.

I began by designing the most intricate set, the main floor of the castle. Certain elements were predetermined by the plan and proportions of the real building and its exterior. The size and height of the French doors had to be the same as the castle on location. Looking out through the windows, we had to provide photographic backings using stills taken on location. The entrance door had to be placed in the same correspondence to the exterior walls as the real building's door. From then on the appearance of the interior was left to me to imagine.

In my conception the entrance hall was the hub of all castle activities. One entered the house there from the terrace; from there the main stairway led to the upper floor and the bedrooms. Also from the hall, another stairway led down toward the kitchen and the servants quarters. On one side the hall opened onto a small sitting room, which had entrances to the large ballroom. On the other side of the entry hall, double doors opened to a gunroom, where guns were stored in glass cases and where the hunters could hang their gear on pegs fixed to the wall. From the gunroom, doors led to a large dining room. In addition to the doors leading from one room to another, I provided a side corridor open to all these rooms, giving Renoir a playing area where he could stage the climactic chase sequence. For this set I planned to open the wall between the two large stages of the Pathé studio, making room for the unusually deep set of the main floor of the castle. I wanted to build all the rooms of this floor on the same set to clarify the visual connections between rooms and allow Jean more fluidity in staging the continuous chase of Modot after the elusive Carette. It would offer a more elegant way of shooting, without obliging the camera to cut from one set to another. By combining the two stages, I would have a useful area of about 150 by 60 feet.

In designing the interiors, I tried to keep the dignity and noble proportions of the original castle. As usual when I began designing sets in any historical style, I visited some important antique dealers, as well as some large wrecking yards whose stock consisted of architectural pieces saved from demolished Parisian buildings. In one of these demolition firms I found a complete stairway, carved in oak. It dated from the early seventeenth century. Each baroque baluster was hand carved, and the entire design of this highly unusual stairway would give an original and individual touch to the entrance hall. As the piece was tremendously heavy, I had to send a large crew of studio carpenters and laborers to load it on the truck. At the studio we unloaded it with a block and tackle and hung it in the middle of the empty stage.

I began designing *Rules of the Game* with my usual collaborator, Max Douy, in this film my co-art director. We studied the stairway and planned the design of the entrance hall around it. As I had done in *Human Beast*, I decided to use real floors in the castle set, as opposed to the French practice of using pasted paper floors with reproductions of stone slabs. I decided to use real parquet in the bathroom and the sitting room and checkered stone slabs on the other floors. They were actually cement paving slabs; but waxed and polished, they had the look of marble.

We designed rough plans for the other sets: the upper floor of the castle, the kitchen and servants quarters, and the Paris house of the marquis.

Armed with these rough drawings, I took the train to La Motte-Beuvron, the closest village to the hunting location. I walked from the village hostelry to the place where I was to meet the shooting company. On the way strange plants sticking up above a hillock attracted my attention. Soon the plants moved, and I realized that they were rabbits, sticking their ears above their holes in the ground. There were thousands and thousands of rabbits. I immediately re-called the problem the Sologne farmers had with this rabbit invasion. Before the First World War, to promote hunting, a clever businessman had imported some strong hares from Yugoslavia and let them loose in the Sologne wilder-ness. During the war, there was almost no hunting and the hares multiplied. These burrowing mammals were so prolific that some years later Sologne was infested with them. Farmers had to put fences around their fields and orchards for protection, but with little effect: the Yugoslavian rabbits ate millions and millions of dollars worth of crops each year. During my walk toward the loca-tion site, I realized that we would have no problem getting animals for our hunting scenes.

On an unusually sunny winter day I met Renoir and the company in a grassy glade. Renoir was rehearsing a scene with Dalio, Gaston Modot, and Carette. In his typical way he shot the scene using a very long and uninter-rupted master shot after a thorough rehearsal. In this picture, more than in others, Renoir favored composition in depth with sharp focus in the back-ground action as well as in the foreground.

The company broke for lunch with the usual sandwiches, sausages, and red wine. I showed Jean the drawings for our future sets and told him of my decision to combine the two stages at the studio. Jean asked me to stay over-

Left: *Music room.*

Below, left: *"The entrance hall . . .
gave an impression of severity to the
chateau at La Ferté Saint-Aubin."*

Servants' dining room.

night in Beuvron so we could study and discuss the set plans at leisure; however, the continual problems of production and the script distracted Jean from his study of the plan. When he returned from the location, weeks later, he was confronted by an almost unfamiliar set, and I had to guide him through the different rooms, stairs, and corridors, as well as potential entrances and exits.

In hunting castles it was quite common to decorate walls with paintings or sculptures of animals. To give our stairway a finishing touch, I asked my friend Donada, a talented sculptor, to carve a small lion in imitation wood to top the newel post. I also asked him to carve some wild animals on corbels supporting the ceiling beams and to carve a life-size deer in imitation marble that I could place on a console against the wall of the entrance hall. It was an extravagant decorative detail, but I thought it reflected the eccentric taste of the marquis. Choosing furnishings in the heavy seventeenth-century baroque style was the fancy at this time of the Parisian *beau monde*, and it was also in character with the marquis's taste and theatrical life-style. This surrealistic theatricality was also a fashionable attitude of a certain Parisian milieu. I mention these details to emphasize the fact that set decoration is not a haphazard affair but a serious concern for a production designer.

The whitewashed entrance hall walls, the antique doors carved in natural oak, the checkered black and white "marble" floor, the carved oak stairway, all gave an impression of severity to the Château de la Ferté Saint-Aubin. Next to the hall, the small intimate sitting room was done in a softer style with its walls in wood-carved paneling and Louis XIV tapestries. The very large ballroom was decorated in a transitional style, with elements of the graceful eighteenth century, its walls covered in white trellis on a light gray background. As the film was shot in black and white, I used photographic enlargements of Watteau paintings for the murals.

The next set to be built was the basement kitchen. It occupied another stage in the Pathé complex of stages. Douy and I decided to place the kitchen under a vaulted ceiling. It was a typical construction in these castles and added visual interest to the set. But the kitchen ceiling was difficult for our builders, and it became a worrisome problem for the art directors. The use of lightweight plastic foam was unknown in studios at this time, so we had to use a complicated frame construction and find a crew of Italian plasterers for these arched vaults.

My general conception for the sets was to keep them clear in color and uncluttered in detail; and I tried to keep the walls as bare as possible. I have always been especially suspicious of last-minute whims of some cameramen or directors who add paintings or other hanging objects to the walls. Uncluttered, light-colored sets form perfect backgrounds for silhouetted movements of actors, making them extremely readable.

As the years pass I am more and more inclined to simplify sets. The idea of simplification came to me before I started to work in films. In 1933 I was designing a ballet for the de Basil Ballet Company in London. At this time their repertoire included *Présages,* Massine's ballet set to the Fifth Symphony of Tchaikovsky. It was designed by Paul Masson, then a well-known painter. The background was an agglomeration of dynamic abstract forms in strong colors. It was very impressive and beautiful in itself, but the dancers' movements were lost in front of it. I decided then and there that I would design, not to obscure dance movements, but to heighten them. From that time to the present I have remained very conscious of keeping backgrounds simple in order to set off actors' movements.

We filled another stage with the upper floor of the castle. It was basically a long corridor leading to many guest rooms.

The last important set we built was the marquis's Paris house. It reflected his taste as owner of the castle but geared to the different demands of worldly life in Parisian society—the snobbish preoccupations of an empty life and the desire to impress friends with extravagant, unusual objects. I tried to keep a certain similarity between the decoration of the Paris house and the castle. I still used the antique furniture and even some similar Louis XVI carved doors, but I set the doors in a modern frame made of mirrors. Also, using the general shape and moldings of some of these doors, I substituted etched mirror panels for wood. It gave his apartment a sophisticated, surrealist chic, a deliberate mixture of antique elements with an ultramodern treatment.

The Marquis de la Chesnaye was also a collector of bizarre musical toys: monkeys that played the cello, dolls that beat on drums, artificial birds that

Above: *Paulette Dubost with Renoir. The upstairs set of the Marquis de la Chesnaye's Parisian apartment.*

Finding focus. Christine (Nora Grégor) and Octave (Jean Renoir).

chirped and whistled. All were placed haphazardly on different pieces of furniture, on bookshelves, or on the floor. For this set I also found an interesting way to do large murals. I took eighteenth-century etchings from a costume ball in a Versailles garden and ordered photographic enlargements that would occupy an entire wall in the marquis's studio. These enlargements from fifteen-inch engravings into twenty-foot murals were hauntingly beautiful and highly original, the eccentric taste of the marquis exactly.

Christine's bedroom consisted of crystal and mirrored furniture, Venetian blackamoors, and, the current rage of Parisian society, excessively large paper flowers made by a Polish refugee.

Finally I designed the greenhouse for the park next to the castle, the place of clandestine meetings, orchids, and crime. It was an appropriate setting for the tragic finale of the bizarre party; the misty light had a diffused underwater look, and from outside, everything appeared mysteriously murky.

My construction crew finished the sets, but the company was delayed in Sologne. Numerous scenes in the hunting sequence were added; they enriched the sequence but shattered the schedule. Then rains further delayed the shooting. If Renoir was annoyed by these delays and preoccupied with money questions, he did not show it. Once he told me, "We don't have to present an account to anyone. It is our own company."

By studio rules we had to keep the basic construction crew till the completion of shooting. To keep them occupied, I asked them to wax and polish the marble and parquet floors, the woodwork, and the stairway every day. We had the shiniest floors I ever saw.

The last days on location were spent in day and night shooting around the terrace of the castle. Then, like a big family, the company returned to the studio.

The first day in Paris Jean and the camera crew acquainted themselves with the set. The ballroom set, with the adjoining corridor at the back, gave Jean definite ideas on how to stage the ball sequence and the beginning of the Schumacher chase. As always in Renoir's way of working, the definite shape of the scene resulted from collaboration with the actors during rehearsals. Renoir didn't imagine the minute details of a sequence beforehand, but let them grow naturally, leaving the reactions of each participant to shape the action. He guided actors, but did not dictate to them. In this way he took full advantage of each actor's personality. His films do not look acted, but alive. I think this way of creation is what makes Renoir's films such a special experience.

Our work in preparing the sets for the next day's shooting usually kept me away from the stage where shooting took place, but I was there for the sometimes hilarious, sometimes macabre sequences of the ball and chase; then, for the scene of the triumphant unveiling by the marquis of his "Limonaire," a mechanical merry-go-round.

Because of an earlier engagement, I had to leave for New York at the end of filming. I left the beginning of May and returned from New York in July to start work with René Clair on his new project, *L'Air pur.* In Paris I attended the premiere of *Rules of the Game* at the Colisée Theater on the Champs Élysées. After the premiere I was walking behind some friends of Renoir's. One of them expressed his negative impression of the film.

"Poor Jean," he said, visibly chagrined that Renoir had produced such a turkey. I couldn't understand his opinion. For me, *Rules of the Game* was a highly moving and very original piece of filmmaking.

However, public opinion was against this picture. The film was not understood at all and was a box-office failure. Soon it was removed from the theater. This remained a severe blow to Renoir, who wasn't vindicated until the second rerelease of the complete version in 1959 when it was triumphantly received at the Venice Film Festival.

Rules of the Game, conceived during Renoir's dark premonitions of impending war, although ostensibly a high-society "entertainment" was in fact a war picture, reflecting the reactions of the characters to the anxiety of their times and their furious rush to live life fully while it was still possible. In this film Jean perceived in the phosphorescent glitter the decaying state of French high society. The film was a daring enterprise, but characteristically, Renoir thrived on daring enterprises. He told me once that he admired an athlete who fails attempting a difficult jump more than a circus clown who easily jumps over a one-foot barrier, the limit of his ambitions.

The Rules of the Game was the last film I worked on with Jean Renoir in France. I was lucky to make four more pictures with him in Hollywood and India *(The River),* but of all of these films, the ones we realized in France left me with the most unforgettable sense of fulfillment. We all worked together with a passionate devotion to the film in its making. Maybe being young played a part in this passion.

In giving me one of his books, Jean inscribed it: "To Gene Lourie, my companion on the road." This feeling of being his companion is always present.

THIS LAND IS MINE

From the early days, aspiring painters were attracted to Paris. The logical destination for filmmakers was Hollywood.

When Paris and half of France were occupied by Nazis in 1941 and the rest of the country was under the rule of the so-called Vichy government—who were in fact German stooges—all cultural life in France came to a stop.

The directors and producers with whom I worked or had contact had left for the United States: Jean Renoir, René Clair, Max Ophuls, Julien Duvivier, André Daven, the Hakim brothers. Other filmmakers were dispersed elsewhere in the world. My goal now became Hollywood, which was attracting filmmakers like a gigantic magnet.

After waiting a year for an American immigration visa, and a succession of many cables to and from American friends, in May 1941 my wife and I boarded a French ship that was sailing from Marseille to La Martinique, where our passage to New York had been arranged. Our trip was interrupted, however, by a forced stay of two months in the port of Casablanca, Morocco. Again it took a lot of patience and many fights with authorities until we found a Portuguese steamer that would take us to New York; the transatlantic passage lasted sixteen long days. In New York I found work designing advertisements for fashion magazines. But we were one step closer to Hollywood . . .

My first film assignment in Hollywood was in 1942 for Warner Brothers' *The Desert Song,* directed by Robert Florey. I had left France with a certain reputation as an art director, and Robert Florey knew me by name. He wanted me to design his picture, but *The Desert Song* had been in preparation for some time and Carlo Novi had already been assigned as art director. Since I had recently spent several months in Morocco, Florey asked if I would work on the film as a technical advisor.

"This way, Gene," he said, "it will serve as a good introduction for you to the ways of Hollywood studios." The work turned out to be useful and enjoyable.

My next job was as art director for a small independent production directed by Fedor Ozep: *Three Russian Girls.* It was a remake of a Russian war film and starred Anna Sten. My work consisted mainly of providing snow exteriors on a stage that would be used to match the master shots of the original Russian film. Very few other sets were needed. As the film was made by an independent producer, I was not required to join the Art Directors Guild.

At this time Jean Renoir and Dudley Nichols had begun preparing *This Land Is Mine* for RKO. It was to be my first art director's credit for a feature film produced by a major Hollywood studio—although officially, I was to be called the film's "production designer."

Having recently escaped from Europe, Jean was well aware of the disturbing events in France. The country was under German domination, and the population was tragically divided—some collaborating with the Nazi invaders, others engaged in some form of resistance. Most people, however, tried to live day by day without taking part on either side. These conditions in prostrated Europe were a springboard for the projected film, which was basically a political melodrama specifically made to educate American audiences on the conditions in Europe. The film also presented a simple moral message about human dignity and praised the blessings of liberty. In spite of the obvious propaganda, *This Land Is Mine* was a very personal story told in human terms.

Charles Laughton played the part of Albert Lory, a middle-aged teacher in a small French town (although Jean and Dudley labeled the town as "somewhere in Europe"). Lory, a timid soul, dominated by his strong-willed mother, is secretly in love with his fellow teacher, Louise Martin (Maureen O'Hara). But Louise is engaged to Georges Lambert (George Sanders), the administrator of an important railroad depot. After sabotage occurs at the depot, the German commander, Major von Keller (Walter Slezak), orders ten town citizens to be taken hostage. They will be shot if the terrorist is not found or denounced. Lory is among the hostages. His mother (Una O'Connor), in a desperate rage, runs to Georges Lambert and tells him she has seen Paul, Louise's brother, sneaking home soon after the explosion. Lambert tells this to von Keller, who sends soldiers after Paul, and he is killed.

Lory is set free, but when he learns that his mother has informed, he rushes to confront Lambert. Lory arrives too late. Lambert, ashamed of his own cowardice, has committed suicide and Lory, found near Lambert's body, is accused of the murder. A jury trial could result in a public forum, so to prevent Lory's public denunciation of Nazi rule, von Keller visits him in prison with a proposal. If Lory keeps quiet at his court hearing, a fake suicide note will be found in Lambert's office, and Lory will be set free. But that same evening, from the prison window, Lory witnesses with horror the cold-blooded execution of the remaining hostages, among them Lory's beloved schoolmaster. The next day in court Lory finds moral strength and strikes out at the Nazi oppressors and their French collaborators. He is allowed to leave the courtroom, and no longer afraid of death, he returns to his classroom to await the arrival of Nazi soldiers who will execute him, not for the death of Lambert, but for his plea of liberty for free people.

Besides this rather simple, thematic situation (reminiscent of Alphonse Daudet's short story, "The Last Lesson"), the moral of the film lies in the personal story of the hero, an ever-frightened coward. Only after experiencing the cruelty and injustice of the oppressive Nazis does he revolt and find the courage to voice his anger. The quiet lamb becomes a battering ram—or, in Laughton's mind, a roaring lion.

The film was shot in the old RKO studio on Gower Street. I believe it was the first time that Dudley Nichols, a well-known screenwriter, assumed production chores for a film.

For some unknown reason, Al D'Agostino, the head of RKO's art department, decided against asking permission to admit me into the Motion Picture Art Directors Guild. Instead he offered me the more prestigious title of production designer, a position not controlled by the Guild. I was indifferent to the title. I only wanted to design and build the production for Renoir. Al d'Agostino explained that because of my inexperience in the Hollywood studio system, he would assign a full-fledged art director as my assistant. He was to be Walter Keller, who agreed to work under my supervision. Walter would share the art direction credits with Al D'Agostino, and my name would appear separately as production designer.

It was all right with me, but not with the Guild. At this time many well-known stage designers from New York were coming to Hollywood to design films. They worked outside Guild jurisdiction and were given a new title, "production designer." Some members of the Art Directors Guild were alarmed at this potential invasion of their profession.

And so one day I received a nice letter inviting me to join the Guild. Thus I became sanctified to work in my profession as an art director.

For me, designing and constructing sets in a Hollywood studio was quite similar to my French experience, but I met different rules. In Hollywood, for example, working drawings could not be handed directly by an art director to the construction department. I didn't have the right to make finished sketches of the sets; rather, the studio assigned a sketch artist or illustrator, so my sketches could be redrawn. In France, however, the art directors alone with their assistants made the working drawings for the set construction, no matter how schematic those drawings were to be. In cases of complicated sets or illustrated details, we occasionally used the help of architectural draftsmen. In all my designing of some fifty feature films in Europe, I do not remember more than twelve or fifteen for which I had to show sketches. These instances were mostly for historical films. In Hollywood productions, however, the presentation of sketches was an established procedure. Thus there evolved a special art of detailed paintings done by sketch artists or set illustrators, highly trained, able professionals, whose time was devoted solely to drawing perfect scene illustrations.

As many of the set details were not decided on at the time the illustrations were made, it was up to the sketch artist to suggest them, so it was crucial that the illustrator understand, almost intuitively, the art director's ideas.

The studios, however, selected the illustrator for a film haphazardly from whoever was available in the art department pool—not a particularly happy way to choose a collaborator for an art director. Set illustration is by no means a dry architectural rendering of walls, doors, and windows, but has to represent the subtle ambience of a set, reflecting the personality and mode of life of its inhabitants. Additionally the set illustration must show the mood of the set and the lighting effects.

Later on in my Hollywood career, I found many illustrators, close collaborators, whose contributions were helpful. I was happy to be able to work with them harmoniously, since the relationship between art director and illustrator, requiring compatibility of taste, cannot be that of boss and supplicant.

In addition to the custom of using set illustrators, the most radical departure in Hollywood from French production practices was the part played by the studio production office in what appeared to me to be basic set-designing decisions.

As an important part of the film *This Land Is Mine* took place in the streets of a small French town, I was confronted by a *dictat* from the production office: "We already have a French town built on our lot. You have to use it."

I was driven to the RKO ranch on Ventura Boulevard, and there I confronted the decaying sets for the medieval French streets built for *The Hunchback of Notre Dame.* The set was highly stylized in a pseudo-Gothic fashion akin to the illustrations of Gustave Doré. I was faced with the dilemma of how to use this set that was so wrong for Renoir's conception of our film, as well as my own. We wanted a nondescript, anonymous, contemporary French town where an average Frenchman lives his ordinary life. Our story was about such a man. And so I was looking for nothing out of the ordinary in a set, especially not an architectural extravaganza of the flamboyant Gothic style.

Across an empty lot from the Gothic church I saw an imposing front of a three-story building in a nondescript Renaissance style that could, in my opinion, be converted into the city hall of our town. The "Notre Dame" district was used only as a faraway roof line of chimneys and tiled roofs. Other houses served as structural supports for new façades I designed. Everyone was happy: the production office had their wishes fulfilled—I used their French town—and Renoir and I were happy at its nondescript look. Dudley was satisfied that by staying within our budget, we had worked for the good of the film.

The week before the start of shooting, Dudley, Jean, the cinematographer, the crew, and the usual production entourage gathered on the set. Some approximations of German tanks were rolling down the pavement. Jean proceeded to plan the action and camera set-ups. For the fluid coverage of German soldiers advancing on the streets, he decided to use a crane.

"But Jean," said Dudley, "I don't think you can have the crane. I didn't put it in the budget and I can't ask for it now."

Jean was definitely ruffled by his friend and producer's veto, but keeping his calm, he said, "Very well, I will change my way of shooting the scene, but to keep the unity of style, I will not use any traveling shots in the film at all."

To me, this interference by a producer in a director's decisions was something new. My own conflict with Dudley came about at the same time. While working, Renoir and I often discussed points of the script. As the theme of the film was sensitive to French consciences, we had some differences of opinion as to how Frenchmen would react to certain facts of the German occupation. I am unable to remember exactly what the discussion was about, but Dudley heard our voices coming from Jean's office. When I came out Dudley stopped me. "Gene," he said, "I do not want you to upset Jean during the preparation of the film. Maybe you shouldn't do the picture." It was an unexpected blow and unwarranted. I went back into Jean's office to tell him of Dudley's remark.

"Do not worry," said Jean. "I will explain to Dudley that sometimes friendly discussions among Frenchmen sound like disagreements."

"Other houses served as structural supports for new façades."

I continued to work on the film.

While I was designing the town street, we had to solve the problem of which language to use for signs and posters. Jean and Dudley opted for English, feeling that as all the French characters in the film spoke English, the signs should follow. Only the Germans in the film would speak their language.

As I remember, the shooting started on the set with the streets empty, as all the inhabitants were hiding behind their locked doors. The heavy steps of the advancing army reverberated on the empty pavement, the German infantry marching, the tanks rolling in front of the town monument to the dead of the previous war. The inscription on the monument was "1914–1918. In memory of those who died to bring peace to the world." It was a painfully ironic comment on the German invasion of 1940.

When I worked in France I had to age sets myself with a spray gun. I decided to do the same in Hollywood. Al D'Agostino was appalled. It was against union regulations. Finally Al agreed on condition that I work late in the afternoon and use a standby studio painter to assist me. One evening we finished our work late. I remained alone to decide which dressing would give the set a lived-in look. I heard the sound of steps coming from the stairway. It was late and no one was supposed to be on the stage. Then I saw Charles Laughton running up and down the steps of the set. When I asked him why he was doing this, he timidly replied that he was getting himself accustomed to the narrow stairway!

I had seldom met an actor who prepared his part so meticulously. On another set, however, his thoroughness created a bit of conflict. The only window in the set of the cell was placed high. Charles had to grab the iron bars of the window to look into the courtyard to see the execution of the hostages. To make the scene more expressive, he decided to shake the iron bars in despair. However the "iron" bars were built of wood. They couldn't withstand Laughton's vigorous shaking. Realizing the problem, he refused to play the scene.

"I cannot play this scene in Gene's flimsy set!"

It took all Renoir's authority to calm him down. Jean said, in essence, that being an actor, Laughton had to act and *pretend* to shake the bars without breaking the set. When Jean smilingly described this episode to me, I told him of my previous encounter with prison bars. It was in the French picture *Les Hommes nouveaux,* and in it Harry Baur was imprisoned in a Moroccan jail. To make the set visually interesting, I had made the jail part of an old vaulted fortress with barred openings between the cells. As usual, Marcel L'Herbier, the director, came to visit the set the day before shooting. He approved the set and liked the open view from one cell to another. Then an idea came to him of how to use the set "creatively."

"Imagine," he said to Alexander Kamenka, our producer, "how interesting it would be to put live lions in the cell next to Harry Baur."

Visibly impressed by L'Herbier's creativity, A. K. asked, "What do you think, Gene?"

I thought the set might collapse under the weight of the lions and the wooden bars might not be strong enough.

"You may have to risk your actor being eaten alive," I answered.

"Then what can be done?" asked A. K. "We have to shoot the scene tomorrow."

It took twenty carpenters all night to fortify the prison cell and install circus cages instead of wooden bars. Next day some mangy lions were brought in. They slept all day long and remained hidden, except at mealtime when they roared so loudly that sound recording became impossible.

This lion episode and the romantic exaggerations of the Moroccan set contrasted with the simple conception of the set in *This Land Is Mine.* It illustrated the basic difference in my approach to set design between the earlier French films and the period of my work with Renoir. In the early pictures, corresponding to the fashion of the time, my accent was on romantic exaggeration. In the later period my sets became more simplified, stripped of useless ornamentation.

In *This Land Is Mine,* I tried not to resort to an easy, pictorially cute "Frenchy" style. My sets reflected the trend of simplification in set design, influenced by a group of Renoir's friends of which I was a part. We simply abhorred the fashionable prettified restaurants done in the so-called "rustic" style, "Ye Old Village Inns" decorated with fake ceiling beams, a profusion of brass utensils, French Provincial sideboards, and checkered tablecloths.

So with the interiors as well as the streets. With Renoir's blessing I underlined simplicity and a sort of neutral nudity in the sets. I didn't want to distract viewers from the somber drama. In this case as in others, anonymous-looking sets better served the dramatic action.

To the distress of my set decorator, I banned all paintings from the walls and bric-a-brac from the mantelpieces. The wall clock was the only prominent prop, because it served Charles Laughton's actions.

An episode in the film called for a scene between Laughton and a young pupil going for a Sunday outing. They picnic in a meadow by a waterhole. Jean didn't want to go on location for such a short scene and asked me to build a landscape on stage, using perspective miniature for the background.

The usual method for a landscape set built on stage is to have some greenery—grass, trees, and bushes—in front of a painted backdrop. However, to paint an adequate backdrop is quite expensive, and Renoir favored my method of using background miniatures. They gave a more accurate feeling of life; the wind could move the leaves and the stage lighting was more controllable.

To build a miniature landscape is very pleasurable, but it also means special problems. It was almost impossible to find miniature trees, such as the bonsai trees grown by Japanese gardeners. Moreover, even the bonsai trees usually have gnarled, bizarrely textured trunks and odd, dwarfish shapes. They can seldom represent normal trees in diminishing scale. But searching very carefully through scores of trees and bushes, you can usually find some small specimens imitating the shape of full-grown trees. The attentive care of the RKO greens department helped me create the distant forest and glades of rural France.

Because of the narrow available stage space, I was obliged to place the actors very close to the miniature background representing, supposedly, a faraway vista. This proximity was a novelty for the art department and for our cinematographer, who feared the subterfuge would not work and the film would show the true distance between actors and the miniature trees.

However, I had previously used miniatures that were placed very close to the live action, and I knew that the visual illusion of distance could be obtained if the set were painted and lit according to the rules used by landscape painters. It is called aerial perspective and basically involves using lighter, more diffuse colors in the background and stronger contrasts in the foreground. I thought that seeing a horse roaming in the distant meadow would enhance the scene. The head of the optical effects department told me he could easily print, onto the meadow, a shot of a real horse reduced in size, and it would look right. For the first time in my designing career, I saw the traveling matte, in which moving objects are filmed against a light blue background. This filmed image is then printed onto a shot made separately—in this case, the miniature land-scape. Later I used this effect many times. It was also the first time I met the stuntman, an occupation that didn't exist in France.

Jean asked me to choose a footbridge above a railway and to stage a scene with a stuntman where he as Paul's double jumps from the bridge to the roof of a moving train. Thus I met a professional stuntman, who is still performing his daredevil acts some thirty years later.

My relations with Walter Keller, my helpful art director, were cordial. We struck a perfect understanding. So were my dealings with Al Fields, the set decorator, who quickly understood my intentions and came out with the right props for the set dressing.

However, some Hollywood procedures seemed strange to my French-trained eyes. In France we were accustomed to improvise solutions on the spur of the moment. For one scene we needed to show the set of an empty office, aban-doned for some time. I wanted dusty desks and asked the prop man who was working on the stage to gather up some dust—the floors were being swept up at this time—and scatter it on the desk tops. "Oh, no," was his answer, "dust-ing is the special effects jurisdiction." He made a telephone call and some twenty minutes later, a special effects man appeared. "What needs to be done?" he inquired. When told it was making some desks dusty, he disappeared and came back with a strange contraption that looked like a blower you would use to start a fire in a fireplace. He blew and out came a cloud of whitish powder that covered the set. It looked bad and had to be cleaned. This effect, which seemed so simple, took hours and became a major operation. To me, it was like hunt-ing a fly with an elephant gun.

I was amazed, though, by the loyalty each film crew had to their respec-tive studio, a Hollywood tradition that was new to me. I met some art direc-tors who remained with the same studio for all their professional lives. They would have found it inconceivable to change studios, to work, so to speak, under another flag. In Europe we tried hard to work with some preferred di-rectors or to choose films interesting in content or visual ambience. But in Hol-lywood I met designers working regardless of the film content, guided only by their loyalty to the studio. In my early Hollywood days studio art directors looked upon their independent colleagues with a condescending suspicion; they made me feel like one of the "irregular" intruders. This attitude changed in later years when the reign of big studios ended.

After our misunderstanding at the start of production, my relations with Dudley Nichols became cordial. He was a sincere, dedicated man who took his writing very seriously and regarded the results of his labor as unalterable. Usually he closeted himself in his office to write or rewrite a scene in a spirit of utter dedication. He emerged looking exhausted, brandishing the pages like Moses bringing the tablets from Mount Sinai. You knew that tampering with his text was impossible.

In spite of the basic difference in their personalities, the friendship between Jean and Dudley was sincere and strong. Charles Laughton also became strongly attached to Jean. Laughton was always on the lookout for him, and very often during lunch break, his voice would boom from his or Jean's dressing room, reciting long passages from Shakespeare or the Bible.

Shooting the film proceeded smoothly. All the actors were dedicated to their parts and genuinely touched by the suffering of characters they were playing. They seemed to be living their parts, following the friendly guidance of Renoir.

This Land Is Mine was finished in record time and released in the spring of 1943. In spite of the somewhat didactic theme, it met with success. The reception in France in 1946, however, was quite hostile. Frenchmen couldn't accept Renoir's description of the occupation, as he had not been there to endure it. They didn't see the intelligent, sincere attempt at comprehending the situation in an occupied country and describing it with sympathy and love. Also, it was probably impossible for a Frenchman to admit that a hero of the Resistance could be, after all, a coward.

For me, this picture was the first important film I worked on in Hollywood and the first with Renoir in the new surroundings of Hollywood studios, where I found the actual techniques of set construction were similar to methods used in France and also similar, as I experienced later, to those used in England, Sweden, Spain, or Italy.

SAHARA

I *was* finishing Jean Renoir's *This Land Is Mine* in 1942, when I got a call from Vincent Korda. Vincent was a very talented art director and practically the head of production at Alexander Korda's company, London Films. We had known each other a long time ago in Paris when we were both aspiring painters. The last time I had seen him was in Paris when he was preparing to leave for London to join his brother, Alex, the producer. Vincent was sad having to abandon Paris and his painting for art directing in London. I met him several times in London at Denham studios after I had also become an art director, having betrayed the "true art" as well. After the invasion of France I saw him in Hollywood, where he had designed *That Hamilton Woman* and *The Jungle Book.* Alex Korda had resumed production in London and asked Vincent to join him there. That was the reason he called me. Zoltan Korda, the youngest of the Korda brothers, was preparing a Hollywood production for Columbia

Pictures. Vincent was obliged to leave this project and would feel relieved if I joined Zoli as a friendly collaborator.

I met Zoltan, a handsome man who reminded me of a somber hero from the romantic era. The meeting was friendly, and he introduced me to his producer and production manager. It was a simple formality. I was also presented to Lionel Banks, the head of Columbia's art department, who was to share with me the credit for art direction. It was a Hollywood custom and quite new to me: the head of the art department would sign all the pictures produced by the studio and the actual art director would be given the title of associate. It really didn't matter to me, as long as I was given freedom of decision in designing the picture.

The idea for *Sahara* came from an episode in World War II during a battle between English troops and Germans during the invasion of North Africa. The story concerned the attempt of one tank and its American crew to escape from the Nazis and rejoin the British troops. On the way, the crew is joined by remnants of defeated English detachments. Their adventurous journey through the desert, their hardships, and their final confrontation with a German detachment form the core of this grim war picture.

As in all war pictures, *Sahara* had to have the immediacy, the stark reality of a newsreel—or of today's television reporting from the battlefront. We saw it also as a film of heroic adventure imbued with romantic feeling, like a quest from the sagas of knighthood. Already in my preliminary conversations with Vincent Korda, I understood that with Zoltan we would have to follow the romantic tradition of his former films—such as *Four Feathers, Drums of India, Thief of Baghdad,* even *The Jungle Book.*

I kept in mind this dual nature of *Sahara* during the first scouting trip to the desert to check out some locations suggested by the production department. I was happy to make the trip with Zoltan Korda and Rudy Maté, whose camera work I had greatly admired in Carl Dreyer's European masterpieces, *The Passion of Joan of Arc* and *The Vampires.*

As we drove into the desert, I knew what we were looking for. We had to find not *any* desert but a *certain* kind of desert, especially akin to our idea of the film—a characteristic difficult to define, since an idea of this sort is intangible. However, all three of us—Zoltan, Rudy Maté, and I—agreed that we were looking for ways to emphasize the insignificance of men against the immensity of the desert: the hostile vastness of sand dunes and the smallness of men; a melancholic vision of an abandoned, half-ruined Moslem shrine—a mere speck lost in a sea of sand.

The most promising location we found was the desert along the Salton Sea. It had grandeur created by a combination of dark rocks and sand dunes, and it was also conveniently close to the town of Brawley where the company could stay.

Our second scouting trip some time later, to pinpoint specific locations, was quite an elaborate affair. We had Zoltan Korda, the director; the production manager, Gordon Griffith; the unit manager, Norman Cook; Lionel Banks; the location men; two assistant directors; the grip master; Freddy Woolf, the special effects master; other assorted technicians; and our three drivers for two limousines and one bus. I was new in Hollywood, and this entourage seemed like a lot of people to me compared with the few we used in Europe, where I would scout alone or with my assistant or sometimes with the director.

Looking for actual locations, we stopped on the highway some thirty miles short of Brawley. From this point on we had to proceed into the desert on foot. Our progress became slow as we came to the sand dunes. Very soon the faint-hearted members of our party were left behind, the eager assistants, the unit manager, and I bravely following the indefatigable Zoli.

Two miles later we were alone, Zoli and I. From a ways back, I saw signals of distress from our unit manager. Choosing a location so far from the highway and in sandy terrain seemed utterly impractical to him. Zoli plowed ahead. However, I remembered that earlier in our walk we had crossed a very sandy depression that was surrounded by black crusty rocks. I guided Zoli back, and to the satisfaction of everyone, we planted our markers there. I still faced the necessity of building a practical road through two miles of sand to accommodate our heavy equipment. But I didn't know then how easy this task would become when the army engineers attached to our film joined us.

I don't know exactly how we got the army's cooperation. It was wartime.

Left: *"I decided to build the set with real adobe bricks."* Lourie's sketch of the abandoned shrine.

The finished shrine.

But I heard that after three days of pleading, Gordon Griffith, the Columbia production manager, persuaded General Patton's staff that our film would be a morale builder and would provide useful, practical training for all the units involved.

We decided, along with Zoli, that the shooting would be done entirely on location. We would build a temporary, tarpaulin-walled, taped-in studio for interiors and shoot there during spells of bad weather.

The main set I had to build was the half-ruined, abandoned Moslem shrine. These desert monuments are usually made of sun-baked bricks, called adobe. When building this type of set on stage, the usual procedure would have been to use cast staff (plaster cast in a wire form) molded as the surface of the adobe walls. I remembered, however, the magnificent look of real adobe ruins in the desert, etched by wind and drifting sand. I couldn't obtain this effect of erosion by using staff.

So I decided to build the set with real adobe bricks, which, by the way, were still the prevailing building material in Mexico and the southwestern states at that time. The bricks would be easy to erode and were easy to make. You mix some clay with straw and water, pack the mixture in wooden forms, and leave them to dry in the sun.

But after conferring, my construction foreman and I realized time was short; it was late in the season and the nights were cold. The adobe would not harden and we wouldn't be ready in time. Then nature came to our rescue. A year earlier the Imperial Valley had suffered a strong earthquake. Many adobe buildings had been destroyed and abandoned. Pretty soon we found ourselves in the demolition business, buying half-destroyed houses and sending our laborers to remove damaged walls, brick by brick. Soon trucks were arriving daily, heavily loaded with our building material, and the construction of the Moslem shrine set progressed nicely. I surrounded the shrine with ruined adobe walls to create protection for the sharpshooters repelling the attacking Germans. I also built niches and recesses, convenient sites for hiding and overhearing secret conversations between German prisoners.

After the shrine set was completed, we erected frames for the temporary tarpaulin stage right behind it.

It was not difficult to build these sets, even though we were working far from studio facilities. Certainly being outdoors all day in the dry desert air was enjoyable. We all felt somehow like Boy Scouts on a merit-badge building project. However, nature played some tricks on us. One morning it seemed more windy than usual. As we drove to the location, the wind became a sandstorm. We all had goggles, but we couldn't walk or even stand erect against the strong gusts of wind. There was no chance of working. The storm lasted three days. When we could finally return to our location, I saw that the entire sand dune, the most important element of our set, had been blown away. Instead of sand there was a hard, dark mica crust on the bare ground. The shiny mica surface was beautiful to look at but impossible for the requirements of our story. Faced with this unexpected problem and the impossibility of changing locations, I decided to haul sand from the shores of the Salton Sea. Four trucks making four trips daily would bring us forty-eight tons of sand a day. In ten days, I calculated, we would have more sand than we started with.

Meanwhile one of the army units assigned to our picture arrived with bulldozers, half-tracks, sixteen men, and Lieutenant Smith from the army engineers. The road to the highway was quickly completed. I learned then to appreciate the working capacity of the bulldozer. One day when I was examining possible shooting angles around the shrine, I noticed that one of the surrounding hillocks hid too much of the desert view. I mentioned this to the lieutenant, who was standing nearby. He said, "We will see what we can do about it." The next evening the entire hillock was removed by the engineers' bulldozers.

At this time, when I was alone in Brawley with the crew, I had very little social contact. Life in the "Grand Hotel" of Brawley was prosaic and monotonous. Once in a while Zoltan visited us to check on the progress of the set. Sometimes, Rudy Maté appeared with his crew and a portable darkroom. He made numerous camera tests using different filters and exposures. Otherwise it was lonesome. Happily the public library was opposite the hotel and open quite late. There I learned all about the history of the Imperial Valley and its desert environment, which offered us a continual change of scene and a great deal of amusement.

We made daily trips to the location in the early morning, always freezingly cold, and on each roadpost we would see a tiny sleeping owl. Our digging in the ground often disturbed sidewinders, small rattlesnakes heavy with winter slumber. We also caught funny little horned toads, bizarre desert lizards shaped like tiny dragons. I heard that Mexican ladies kept them as house pets. I didn't try that, but I often held the lizards, and they did remain amazingly quiet in the palm of my hand. Then, as always after the heavy winter dews, solitary flowers popped out of the sand.

When I needed a place to work, I transformed the table in my hotel room into a primitive drawing board. Evenings I usually spent in the library across the street or at the local cinema house, watching Mexican movies without understanding the dialogue. It was there I became acquainted with Cantinflas, whose brazen naïveté reminded me so much of Charlie Chaplin.

Weekend trips to Los Angeles were not taken often. Sometimes Mike, my construction foreman, was drunk on weekends. At those times he became talkative and sentimental. Coming back from the cinema one evening, I ran into him. He had some flowers in his hand, and he was going to the open desert, some twenty miles from town, to gather more flowers that were growing in the moonlit dunes.

"Gene," he said, "the desert is so beautiful at night."

I also went for some rides in a tank, and for weeks I wore black marks on my ribs, bruises I got when the tank driver convinced me of the pleasure of traveling in a tank over desert ridges and gullies.

Soon more and more technicians reported to Brawley. The special effects crew established its workshop. Grips stretched tarps on the frame of the temporary stage.

The shrine was in the final stage of construction—the delicate task of building the rounded dome. This was a tricky job. We had to make the dome self-supporting without internal wooden bracings, since the script called for an explosion and partial destruction of the shrine to be seen in action and I couldn't risk the discovery of the wooden skeleton while the dome was collapsing.

For many sequences inside the tank we decided to build a mock-up of the tank's interior. Military regulations were strict. No still pictures were allowed

Eugene Lourie with one of his carpenters. The desert along the Salton Sea near Brawley, California, in 1943.

of the tank's interior. Drawings, yes; photographs, no. I telephoned Lionel Banks and he dispatched a draftsman to Brawley, who carefully measured and designed every detail inside the tank. The studio prop shop had to duplicate the complicated agglomeration of screws, bolts, wires, manometers, and levers. As it happened, when the finished mock-up arrived some five weeks later, one look was sufficient to see that we couldn't possibly use it. It was impossible for studio technicians to reproduce the fine metal details in wood. Every detail was thicker than the original. But somehow we managed to get around the difficulty. You see, while the regulations wouldn't allow *still* pictures, they made no mention of *motion* pictures. The usual paradox of military regulations. So we shot all the interior scenes inside the real tank on our tarped-in stage. We had some difficulties lighting the confined space, but there were no concessions to the reality of the tank's interior.

We were finishing the set construction ahead of schedule, and I was satisfied with the amount of sand covering all approaches to the shrine, when we were hit by a second sandstorm. Once more all the sand was blown away. The interminable procession of trucks started again—bringing sand, bringing sand.

Meanwhile I chose the location for the early scene of the desolated battlefield covered with useless heaps of disabled tanks and equipment. I made a scale map and marked on it the placements of disabled cannons, destroyed military vehicles, and half-burned, mangled corpses. I also very carefully marked and numbered the exact places of the explosions and traced the path that Humphrey Bogart and Bruce Bennett would have to take when they ran from their hiding place beneath the overturned truck to their tank.

Zoli was now permanently in Brawley. He okayed my disposition of the battlefield, and with the special effects men I proceeded to place markers on the spots assigned on my drawings. With army cooperation guns and equipment were put into places. Laborers dug holes in the ground and special effects men buried mortars for explosives, then pulled innumerable wires from their control boards to each explosion site.

All the technicians and actors were now in Brawley. Finally Bogart appeared with his ironic grin and slightly tipsy wife. The next day we had our final rehearsals with explosions, smoke, and all the effects. Then we put the cameras in place. Zoli was on a platform, dominating the battlefield like a captain on his bridge. In front of him was my map of the field with the numbers of the explosions marked. Next to him was the electrical board for Freddy Woolf, the head of special effects.

He explained to Zoli, "It's like playing the piano. You hit the number and the explosion goes."

Zoli said, "Let's rehearse with the principals. Are you ready, Rudy?"

Bogie and Bruce took their places and rehearsed again the secure path they would be taking amidst the explosions. The timing and placing of the explosions were carefully worked out to look dangerous, without really being dangerous. It looked perfect, in theory.

It was time to shoot the scene. Everything was ready, everyone in his place. The assistant shouted, "Camera!" Zoli shouted, "Action!"

Bogie and Bruce started running.

Zoli said, "Explosion number three!"

Number seven exploded, just in front of the running actors, peppering them with debris and almost blowing off their legs.

Red-faced, the special effects crew could not explain this accident, but it was clear it would take several days to recheck and rewire the entire battlefield. At that point, Zoli decided the shooting next day would start with another sequence, without explosions.

According to the new schedule, the first day of shooting would be of the film's final scene where the German prisoners, escorted by the tank, met the English rescue column. Apart from the principals, the shot included tanks, half-tracks, and some 400 extras as marching soldiers.

Everyone assembled in the morning, and Korda wanted to begin shooting; but Rudy Maté was not satisfied with the flat light on the dunes. He wanted to shoot much later in the day, when the shadows would give relief to the desert. Zoli was adamant. He could not wait, not on the first day of shooting. The results of this first day were too important to him because he had unfortunately made some powerful enemies in the hierarchy of Columbia, including his star, Bogie. Bogie in fact was not on speaking terms with him—and Zoli knew the reason. As I heard later, Bogart had promised the direction of *Sahara* to a friend of his, a Hungarian director. But despite Bogart's high standing and influence at Columbia, he was unable to switch directors for the film, since Korda had the legal rights to the story. The rumor was that Bogart's director friend had his suitcases packed and he was ready to come to Brawley at a moment's notice to replace Zoli. Therefore it was important for Zoli to show good results of the first day of shooting. Production heads were usually poor judges of film quality, especially when they saw only the rushes. The important thing to them was, "How many pages of script has this director shot today?"

Rudy, still dissatisfied with the flatness of light on the dunes, decided to paint shadows. And so we observed the strange spectacle of two painters advancing farther and farther into the desert painting shadows with a Hudson spray gun as some 500 actors, extras, and technicians watched. Zoli bit his lip and looked at his watch as the time passed. Finally shooting started and proceeded very smoothly and successfully. The British column met with the victorious tank. Shots, close shots, reverses, everything in the schedule was accomplished before the winter sun went down.

Meanwhile life became organized in the *Sahara* colony, having changed considerably when actors and technicians arrived. Living in faraway Brawley knit us together. Queuing up in front of the lunch wagon or waiting in the sun between takes made us friendly and communicative. We were like strangers on a train, telling each other our life stories on our short trip together. But in the evenings social life was quite limited. The hours were often passed in the bowling alley or around a billiard table in the bareness of a Mexican bar.

Zoltan, most of the technicians, and all the actors were lodged in the "Grand Hotel" of Brawley, except for Rex Ingram. Being a black, Rex was not welcome in the hotel. Times were different then. The production rented a bungalow for Rex. It was a charming place and I think he had a better deal than we did. His stand-in kept him company and took care of the cooking. Sometimes Zoltan and I had delightful dinners there.

The atmosphere in the hotel was not as peaceful. Bogart was often "under the influence" and brawls between him and Mayo Methot, his wife, often reverberated in the hotel corridors. Bogie openly despised Zoli, which certainly didn't help to create a congenial atmosphere.

But shooting of the film continued. While the special effects crew was still rewiring the battlefield, we shot scenes of the escaping tank and its meeting with the first group of defeated British troops.

In the dark twilight of the desert, the tank is stopped by a group of stragglers. In the fading light we can make out the gangling silhouette of an English major and some stooped figures of exhausted British soldiers.

Thus started the odyssey of the escaping tank and its diverse crew. The lighting of this sequence suggested a somber premonition of the hazardous adventure; and on the following days, we made montage shots, repeated passages of the tank advancing through the murky air and sand drifts—a strange silhouette overloaded with injured or dying soldiers on its top and gun turrets. These images were a result of the brilliant camera work of Rudy Maté whose subtle use of lighting, filters, and diffusions made his chiaroscuro composition like a Rembrandt painting. And the quality of his black and white camera work kept the same pictorial intensity throughout the film. I understood then the reasons for Maté's repeated trips to the desert for photographic tests. In *Sahara,* more than in any other film, I worked for every set-up in close concert with the director and cameraman.

We finally shot the battlefield sequence. Bogart and Bruce Bennett ran heroically between the explosions as extras lay scattered here and there, realistically imitating dead soldiers. All the explosions and smoke went off on the right signal. The take was perfect. The next day the army took possession of the guns and gear and departed, leaving us with our tank, a reduced number of engineers, and Lieutenant Smith. The company moved to the principal location, the ancient grave and our tarped-in studio.

Working on location, living in the same hotel, and eating from the same caterer's wagon, as I've mentioned, created a bond among all of us. The only thing that spoiled this idyllic life during the first weeks of shooting was the continuing animosity between Bogart and Zoli. Communication between them was usually through an assistant. One day Bogart told an assistant, "Ask that little man"—meaning Zoli—"ask that little man where I must move for this shot." Zoli overheard him. Losing his self-control, he took out his pocketknife. It was a big Hungarian knife that Zoli usually used for whittling. Zoli looked straight at Bogie and said loudly, "Bogie, the next time I hear you speaking about me like that, I will cut you to pieces. I will cut you like I am cutting a Hungarian sausage!" He sounded very menacing and terribly serious. Bogie was probably taken aback. Anyhow, from this moment on his attitude changed.

The day after this confrontation Zoli was seated at his chessboard waiting for the camera crew to prepare the next set-up. Bogie, also a chess addict, observed with interest. "Zoli," he said, "would you like to play a game with me?" They played all day long, between each take. They continued playing back at the hotel. You see, Bogie was losing every game and the more he lost, the more he was determined to show his mastery. From this day on they played chess often. Peace prevailed.

In the movie the entire tank journey is made in quest of the well. The men finally find it next to the abandoned shrine, but the well is almost dry. Only a few drops of water ooze from the walls of the well from time to time. It is quite a sequence with many set-ups. We had to show the sergeant, played by Rex Ingram, climbing down the deep, dark well; we had to shoot inside at the bottom of the well where he looked for water, and we had to shoot up from the bottom to show other members of the party looking down into the well. In short, we had to be able to shoot up and down inside the well. Using normal studio technique, we would have built a high scaffolding to support the armature of the shaft. The surface of the shaft would then be covered with sheets of staff, imitating the rough dirt texture. A solid platform on top of this construction would serve for the group of actors seen from the bottom of the well, silhouetted against the sky.

Mike, my construction foreman, started to calculate how much lumber we would need for the well's construction. I had, however, a much simpler idea. Not far from our shrine were several hillocks, about forty feet high. By gouging out a shaft from the flank of a hillock, I had a ready-made well shaft of dug-out earth. The upper part of the shaft was finished all around with a sort of wicker basket, as is done in Africa to protect shafts from collapsing and from drifting sand. Thus we no longer needed complicated scaffolding to support a platform for actors and cameras on top of the wall. We built a simple platform on top of the hillock above the well shaft. The sides of the shaft were open so that we could follow, with the camera, the actor climbing down. The lower part of the well on the ground level was also open to the camera, but tarped in and mysteriously dark. Creating the dripping water was the easiest part of the problem. The interior of the well was built conveniently close to the exterior of the shrine. The top view of the mouth of the well was dug out separately from the shaft near the shrine, for which we dug a hole in the ground about eight feet deep, allowing the sergeant to start climbing down the well.

For the dramatic episode where Bruce Bennett has to abandon his jeep on his way to seek the British positions and later gets lost in drifting sand, I couldn't find nearby the sort of high, impressive sand dunes needed for the sequence. I went to the famous dunes at Yuma, Arizona, a classic location for Hollywood desert scenes and about a two-hour drive from Brawley. I found the right place for the sequence, and later on the company arrived with wind machines. We shot the sequence where Bruce painfully crawls up against the sand, collapses exhausted, and is finally rescued by a passing British patrol.

Now we had to shoot the scene where the tank arrived at the shrine during a sandstorm. In addition to the two strong sandstorms during the construction of the set, we had one more during the shooting, two days of heavy storm. In fact, our idea of using the tarped-in stage for shooting during bad weather didn't work. The storm was too strong to allow us to travel to our location, and the noise of the wind was overpowering. I asked Rudy Maté if we could take advantage of this impressive storm and shoot it.

"Definitely not. I will not take the camera out of the case. The lenses would be spoiled forever." When the weather was quiet and the desert serene, we had to create our own controlled storm, blowing sand—sawdust—exactly where we wanted it to blow. I met an almost similar problem years later when I was shooting a sequence of *Gorgo* in Ireland. I was marooned with Freddy Young, our cameraman, and all his crew in a lighthouse at the end of a jetty in the port of Dun Laoghaire near Dublin. The storm was terrific. Waves splashed high above the jetty. The port authorities ordered us to stay put until the storm and tides subsided. Tossed impressively by the mountainous waves, a freighter tried to approach the port. It was exactly like a scene described in the script. I thought it would be a good chance to catch the scene. "No way," was Freddy's reply. Later on I had to shoot the scene with a miniature ship in a studio tank.

I found that if actors had to show some physical difficulty, as if moving against wind, for instance, the art director could help by creating a real obstacle for them to move against. In the scene of the tank arriving during the sandstorm, we artificially created such a strong storm that actors really had to fight for each step against sand whipped up by our seven airplane propellers. Each propeller had a chute feeding a continuous flow of sand and sawdust. Four laborers per machine were constantly shoveling sand into the wind. The result was more effective than a real storm, but limited in the area and direction of the wind. The actors really had a hard time fighting their way against the sand, but Rudy's lenses remained intact.

I also learned how to use the airplane propellers as a tool for effectively aging the desert set. Instead of throwing sand with shovels to simulate drifted dunes, I used the wind machines. In this way I partially buried the tank and created hillocks of sand against the walls of the shrine. Blown by the wind, the sand shaped itself very naturally, and blown into crevices between eroded adobe bricks, created desert aging.

Including the preliminary time we spent in the desert, it took almost five months to film *Sahara*. It was the first time I had been on location for an entire picture.

During the months of filming, after the peace overture of the first chess game, Bogart and Zoltan spent many evenings and sometimes nights around the chessboard. My boyhood recollections of Russian Revolutionary days drew smiles from Bogie and provoked Zoltan to long conversations.

In our isolation in the Salton Sea desert, we were not unlike the diverse crew of the tank in our film. The same kind of conversations occurred among the film crew as among the dregs of the battlefields assembled on our lost tank. My carpenter expressed bewilderment about the aims of the raging war as did the Italian prisoner, played in the film by Carrol Naish, who refused to understand why at the end of his life he had to run limping in the blazing desert like some rabbit, instead of sitting in his village in front of a bottle of wine.

However temporary, friendships grew warm between members of our company.

But the most rewarding result of our toiling together was my relationship with Zoli and my confidence in him. Our friendship grew and remained strong in the years to come. Zoltan's method of working with actors was characterized by unobtrusive suggestion and encouragement. At this time he suffered from severe back pains. But they didn't alter his patience, perseverance, and meticulous attention to detail.

Remaining his friend was rewarding. I kept the privilege of his confidence, and we often discussed the projects of films he had in mind: *Cry the Beloved Country, The Macomber Affair,* and others.

I was amazed by his self-inflicted sufferings in trying to solve some particularly recalcitrant script problems. He approached these scripts with the same tenacity he applied to chess problems. I remember many months discussing the improbable solution of *The King's General* by Daphne du Maurier, a story unsolvable because of its basic premises. Prodded by difficulties, Zoltan stubbornly looked for solutions.

In spite of our mutual desire to work together on another film, the occasion came only much later when I designed the production of a film based on Aldous Huxley's story, *The Giaconda Smile,* which Universal pundits later entitled *A Woman's Vengeance.*

7

THE IMPOSTER

My *involvement* with *The Imposter* has an ironic prologue. Before the war Julien Duvivier was one of the most interesting and best-known directors in France. I had often met with him, but we had never worked together. After the Nazi invasion of France, when I finally arrived in New York, my prospects for the future were uncertain. I had already become a well-established art director in France, and Hollywood seemed to be my logical destination. But in New York I was able to find work, and was successfully designing advertisements for *Vogue* and similar publications. But I still wanted to go to Hollywood. Duvivier was also in New York, so I met with him and asked his advice on finding work in Hollywood. He sincerely dissuaded me. "Hollywood is a terrible place. They will not let you in the union. You will be lost there certainly. Believe me. Hollywood will be a deception." That conversation took place in November 1941 . . .

Less than two years later I was sitting in Duvivier's office at Universal Pictures where he asked me to design his next picture, *The Imposter*.

The story takes place in France at the beginning of the war. A guillotine is being erected in a prison yard. A man will be executed at dawn for murder. The prisoner, Jean Gabin, is awakened and led to a cell where he meets with the warden, a guard, and a priest. He spitefully refuses the spiritual help of the priest. The guard cuts off the prisoner's shirt collar, the usual ritual before a beheading. German airplanes bombard the town. A bomb destroys the prison, burying the warden, the guard, and the priest under the stone debris. The prisoner is alive. He climbs down the smoking ruins, escapes from the prison, and flees the town during the panicky turmoil in the streets.

Alone on a country road, he is given a ride in a military truck filled with soldiers of the departing French army. They are going south with the hope of embarking for Africa where the French resistance is being organized against the German invasion. German planes strafe the roads. The truck is hit, and once again the prisoner is miraculously saved. He climbs out of the overturned truck amid the corpses of the soldiers. Alive, alone. He decides to shed his identity, dresses in a dead soldier's uniform, and steals his identification papers.

The waterfront in the port city of Saint-Jean de Luz is crowded with disorganized French soldiers. Gabin embarks with the other soldiers, feeling security in the crowd. Once in Africa he plans to go his own way. However, without any money, he finds himself once again in the company of soldiers and is sent with a small detachment to man a solitary post somewhere in the jungles of equatorial Africa. Reluctantly at first he joins the life of his companions and little by little finds friendship with the men and respect for himself. He saves the life of his commanding officer and is promoted. Now it seems that he can make a new identity for himself.

However, he cannot escape the past. He is denounced as an imposter by a friend of the soldier whose identification papers he stole. He decides not to try a possible escape that is offered to him. Judged and demoted in rank, he voluntarily joins an advance combat unit and is killed.

This plot sounds like a highly melodramatic soap opera. But directed real-

THE IMPOSTER. *Gabin as Clement.*

Ralph Morgan (extreme left); Julien Duvivier (third from left); Gabin; Michael Kalatzov, a representative from the Soviet Union (fourth from right); Lourie; Paul Ivano (second from right); Levi Strauss, associate producer (extreme right).

istically by Duvivier with sensitive detailing of characters, it comes alive. In fact, it bears the typical Duvivier touch—the exploitation of outrageous situations in a vein similar to that of Victor Hugo's novels. And I must say, I think Duvivier wrote much of the script himself because it had all the touches of his writing. He was a very sentimental man beneath his gruff exterior.

The production of the film presented many problems. Universal's production department estimated the cost of filming the first draft of the script, then returned it to Julien for drastic revisions. They simply would not make the picture unless they could do it much less expensively.

Julien said he was happy to have me on board and told me about the budgeting problems. He was eager to make this picture, but he didn't want to change the script at all. He asked me to work out practical solutions to the problem sequences. In other words, he didn't want to change the substance of the film, but he wanted to find a cheaper way of shooting.

It happens very often in Hollywood that when studio production departments make preliminary estimates of new projects, they often inflate them to protect themselves, not yet knowing how the problems can be solved practically. That is probably what happened with *The Imposter.* They read, for example, that "the streets of French towns were crowded with incessantly moving soldiers and equipment"; that "the waterfront of Saint-Jean de Luz was filled with soldiers, trucks, and equipment waiting to be boarded, the steamers moored to the wharf or anchored in the roads." Reading such a sequence alone would terrify any production department.

It was my task to find ways to shoot this sequence without inflating the budget or sacrificing the visual content of the scenes. I presented my ideas to Julien. We analyzed them, found them workable, and came up with estimates much lower than the projected figures. We had a meeting with Frank Murphy, the studio manager; John Goodman, the sympathetic head of the art department; and others. Soon we got the green light for the project. *The Imposter* was on its way.

To arrive at a realistic budget for the problem sequence just mentioned, I analyzed it and divided it into separate parts. First was the French town crowded with the military exodus. I decided to use one of the existing Universal sets in its outdoor complex of so-called "European streets." The houses on these streets were in a bad state of repair and would require carpentry, paintwork, and new signs. But by placing the camera high, you wouldn't see the major defects of the streets. You would only see the cobblestone pavement and the narrow, crooked outlines. We decided to place the camera on a forty-foot tower. I also left the roofs as they were; they didn't bother me since I had decided to complete the frame of the set beyond the outline of the street, using a painted matte of the roof view of a small French town with a smoke-filled horizon.

The second part, the waterfront of Saint-Jean de Luz, was the budget's main stumbling block. The "European street" had an arched plaza that was somewhat similar to the plaza of the French town. Again I planned to put the camera on a high platform. In fact, for this shot we used the roof of one of the adjacent buildings. The plaza was to be filled to capacity with soldiers and military trucks. Seen from above, the tarp-covered trucks did not require any semblance of authenticity. The entire view, shot with a wide-angle lens, would occupy the bottom quarter of the frame. In other words, this complete frame would be reduced to occupy one-quarter of the frame. Then, after moving the camera but keeping the required perspective, we would again shoot the same view, the same vehicles and soldiers, in a slightly different position. This view would occupy the second quarter of the frame. Thus the lower half of our frame, the two quarters, would be filled with a double amount of extras and vehicles. The upper half of the frame would be completed by a painted matte of the sea and ships, with drifting smoke added to create movement.

In the final editing of the film this scene is quite short, but essential in establishing the locale. The shot was composed like a mosaic: inserting elements of live shots and adding a painted matte. It successfully served its purpose; a complex scene could be shot within the limits of our budget. It goes without saying that had this sequence been realized on location, with real ships moored in the harbor, with thousands of soldiers and authentic military vehicles, it could have been shot with much more camera coverage and detail. Cameras could have moved through the crowd, and the director could have satisfied his ego by inventing new angles on traveling cranes. In conceiving and realizing *The Imposter,* we were bound by the discipline of cameras placed in one spot.

Sketch of the French street. The roadway was shot on the Universal back lot, then the town's roofs were added later with a matte shot.

Duvivier knew exactly what he wanted and the resulting shot was all that was necessary for this short scene. At this time the superfluous luxury of unlimited budgets was not yet in fashion.

The third portion of the scene was the shot of the embarking soldiers climbing the gangplank. We decided to use extras and shoot the scene on location in San Pedro with real shops and real gangplanks.

But the action on the deck of the ship was to be shot on the Universal lot against a sky backing or with a traveling matte background of the rolling sea. This sequence was subsequently shot as planned.

Another problem scene occurred at the beginning of the picture: the explosion and destruction of the prison and Gabin's escape. Again I divided the scene into components. First was the set of the cell, where the shirt-collar cutting ritual took place. This set was built on stage, like a normal set. The action here would continue through the explosion. When the entire scene was obliterated by smoke and falling debris, we would make a lap dissolve to another set that was already built, a similar cell but partially destroyed and covered with debris. This set was to be built high on the top of the multileveled ruins of the prison because Duvivier wanted to make Gabin's escape more dramatic. Gabin doesn't just step out of the ruins of his cell; he has to climb down the ruins of the prison to escape.

The action would start with the overlapping explosions and Gabin would be found alive in the destroyed cell. He would then climb down the smoky ruins of the prison to the floor level, where in the background would be a backing that showed the burning street.

At this time Universal studios had a very relaxed atmosphere, like a country club. Art directors, a friendly bunch, were dispersed in different buildings and cubicles of the studio. My office was in an old building called "The Bullpen." Bob Florey had the same office years earlier, and he told me how he used to inspect the office every morning and sometimes chase out a rattlesnake.

The drafting room occupied a large office on the ground floor facing the main passageway of the studio. At the time we were preparing *The Imposter*, young Shelley Winters would often run between the dressing rooms and the stage. The draftsmen would abandon their boards, rush to the window, and whistle in unison.

The cafeteria was open all day long, and the barbershop offered both haircuts and tips on horseraces.

Working with Duvivier was fun; he quickly understood my proposed shortcuts in set conceptions and accepted them. His associate producer, Levi-Strauss, an even-tempered, portly man, would smooth relations with the production office, as well as obtain the stages and facilities.

Jean Gabin was an old acquaintance from France and we had worked on several films together, including *The Lower Depths, Grand Illusion,* and *The Human Beast.*

The jungle compound was one of our most important sets. Out of many possible locations, we chose the so-called "Sherwood Forest" set in the San Fernando Valley. It was profusely wooded. I liked the constant back light on this location, which would give us the mysterious mood of the jungle. However, to create a steaming, tropical jungle out of this growth of green oaks presented a problem. We had to order some thirty large tree ferns from Hawaii, as they were unavailable in California. We had to manufacture hundreds and hundreds of yards of artificial lianas and wild orchids. We gathered every kind of tropical plant available for rental. I decided to have in the glade a bamboo grove that would catch the strong sunlight. It would create contrast between the light bamboo and the dark of the trees. As we were shooting in black and white, I had to think constantly about the interplay between the dark tones of the shadowed areas and the contrasts of the sunlit branches of light foliage. In color photography, the difference in colors makes the picture; in black and white, it is the difference between dark and light areas.

In the 1980s we are accustomed to seeing color; to look at black and white photography has become a novelty. In fact, many directors today seem to use black and white to give a special feeling to their films.

I decided to build some huge banyan tree trunks, with their complicated hanging and crawling roots. And finally we had to build the isolated military post, "Camp De Gaulle." Building a green set demands constant supervision.

The preliminary drafting can only indicate the approximate placement of trees and plants. Obviously trees come in different shapes and sizes. You have to improvise continually, composing and arranging the greens in relation to the light and to each other. You have to create zones of darkness and play the light elements against them. You have to hang lianas in front of dark masses of foliage, for example. During the construction of the jungle set, I had to leave early each morning to work with the construction crew.

Between Universal studios and our location ran Ventura Boulevard, a forty-minute drive along continuous walnut orchards. There were no houses then. Along the entire way I remember only one small coffee shop where we stopped, shivering, at seven in the morning.

By being on location every day from early morning until late afternoon, I could observe the changing light in the forest. I felt the darkness of certain hours was too much for the camera, so I decided to make photographic tests.

One morning we set out with Paul Ivano, our cameraman, his crew, and some special effects men. Our jungle was definitely too dark and the succession of plants had become one single mass. We decided to use low-lying ground fog to soften the background and create more separation between the trees. Using fog was like putting a separation filter between one layer of trees and another. It became an invaluable asset to our black and white photography. The jungle acquired depth and mystery. Sometimes I even added hanging cobwebs to create a natural-looking screen.

One of the first scenes in the jungle set was the arrival of our soldiers. The scene starts with a close shot of three monkeys on a branch, shot from a high camera. The monkeys, visibly excited by the unusual happening, had to chatter excitedly. The camera had to pan down toward the advancing column of trucks proceeding through the jungle. It looked very easy on paper. However, the monkeys decided otherwise. Despite the wild gesturing and shouting of their trainer, the monkeys did not react. They didn't chatter. They weren't excited. They totally ignored everything. Time passed and the light changed. Paul Ivano had to change the position of the reflectors; the electricians had to change the carbons in their arcs; Julien looked at his watch and decided to change his way of shooting the scene. The camera would shoot the advancing trucks from the point of view of the monkeys. The monkey reaction shot would be done at another time without involving the entire column of trucks and actors. It was decided to do the monkey shot the next day with some new monkeys to replace the reluctant ones. Julien asked me to take care of it. This monkey business was to become my first directorial assignment. I took the shot first thing the next morning.

Duvivier and I understood each other instantly, and his grasp of my proposals simplified our work and made our collaboration enjoyable. Strangely enough, however, Duvivier had the reputation of being a misanthrope, difficult to deal with, cuttingly sardonic, and dictatorial in his treatment of actors and technicians.

I think one reason for this reputation was his impatience with people who didn't immediately understand his decisions or the reasons behind them. Maybe his harsh exterior was a way of protecting his privacy. But under this hard shell was a soft, sentimental, and sensitive being.

Anyhow, I didn't have the time to think about Julien's reactions to other people. We had to produce quite a large number of sets. The sequences in each set were short, so the succession of sets moved rapidly.

Some problems were difficult to resolve. For instance, where do you find a French-looking country road? Once during a drive I had spotted a secondary road with rows of tall poplar trees in the San Fernando Valley. It took a trip in a helicopter to find this road again.

Next problem: how to hack out a path in the jungle and discover, in the very same shot, an airstrip being prepared in a glade. I explained to Julien how I proposed to realize the shot. I wanted fifty or more strong-looking men from the French colony of Senegal. Each man would hold a thick bunch of cut bamboo in one hand, a machete in the other. One row of men would be placed across the frame, then there would be several rows, one behind the other, and so on in depth. First you would see a close shot of a wall of bamboo and hands swinging machetes, seemingly cutting the bamboo. As the bamboo fell down toward the camera, you would discover the second row of men, then the third, and so on until all the bamboo was cleared, and you would find yourself on the freshly cut path. At the end of this opening, you would see the airfield being finished. For that shot we found a place in the San Fernando Valley, a clearing for our airfield. In this clearing we put the camera in position to shoot the airfield scene and in front of that, the rows of bamboo and soldiers. And that was that. The actual shot was shorter than my description.

"Gene, I think your idea is good," said Duvivier. "Instead of going there with a second-unit director and trying to explain to him how to shoot the scene, you go there yourself and direct the second unit. I will even find more shots for you to do." After the monkeys this was my second directorial assignment.

To give my African interior sets unity, I adopted a typical mode of construction by using whitewashed bricks. Instead of windows I built geometrically spaced ornamental openings in the brick walls. These were true to the location because very often African buildings had no windows. Also, these openings created the opportunity for an intricate play of light and shade. I softened the harshness of the light by using gauze mosquito netting. Adopting this standardized construction allowed me to easily remodel one African set into another—from a military office to a hospital room to a club room in Brazzaville.

White walls, deep shadows, strong patches of sunlight, semitransparent mosquito netting swaying in the wind, all of this gave our picture a unified quality and quite a tropical feeling.

For the stark scenes during the military tribunal, I wanted utter simplicity. The room was deep and narrow, with plain whitewashed walls and a visible, dark ceiling built of palm logs. To make this ceiling more prominent, I built it in forced perspective, dropping the ceiling lower and lower as it moved toward the back end of the set. Using this technique emphasized the depth of the room and the visual importance of the log ceiling. To take full advantage of the set and the forced perspective, I planned to shoot the set in the same direction, even though the shots would represent opposite ends of the room. In other words, we would shoot the master angle first, from the back of the audience toward the tribunal. The reverse shot, from the view of the tribunal toward the audience, was to be shot in the same direction of the set but reversing the placement of the benches and the participants' seats. The walls of the whitewashed room were similar on both sides. This kind of shooting is possible with those few directors who can easily orient themselves in reversing the direction of action. The pleasure of working with Duvivier was his quick understanding of technique. He was eager to use his ability to adapt himself mentally to this change of direction. He appreciated its simplification and the economy. In his mind the shooting for the entire film was clearly preplanned, and with him I never had to build a nonusable portion of a set. When we studied the proposed floor plan of a set, his usual remark was, "Gene, I will not need this or that portion of the set. Don't build it."

When Paul Ivano first saw the tribunal set, he voiced strong objections. "How can I light this set with no recesses in the walls and with a complete ceiling?" Duvivier cut him short. "If you are a good cameraman, and I think you are, you will start lighting this impressive set instead of wailing. And make it look impressive." I often notice that the more lighting problems a set presents, the more a cameraman is compelled to use his ingenuity.

One of the last sequences of the picture and the last one on our shooting schedule was the battle scene in the palm oasis, the sequence where Gabin dies heroically. Apart from Gabin no other actors were involved, so it was scheduled almost as postproduction after we had finished our principal photography. I left for Palm Springs in the morning with Joe MacDonald, our first assistant, functioning in this sequence as unit manager. We arrived early and had to scout and decide on a possible shooting location for the next morning. We visited many palm gardens close to the town. All had the manicured look of planned orchards. None, in my opinion, was adequate for our needs.

However, a little farther down the road, we found a site called 1,001 Palms, which was less cultivated. It was situated on a small hillock surrounded by an unobstructed view of the desert and looked like a logical place for the Germans in our script to occupy a position. However, Joe objected to this location as being too far from Palm Springs. "Gene," he said, "please do not even mention this location to Julien. He surely can shoot the scene at one of the more accessible locations we visited earlier. Our equipment will arrive in Palm Springs and it will be more handy there." Duvivier arrived in the afternoon but when he saw the conveniently close location, he exploded.

"It's pure garbage!" Actually he used a much stronger French word, *merde.*
"Is that all you boys were able to find?"

I timidly remarked that there was another possible location, but it was too far away. "Let's see it," he said.

In the late afternoon 1,001 Palms looked amazingly right for the scene. Joe's objections were overruled. Julien suggested we find some tractors to help with transportation and that the crew start earlier in the morning. The name of the owner of this stand of palms was conveniently painted on the remnants of a gate. But in our rush of preparations the formality of obtaining permission from the owner was postponed to the next morning and probably forgotten in the turmoil of organizing the shooting.

The departure of the company in the early morning darkness was very impressive. It was still new to me and amazing—the cumbersome caravan accompanying the Hollywood shooting company. Grips with their own heavy truck, another truck for special effects, one for electrical equipment, the heavy generator, the caterer's wagon, the trailer with dressing rooms and toilets, buses for the crew and the extras, and so many cars with the director, actors, and staff members.

Visually the location was ideal—a desolate hillock shaded by tall palms. The action called for the German-occupied hillock to be attacked by the French soldiers, advancing on all sides. The camera was placed under the palms, in the middle of the German position. In the foreground the German machine gunners repelled the advancing Frenchmen, who fell on the desert floor. Exploding shells and drifting smoke completed this sequence. It took time to organize all this activity—the cameras, the lights, the explosions. We were ready to shoot at about 1 P.M. With our early start the crew was on "meal penalty" and being paid double time, to the distress of the assistants.

Suddenly the wind changed and the smoke drifted in the wrong direction, away from the shot. Impatient, Duvivier shouted for the special effects men to change their placement of the smoke trays. Hungry and angry men carried the asbestos sheets and metal trays with smoke pots to new positions. Finally all was ready, and the shot was completed. Explosions exploded, smoke drifted, machine guns chattered. Everything worked to perfection. Satisfied, Julien called,

"Cut!" and the assistant shouted, "Lunch! One hour!" There was a mad rush down the hill to the caterer's wagon. I lingered behind, while the camera crew arranged their equipment.

I smelled smoke, and soon detected it coming from below one of the metal trays. In their rush to change the placement of the smoke trays, a special effects man had forgotten to place asbestos under one of the trays. The hot metal ignited the thick layer of dry palm leaves covering the ground. From then on everything happened at incredible speed. Cameras and electrical equipment were loaded and saved in the nick of time. Extinguishers proved useless and the beautiful orange flames spread quickly. It is amazing how fast dry palm trees catch fire. One palm tree after another became a spectacular torch, shooting flames high in the sky. With the incomprehensible logic of their profession, the special effects men decided to dynamite a row of trees, creating an improvised firebreak. The explosions were spectacular and so was the fire. All hell broke loose and the fire jumped from one tree to another. It took altogether less than two hours to consume all of the "1,001 Palms." During this time, the Palm Springs firemen were bogged down in the sand. When they finally arrived, there was not enough water to sprinkle on the ashes.

Back in Palm Springs we assessed the situation. As Universal didn't have a contract for the use of the property, they weren't covered by insurance. The responsibility fell on the shoulders of Joe, our assistant. He took it very hard. A day later he had a heart attack. Happily, he recovered, and amazingly, the owner of the burned 1,001 Palms was satisfied with a very small indemnity for his loss.

8

THE SOUTHERNER

Working with Jean Renoir was always a special and uplifting creative adventure. I often bypassed other opportunities for the chance to work with him.

In 1944 I was finishing a picture at Universal (*The Strange Affair of Uncle Harry,* directed by Robert Siodmak), and I had already received my next assignment. One evening I got a call from Jean.

"Gene, I will have a film to do. Could you join me? I will drop the novel by, read it." Hugo Butler, a screenwriter, brought me the book, along with the first draft of the script. The book, *Hold Autumn in Your Hand* by George Sessions Perry, was almost a journalistic account, its characters real people that he had known. The prospect of another film with Renoir was alluring, and I asked Frank Murphy, head of production at Universal, to release me from my previous commitment.

The film, to be entitled *The Southerner,* was about one year in the life of a family of Texas sharecroppers. A young farmhand, Sam Tucker (Zachary Scott) seeking independence as his own boss, moves to a rundown farm on which he will work as a sharecropper. His trials, tribulations, and heartbreaking attempts to care for his family are the gist of the story.

Nona, his wife (Betty Fields), shares with him the joys and sorrows of their existence. Their two small children are with them, as well as Sam's old Granny (Beulah Bondi). When finally he sees the promise of a full harvest from the cotton he has grown, a storm and flood ruin the fruits of his labor. His friend Tim (Charles Kemper) suggests that he take an easy factory job in the city, but Sam stubbornly decides to start the farming anew. (This decision to stay on the farm was a switch from the original story, where Sam, downhearted, abandons the farm for the city job.)

There would be many production problems involved in *The Southerner,* since the story dealt with a cotton field in every season of the year and in all conditions. First we would have to show the clearing of wild grass from the overgrown field; after that the plowing and sowing; then the field with cotton blooming, ripening, and finally being destroyed by the flood. This cotton field had to adjoin the house, which was next to a river.

Jean was busy with the screenplay, and he asked me to go to Texas to see the little town where Perry had lived, to visit the actual sharecropper's house, and perhaps meet some of the people described in the book.

Starting from Los Angeles, I drove to Texas with the assistant production manager. Wartime regulations and gas rationing forced us to use a rented car, since somehow rentals could have unlimited gasoline instead of having to use ration coupons.

It was summer and terribly hot as we drove toward Yuma. In El Centro it was 115 degrees. After lunching in an air-conditioned restaurant, I stepped outside and fainted in the heat. Ten miles later we had a blowout and had to use our only spare tire. Fearfully we drove to Phoenix, Arizona, and I decided not to go farther without a spare. I didn't want to be stuck in the desert in this heat. For three days we waited in a Phoenix hotel until the tire arrived from Los Angeles. Wartime regulations!

Jean had asked me to take a sixteen-millimeter camera to capture the atmosphere of the small Texas community, especially on Saturday, the usual marketing day for local farmers. He also asked me to investigate the possibility of filming in Texas. "If the actual sharecropper's house is convenient, maybe we can shoot the film there," said Jean. Production plans were very tentative at this time. We did not know yet how and where we would shoot the picture.

Our destination was a little town about seventy miles southeast of Austin called Rockdale, where we had a contact to show us around. In Rockdale I met Sam Tucker's friend Tim, the man described in the book as working in the factory. He was now a mortician. We had a strange encounter in his funeral parlor.

He offered me some beer and said, "Listen. If you are interested, I can show you the biggest corpse I've ever had. He is in the next room. I'm building a special coffin for him."

Well, I was not interested in this special corpse!

The next morning we saw the actual sharecropper's house that Perry had described. But truth is often deceptive. The house did not correspond to the image that a reader would derive from the book. Perry had described the house as being next to the river and the cotton field. In reality, the field was a twenty-minute walk from the house, and the river was not so close either. Moreover, in Texas many rivers are in deep ravines and surrounded by trees. So from the house one couldn't see the field or the river. The poor sharecropper's home looked like a typical middle-class California bungalow. I thought to myself, "This will not do." The field, the house, the river, all were the real places presented in the original story. But in this case, as in many others I had encountered, exact reality could not be used in the film—it did not work.

My attitude toward "reality" in motion picture settings dated back many years to my work as a painter and scene designer. While painting, the artist doesn't strive to achieve a photographic likeness in a portrait or to slavishly copy a landscape. He tries to express a deeper reality, a perception of the essence of his subject. (It is amazing how some painted portraits look real compared with, say, the empty smile of a photographic likeness.) I approach film settings the same way, and my attitude is shared by most of my art director friends. We seek not an exact copy of this or that setting but the expression of our perception of the setting. It doesn't mean we are in the realm of fantasy. We think in realistic terms, we use all real elements, but we eliminate useless details and compose the essential elements to underscore our idea of the setting. Our sets are true to life, often truer than the real settings. In willingly *choosing* what to show, we do not betray the spirit of the truth.

Such deliberate choice is, in my opinion, the key to all artistic creation. It is true of visual art and applies as well to film settings, whether predesigned and built or shot entirely on location. In all cases the production designer or the director selects and rearranges elements according to ideas he wants to convey.

For two days we traveled in the Texas cotton belt and saw innumerable small farms. Many were miserable shacks, makeshift houses built with old boards and flattened tin cans. Some were gaudily disguised, covered with plastic sheets of imitation bright red bricks. Cotton had been abundant the year before and some farmers made good money, allowing them the luxury of pretending their huts were built with real bricks.

Sometimes I was shocked by the reaction of poor black farmers to our presence. Once, seeing the big limousine stopping in front of their house and four jovial white men stepping out, the black men quickly retreated inside, shutting the door.

But I was able to film a typical Saturday in Rockdale: farmers idling with their beer in a bar while their wives did errands in stores; men sitting on the sidewalks or leaning against walls, smoking or munching on "chickenburgers."

Then I got an urgent message from our production manager in Hollywood, Carl Harriman.

"Gene, you have to come back. We are losing time, we have to start, and we must decide how and where we will shoot. Leave the car there with the assistant and fly home."

As fast as I could I completed my research on cotton fields and sharecroppers and was soon back in Harriman's office.

"We absolutely cannot shoot there," I told him.

"I am glad you told me that," he replied, "for wartime restrictions would make it impossible. I have my own plan. We will do it all in the studio." He had contracted the General Service studios on Las Palmas. There were four stages, and Carl continued:

"We will use the largest stage and bring in truckloads of dirt. With a bulldozer you can contour the land."

"But what about the cotton plants?" I asked.

"The problem is solved. My prop man has prepared a cotton plant."

He showed me a rosebush with pieces of cotton stuck between the thorns. "This looks exactly like cotton," he said.

"Well," I said, "Carly, maybe this is cotton for you, but not for me. Moreover, you may know how to do this picture on stage; I really don't." Carly's solution was no more acceptable to Renoir than to me. But I had to move quickly and find suitable locations in California.

I learned that cotton was grown near Bakersfield and Fresno. With another assistant production manager (the first one was still driving back from Texas), in another rented car, we went to Bakersfield. It was dismal and I found nothing suitable. We went farther on to Fresno, hoping for a better site. And we found it.

Next to the beautiful San Joaquin River was a cotton field, and close to the riverbank, an ideal place to build our sharecropper's house. It was a perfect location.

Our next problem was a human problem. This whole tract was in the hands of Russian farmers, members of a strange religious sect. They didn't shave, drink, or smoke, and considered theater and motion pictures to be the inventions of Satan. The owner of the farm was an engaging young fellow with bright white teeth and a luxurious black beard. Quite unexpectedly, he quickly agreed to rent his land and cotton field. I called Gilpin, the new production manager, from Fresno. (Carl Harriman had resigned, probably offended by my refusal to use his rosebush as a cotton plant.) Gilpin arrived the next day, the lease was signed, and the farmer accepted his advance of $2,000.

But two days later the farmer appeared in Hollywood.

"I bring you back the money. I cannot take it. My father would disavow me. I cannot rent anything to motion pictures. It's a sin!"

Our production manager acted tough.

"We have a contract, you know, signed by you, and if you break it, we will sue you. It could cost you one hundred, maybe two hundred thousand."

This was a visible blow, and the farmer rushed back to Fresno to confer with his father, one of the church elders. The cunning father found a solution. In order not to offend his religious principles and deal with the "unholy" motion picture industry, he found a poor farm worker, also Russian, but not a member of the sect, to whom he "sold" the farm and our contract. Later on I heard that the deal was a set-up; as soon as our company departed, the new owner had to "sell" the farm back to the religious father.

Next I had to plan how to build our set there. The cotton was already in flower, but at the beginning of the picture we had to show the field overgrown with wild grass. Next to our cotton field was an almost identical but uncultivated field. I decided to build the house on skids, placing it first on the wild field and later towing it to the flowering cotton field.

Another problem: in wartime, wood was difficult to buy in any quantity. I went with my assistant to look for old barns we could dismantle. We were very lucky. In Oxnard we found a very old barn—all weathered, every board like a portrait of an old man, etched with wrinkles. Each plank was a masterpiece of aging.

Because rain and night interior sequences would be impractical to shoot on location, I decided to build the set so the entire house could be removed to the stage.

By then I was happy that we hadn't been able to use the house in Texas. Familiar with the Fresno location, I could now conceive and build our set based on a clear picture of the location in my mind. It was much more satisfying than adapting an existing structure. It confirmed my belief from my days as a stage designer that sets have to be created especially for each picture. When the designer prepares a film he has an impression of what the setting should look like; he is guided by the overall visual style he and the director are seeking and by the image he has formed in his mind. The problem with most Hollywood pictures is the reuse of existing sets. It's like the difference between ready-made clothes and garments made to order. Custom clothes fit much better. At any rate I was very happy with our "custom-made" solution.

One of Lourie's sketches for the Tuckers' cabin.

The cabin as it was finally realized.

Soon the set for *The Southerner* began to take shape, acquiring character and individuality as building progressed. I had time to think about additions and details that would enhance the original conception. Was something lacking in the set? I would find the missing detail, the final accent I was looking for. In this instance, washed up on the bank of the river, I saw a dried, crooked tree. Here it was, the final touch I needed. The tree was placed next to the house. Against the sky it became a strong graphic silhouette, like the foreground of a Japanese print.

Production problems and design problems sometimes must be solved concurrently. We had to house our crew. Fresno, the closest town, was thirty miles from our location. Transporting the crew to and from there was costly and time consuming. Our production manager decided to build a camp in close proximity to the set and delegated me to find a place as close as possible without its interfering with the shooting.

To construct the camp we hired Anderson's Camps, a very efficient organization, which had built and was managing a camp for some 5,000 construction workers at Boulder Dam. I went with their technicians to scout and organize the location for our camp. In four weeks' time they had erected it: twenty-six individual cabin-tents, each for four people, complete with toilets, showers, hot and cold running water, and a sewer system. There was a separate canteen and bar and a huge tent restaurant that served 120 people at one sitting. It was quite like a comfortable country hotel, convenient to both our set and the river, where we could take a daily swim. We even put up a large screen outdoors and twice a week projected films for the crew and some neighboring farmers.

The Southerner required a second set, the farm of Sam Tucker's neighbor (played by J. Carrol Naish) and his nephew, Norman Lloyd. This farm was supposed to be on the same bank of the river as Sam's. We were unable to find a suitable location near our main set, and finally decided to build the farm within driving distance of Hollywood, close to Malibu Lake. It was a nice little glade on the bank of a large stream. I built a dam so the stream became wider and could pass visually for a river. There I built a farmhouse, a barn, a workshop, an enclosure for the pigs, and the well, so prominent in the plot of the picture. We started filming at this set, close to home.

The Tucker clan moving in with Granny (Beulah Bondi)
sitting in the back of the pick-up.

Meanwhile the Tucker set was completed and the company left for Fresno. The house was now on the neighboring empty lot for the first scenes of the family's dusty arrival at the unkempt, half-destroyed cabin. After shooting the first plowing of the field, we towed the house to the main location where the cotton was already in bloom.

Working in sequence as necessary, we added a vegetable garden, then shot the destruction of this garden under the hooves of the cattle driven by the villain, Norman Lloyd. The fishing sequence when "Lead Pencils," a giant catfish, is caught, was made close by the house on the river. Renoir staged the entire fishing sequence there, finishing the scene with the actors looking down at the fish on the ground. But their point of view, the gigantic catfish, was shot some 2,000 miles east, in Louisiana, with the bare feet of doubles "standing in."

Next I had to prepare the flood sequence. The company left for some cotton fields about ten miles away to shoot the beginning of the picture: the cotton-picking scene where the old uncle dies, the migrant workers' camp; and the departure of the Tucker family in a dilapidated truck loaded with their belongings, including Granny, who sits atop the load, unruffled, in her chair. During this time, my construction crew built an embankment some two to three feet high around the area of the house. We opened all the irrigation pumps until the dammed area was under two feet of water. Filled with broken and floating cotton bushes, it gave the right feeling of disaster.

For the scene where Sam and his friend try to rescue Sam's cow from the floodwaters, I built the set in the river itself. The river was wide and very swift, but shallow at the banks. I brought some old buildings and fences and we pushed them into the river with the tractor. During the scene I released a lot of broken boards, patches of grass, and live chickens. Carried by the swift current, they floated by, contributing to the effect of a very convincing flood.

The flood scene. Renoir is at far right, Lourie at far left. Wearing the whistle is Assistant Director Robert Aldrich; the DP, Lucien Andriot, stands behind the camera, which has been blimped.

With location work finished in Fresno, the company came back to Hollywood. The set of Sam Tucker's house was transported from the location and rebuilt on the large stage. Simultaneously, other interiors were built on the other stages. While construction progressed, the company went to a nearby location in the San Fernando Valley to shoot the uncle's funeral and the return from the cemetery. The now populous San Fernando Valley was then mostly vast fields of brush, wildflowers, and berries, all crisscrossed by narrow dirt roads.

Next we moved to the old RKO ranch on Ventura Boulevard, a rambling collection of decaying sets, medieval French streets left over from *The Hunchback of Notre Dame,* and remnants of a midwestern town that I remodeled for our small-town Texas street. This included the exterior of the bar, Harvey's Store, and a doctor's office, from where you could see the Saturday activities on the street.

The Tucker house was ready on stage. Our decision to shoot as much as possible on stage was made for many reasons. One was the difficulty of shooting a rain sequence on location. It would have been costly and cumbersome to create a cloudy, rainy atmosphere in the blazing sun of the Central Valley. Then too, there were problems in shooting the night interiors and working with children on location. But the main reason we filmed on the stage was because Renoir preferred to work under controlled conditions. He found it disturbing for actors to perform outside, where birds sang, the light changed, and so on. The rain sequence, the scene with Granny in her rocking chair on top of the truck, required a large shooting space in front of the house. I needed all the available space on the stage. For the view of the surrounding landscape, I had the choice of making a gigantic painted backdrop of some 15,000 square feet, or building a three-dimensional miniature backing. As usual, I chose the latter solution. It is more economical and gives better control of lighting and mechanical effects. To create the impression of perspective, the ground was raked up gently toward the horizon. To imitate faraway trees silhouetted against the sky, I accumulated tumbleweed. Armed with garden shears and photographs of the actual tree line on location, I carved the tumbleweed to achieve this effect. A standard rented sky backing completed the set. With added ground fog the illusion was perfect. Nobody could detect what was shot on location and what on stage. In cinema, reality can be obtained by illusion. "Cheating" is a wonderful weapon in the art director's arsenal.

In this interior-exterior set Renoir staged the rain sequence when the family first arrives at the desolate farm and takes possession of the cabin. Granny sitting in her rocking chair atop the truck stubbornly refuses to come down and move into the dilapidated hut. Then we did the night interior scene where some of the family discussions take place—conflicts between sulking Granny, hungry children, and tired Nona. Here too were filmed the warm indoor scenes of the first fire in the stove; the first meat dinner, when Sam killed a possum; and a confection of a scene when Sam gives a winter coat cut out of Granny's warm blanket to his daughter, in spite of Granny's indignation.

Then there were other sets constructed on the stage. In planning a bar set, I wanted to show bare walls without any pretense of decoration, characteristic of bars in small American farm towns. Another scene depicted a wedding party in the back room of a country store, with the usual pranks and square dances. It was amusing to watch Renoir, the jovial Frenchman, directing with gusto a purely American traditional scene. The drunken wedding party finishes in the gray hours of the morning as incessant rain floods the little town and foreshad-

Renoir and Lourie in 1945.

ows the disaster to Tucker's cotton crop. Arriving home, Sam finds the cabin partly destroyed by the storm, the crop lost. He barely prevents the cow from drowning. But Sam refuses to submit and move to town where wartime factory work would be easy to get.

The original script ended differently. In Butler's script Sam Tucker chose the factory, giving up the farm. Reading this, Renoir said, "I feel uneasy about this ending. Do you, Gene?"

"Yes," I replied. "I doubt that any farmer I met in Texas would change his ways. They are accustomed to catastrophes and always believe that the next year will be better."

"I am happy you have that impression," Jean said, "because it confirms my opinion. Tucker has to stay on the farm."

Renoir rewrote the screenplay with William Faulkner. I don't think Faulkner received credit because he was under exclusive contract with another studio at the time. But some of his dialogue is unmistakable, as tasty as home-baked bread. I still remember the scene where Tucker, grieving for the health of his son stricken with spring sickness, waves his fist in the air and speaks to God:

"Why did you create the sky so beautiful and the earth so miserable?"

Or the scene where Granny says she will die soon and Sam's wife answers:

"You promise, but you never deliver the goods."

By the time of *The Southerner*, Renoir's talent was fully mature and his storytelling was deceptively simple. However, some virtuoso stylistic touches were there, as in the sequence when Tucker's family explores the rundown house. They are heard but not seen as the camera moves around the cabin. This traveling shot through the empty set was valid because the set fully revealed the character of the house, becoming a silent player, acting out its part in the drama. Recent tests show that a film audience absorbs more information visually through images than aurally through the soundtrack. Film remains very much a visual art.

I had one more exterior set constructed on the stage, a winter scene where Tucker hunts a possum in the woods. I built it on multileveled platforms to give the impression of uneven ground levels. The set was full of bare trees, dry brush, and dry grass. I found an impressive, crooked tree with a hollow trunk in which the possum could hide. I added low-hanging ground mist and with the dim lighting, it looked like a real forest and had tremendous depth.

In one of his books André Bazin says that *The Southerner* leaves the audience with surreal images. I thought the film was highly realistic, but "surreal" means different things to different people. However, I agree with Bazin if by "surreal" he means that in *The Southerner* I molded reality. I wanted to go beyond outer appearances to find the essence, to reveal the poetic feeling, to express the same lyricism that characterized Renoir's vision of this picture.

When is reality real? You will remember that I traveled to the little town of Rockdale, Texas, to visit the place where the novel was written. I saw the house that was supposedly described in the book, and it was not convincing at all. The reality was not real. When the designer prepares a set, he is guided by the needs of the dramatic action and by the image he has formed in his mind. In *The Southerner* you accept the house of Sam Tucker as the only convincing reality. Film reality, fit for this film. I do not remember which writer called it—"the poetic reality."

I believe also that a motion picture setting does not exist as a separate entity; its function is to play a part in a film; and it must be used as an integral part of the action in the film.

The work of a production designer or art director in making a film is often misunderstood. Contrary to widespread belief, his work is not simply limited to delivering his sketches to the director. The real work begins only then: preparing working drawings, supervising construction, choosing materials, selecting colors, directing the set dressing, and preparing sets for shooting. Often an art director helps the director through the mechanics of shooting certain sequences. He also collaborates very closely with the cinematographer.

However, this harmonious collaboration is an ideal seldom achieved in the industrial system of film production. Too often individuals making the same motion picture work their separate ways. Sometimes I prepared pictures without meeting the director until the very last moment. How often I have seen directors trying to fan their enthusiasm for a script in which they don't believe. How often the designer works on his own; the composer counts only how many minutes of music he must produce. It is a small miracle that these separate efforts yield a picture that holds together. However, when real congenial collaboration occurs, what a satisfying experience it is to make a picture.

The motion picture is a collective art. Luis Buñuel has said that this collaboration should be anonymous, like the building of medieval cathedrals. Those artisans, stonemasons, sculptors, painters, and architects didn't sign their work. Only the cathedral counted.

I was lucky to have the privilege of complete, absorbing collaboration many times in my career, especially on my eight pictures with Jean Renoir. I think our work on *The Southerner* is the best reflection of our team's happy dedication.

THE LONG NIGHT

The Hakim brothers, Robert and Raymond, were ambitious and successful producers in France where they had produced Renoir's *La Bête humaine,* among others. Now in Hollywood, they had a multifilm contract with RKO. One of their projects was a new version of *Madame Bovary,* the novel by Gustave Flaubert. They made Jean Renoir an offer to write the adaptation and direct the film; this would be his second adaptation, as he had already done a silent version. He agreed to handle the project on the condition that he would direct only if completely satisfied with his treatment.

In 1946 I had been working with Jean from the beginning of the *Madame Bovary* project. As a result of my preparation, I gained a wonderful photographic collection of locations in French Normandy. However, Jean became convinced that it would be impossible for him to return to the Flaubert masterpiece, and he regretfully declined to do the film.

Immediately Robert Hakim put the second project he had in mind to work. It was a remake of the successful French film *Le Jour se lève*, with Jean Gabin. Anatole Litvak signed to direct the film; Henry Fonda and Barbara Bel Geddes would star.

Robert asked me if I would agree to switch from Renoir's film to this new project, now titled, *The Long Night.* The prospect of working with Litvak was interesting, and the first draft of the script, by John Wexley, was pleasurable reading. You could almost taste John's rich dialogue; it was like eating a slice of good bread.

The story followed the French film closely. It told about the love of a sincere young worker (Henry Fonda) in a small Pennsylvania steel mill town for a naive young girl (Barbara Bel Geddes) who is seduced by a suave actor (Vincent Price). In a fatal encounter the worker kills the seducer, locks himself in a top-floor room of a boarding house, and waits for the police to come and get him. A barricade is set up. Tommyguns are fired from across the street. Then tear gas is sent for, and during the delay, the events that led to the killing flash through the young man's mind.

If the picture were made today, the producers would probably insist that we choose an appropriate small town where we would shoot at least the exterior scenes, if not the whole film. They would incur enormous costs in bringing in actors, technicians, and construction and shooting crews, who would need the accommodations of trucks, trailers, and dressing rooms. All this activity would disrupt the normal existence of the town for the sole purpose of conforming to the new mystique of shooting films at real sites on the false assumption that it is more expensive to build sets and shoot films in a studio.

When we prepared *The Long Night,* this way of production was not yet in fashion and Litvak, like other directors of that time, preferred building streets and other sets for the film, fitting the moods and needs of the story. We were sure, for example, that the street sets in the original film, *Le Jour se lève,* were more expressive than any real street, where Alex Trauner, the art director, had succeeded in realizing the quintessence of a sad French town. Our ambition had been to achieve the feeling of a similarly dreary American town. And so we presumed that our sets for *The Long Night* would be dramatically more expres-

Henry Fonda and Barbara Bel Geddes in THE LONG NIGHT.

sive than any Pennsylvania town street. Moreover, they would give the director
the freedom of staging action and planning camera positions without the additional headaches of shooting on location.

And so from the very beginning of this project, it was clear to me that
we would build our own town. We didn't plan to eliminate reality; we wanted
to create the most suitable reality for the film. By omitting certain useless details, by underlining some others, by conveying the mood by lighting, colors,
shapes, and linear composition, the designer could make the sets much more
expressive than real locations. They could become more real than real. A poetic
reality, a reality with a soul. Our town, built on the set, would be a created
reality, as when a writer tells a story and creates a projection of real life.

I had first met Tola Litvak in New York in 1941. We met at the Russian
Tea Room on 57th Street, the favorite hangout of actors, writers, and musicians. He was friendly, but as did Julian Duvivier earlier, he strongly dissuaded
me from going to Hollywood, telling me to be careful or I would be crushed
by the Hollywood "inhuman machine."

In our meeting at Robert Hakim's office at RKO, he expressed pleasure
at our collaboration. He was a well-organized director who thoroughly re-
searched the background and atmosphere of the action. Soon I was able to meet
him in New York and drive with him to small towns in Pennsylvania where
we would do research. This scouting trip gave us ample time to discuss the
problems of *The Long Night*. We mutually agreed that I would try to build the
main street on the studio lot and the second street of an old-fashioned suburb
on a stage. I told him of my plans to include a view of the somber silhouette
of the steel plant that dominated the town in the set. I preferred building the
steel mill in miniature, as opposed to a painted backdrop. Apart from my personal preference for three-dimensional miniatures to flat painting, I felt this
method offered an advantage, as we had to shoot both day and night scenes,
which would necessitate painting two separate backdrops, a very expensive
proposition if they were made full size. Also since the scenic artists would paint
their backdrops before the cameraman would light the set, the painting could
be wrong in its mood and direction of light. A miniature backing could be lit
along with the rest of the set, creating the same mood and unity of lighting.

"Our town, built on the set, would be a created reality, as when a writer tells a story and creates a projection of real life."

Below, left: *Fonda in front of a miniature background. The miniature has not yet been tied in to the foreground with lighting.*

Below, right: *Lourie's three-dimensional, working, miniature background is clearly evident.*

Floor plan and set-up sketches drawn by studio artist Dorothea Redman.

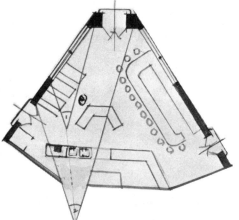

Below: *Another of Redman's renderings for* THE LONG NIGHT.

We could also add life and movement to the miniature set by showing smoke and flames escaping from the smokestacks, some moving trucks, and flickering lights.

After spending two days together in Pennsylvania, Tola left for Hollywood, and I remained to photograph streets and architectural details.

The large exterior set to be built on the studio lot had to represent a busy intersection, the downtown of the town. There was to be the entrance of the Traveler's Hotel; the corner drugstore with a utilitarian interior; a square with a monument of a soldier from the last war; and the four-story rooming house, where Fonda lived on the top floor. I decided to build this street on the studio lot, the so-called "Forty Acres" lot adjacent to the Culver City studio. In a corner of this lot were the half-ruined sets of the railroad depot from *Gone with the Wind*. I used this depot as a convenient distant backing for my street.

For the tall rooming house Tola asked me to build a practical interior of the stairway with four landings and make it possible to shoot inside Fonda's room and the view of the square from his window. To make this all possible, I had to build an elevator that could accommodate the camera crew, the director, and the script girl. It was built behind the removable back wall of the stairway, and it allowed us to make a continuous shot of someone entering on the street level, going up four flights, and arriving on the upper landing.

The actual building of this set became unexpectedly difficult. The memorable studio construction crew strike of 1946–47 started at the same time our set building began. Instead of professional carpenters, I had to rely on the so-called "set erectors," a haphazardly assembled crew, some of whom could not handle a hammer or handsaw. Each piece of lumber had to be cut out many times until it was the right size. Construction dragged on for days, then weeks.

The second exterior set was built on the stage. It was a modest residential street on the outskirts of town. There in a flower shop Barbara Bel Geddes lived and worked. At the end of this street I decided to build the view of the steel mill that dominated the town. The miniature backing was impressive; its chimneys and ducts spit flames, smoke, and steam. The expert photography of Sol Polito gave the right feeling of distant perspective. For this set I used the two largest stages of the Culver City studio, then known as RKO-Pathé. The two stages had a removable wall between them, making the entire area one of the largest stages in Hollywood. As my set occupied the whole depth of the two stages, to be able to show a continuous sky backing (without seeing any overhead scaffoldings at the far end of the stage), we hung a teaser—a horizontal piece of canvas painted in exactly the same color as the sky—across the set. It was a procedure often used in theaters but seldom in films because it was difficult for cameramen to obtain uniform lighting across the entire sky.

Some scenes in the picture required falling snow. At this time one of the RKO special effects masters invented a new snow-projecting machine that produced a very realistic snow that fell in light flakes. As I remember, it consisted of a small electric fan that blew out a light foam normally used for insulation. Litvak fell absolutely in love with the effect and we rarely shot a scene on this set without the snowfall and the effect of a train passing in the background. The train itself was not visible but was concealed behind a hilly terrain. You could only see the rhythmically moving puffs of steam from the engine and hear the sound of it chugging past. These effects were always seen behind a half-frozen Fonda, waiting for Bel Geddes to appear on the snowy porch of her flower shop.

For the set of the sand-blasting shed, Litvak asked me to provide a back-projected image on two sides of the set simultaneously. When the front door of the shed was open, he wanted to see the plant yard with its usual activity, and facing toward the side window, he wanted another view of the side yard. I explained that using back projection process on two sides of the set would mean building a long and cumbersome tunnel for the projection, but Tola remained adamant. I understood that I was dealing with a strong-willed director. We built a back projection on two sides of the set.

During the set construction I became acquainted with Tola's strong determination to disregard the budget and insist on changes he deemed necessary. In our downtown street set I placed a row of telephone poles alongside the street at a normal distance from the houses. They were already in place when Tola visited the set and asked me to place them closer to the front of the houses to create a more crowded feeling. I was obliged to order new holes dug and moved each pole over a mere twelve inches. Nevertheless, our relations remained very cordial, and he often expressed his appreciation for my creating the right atmosphere for this dull industrial town.

In the film there is an important scene where Fonda sits on his bed against the wall, barricaded against the police who fire bullets into his room. Huddled on his bed in the corner, smoking one cigarette after another, surrounded by souvenirs of his army days and his romance with Bel Geddes, he thinks back to how it all started.

Knowing Litvak's habit of shooting many takes of the same scene, I prepared eight sets of interchangeable walls for this set. For each new take, the bullet-pocked wall was removed and replaced by a new wall with the same wallpaper and painted age spots.

We had enough walls to shoot the scene nine times. However, shooting went on and on, again and again. Without explaining exactly what he wanted, Litvak demanded improvement with each new take. Finally, as I recall, the scene was shot seventy times. A crew of painters was continually repairing the old walls, pasting on the wallpaper again and again. The shooting of this memorable scene took a full two days. After the last take the exhausted director turned to the equally exhausted script girl and said, "Print takes two and four."

Vincent Price played the part of a cheap performer whose flamboyance and eloquence seduced the naive girl, leading to the final tragedy of the film. Vincent performed his conjuring act on the set of an auditorium, which had once been a large garage. I decorated the walls with a collection of old automobile registration plates from different states. Vincent found this detail characteristically right. He asked me, "Gene, how can you, a Frenchman, invent such a detail of a small American town?"

"Frenchmen," I answered, "sometimes have good eyes, good memories, and often, good assistants."

I don't have many specific recollections of the shooting of this film. Litvak was an interesting director to work with, however demanding of his crew and of himself. Apart from the seventy takes of the bullet-pocked wall scene, I remember three exhausting weeks of continual night shooting on the street outside Fonda's rooming house. Litvak and I parted on very friendly terms. Years later I met him in Paris, and he asked me to design his upcoming *Night of the*

Artist's rendering of bedroom.

The bedroom as it appears in the film with Sol Polito's dramatic lighting.

Generals. I had to decline the offer because at this time I was directing the second unit of Sacha Guitry's *Napoleon.*

A remake of a film is always a difficult enterprise, especially if the original film was a success. You can't help but compare scenes; the director and actors unconsciously compete with the original film. But this is unfair, as in our case where Henry Fonda was completely different from Jean Gabin and Vincent Price was nothing like the jaunty Jules Berry in the French film. As for the sets, I did not and could not copy the moody streets of Alex Trauner for my typical American small town. But fair or not, the enlightened audiences who have seen *Le Jour se lève* involuntarily compare the two. But the largest audiences did not see the French film. If their judgment is measured by the box office receipts, *The Long Night* was not a resounding success, and Litvak was lucky to have started work on *The Snake Pit* before the final figures from *The Long Night* were added up.

THE RIVER

In late October of 1949, I was on a plane flying in the black Indian sky. Below us, intermittent lightning from a thunderstorm lit the disheveled clouds.

In the predawn morning we landed in the eerie steaming lights of the airfield. Exhausted from the twenty-two hour flight from London, we stepped out into the oppressive humid heat of Calcutta. Someone greeted me smilingly and put a garland of fragrant flowers around my neck. White friendly smiles on dark faces. They belonged to Ram, our cameraman, and Hari Das Gupta, Renoir's future assistant. Thus *The River* began for me.

It had started more than a year earlier. Jean Renoir had given me a book by Rumer Godden, *The River,* one of those books you either put aside indifferently or fall in love with. I found it a mixture of sentiment and enchantment, a warm story of a girl from an English family growing up in India. Though seemingly isolated behind their garden wall, the family's life is actually closely integrated with the fascinating humanity of India and with the Indian belief that people must accept everything that happens to them, just as they accept the continuous flow of the river.

I agreed wholeheartedly with Jean that the book presented a wonderful subject for a motion picture, one we could sink our teeth into. Soon Jean had secured an option for the book rights. Jean's plan was to shoot the backgrounds in India and make the picture in the United States, probably building the set of the family house on the banks of the Mississippi River. But Hollywood producers had a different concept of an "Indian" picture. To them, India was an exotic land of Bengal lancers, tiger hunting from the backs of elephants, and sultry girls dancing for maharajas. Our *River* was not appreciated.

It happened, however, that a newcomer to the roster of Hollywood producers, Ken McEldowney, had just organized a company, Oriental-International, for the purpose of making pictures in India. He had heard about Rumer Godden's new book and the possibility of its being made into a film.

Eugene Lourie.

Jean Renoir had the rights to the book and a loving determination to realize the picture, and Ken McEldowney had the financial backing and the indomitable energy to produce a picture in India. And so it happened.

At this time shooting American pictures in a distant foreign country was an adventure, a leap into the unknown. Soon I found myself at the Los Angeles Airport bidding good-bye to Jean and Dido Renoir as they left for a preliminary scouting trip to India. McEldowney was in India participating in an elephant *kedda,* a round-up of wild elephants that took place every four years in the state of Mysore. As McEldowney's pet idea was to make a film about the *kedda,* he had taken along a camera crew. Jean, helped by McEldowney and the camera crew, was able to do some preliminary groundwork in Calcutta, and on Jean's return to the United States it was decided that the picture would be filmed near Calcutta, on the banks of the Hooghly River, one of the arms of water leading to the Ganges Delta.

It was to be the first Technicolor feature film made entirely in India. It was to be shot with the old, cumbersome three-strip negative camera and required special sturdy grip equipment. The process would also require arc lights and strong electric generators, then unavailable in India. All this equipment was ordered by Ken in London and had to be shipped by boat to Calcutta.

Ken had decided to use an English technical crew, with the exception of Claude Renoir, Jean's nephew, as director of photography, and myself as the production designer. During the photographic tests Jean made in Calcutta, where he interviewed about a hundred adolescent girls for the part of Harriet, Jean noticed the precise handling of the camera by a young Indian, Ram Sen Gupta, and decided to hire him as a camera operator. As neither Claude nor Ram were familiar with the Technicolor cameras, both had to be sent to London to spend two weeks at the Technicolor plant.

Meanwhile Rumer Godden came to Hollywood to work with Jean on the screenplay. She had been raised in India and spent much of her life there, which made her collaboration invaluable. Two of her sisters still lived in Calcutta, and later they helped me organize shooting and solved many day-to-day problems. But for the time being, our only guide was Rumer Godden's novel. I was to receive the final script in Calcutta, some five months later.

The film as it finally evolved told about the way life was lived in Bengal, India, along the banks of the Ganges River. Like the novel, the story focused on an English family that lived by the river, telling about young people growing up and discovering life, about first love and tragedy, about the currents and flow of life symbolized by the river.

The father of the family is foreman at a jute press. The mother is a gracious woman, devoted to her family of six children—all girls except for one boy named Bogey. The eldest daughter, Harriet (who wants to be a writer), is fourteen, an adolescent "running away from childhood, rushing toward love." Harriet has two close friends: Valerie, seventeen (whose father owns the jute press), an only child who knows exactly what she wants from life, and Melanie, the daughter of a neighbor, Mr. John, a man who has lived most of his life in India and is married to an Indian woman. Although at peace with the world, Mr. John realizes his daughter has yet to find her place in it because of her mixed heritage.

Into this setting comes a stranger, Captain John (Thomas Breen), a young man from America who has lost a leg in the war. He comes to visit his cousin, Mr. John. Not caring much where he goes, Captain John is just drifting because he has not been able to regain his faith and purpose in life.

All three girls fall irresistibly in love with the handsome young captain, and each in her way brings him new values—as does India itself as it reveals the meaning of its unchanging traditions. To the girls, the captain brings their first experience of love and the inevitable clash between reality and dreams.

During the time of Captain John's visit, death, jealousy, sadness, happiness, and love enter their lives. Each girl becomes a little more of a woman, and the young captain finds that "with everything that happens to you—with everyone you meet who is important to you—you die a little bit, or are born."

Since Jean was busy working on the script and with casting problems, and Ken was fully occupied with organizing the production, they asked me to proceed to London to interview technicians, to check on equipment, and to help Claude and Ram at the London Technicolor plant. I was assisted by an energetic agent who represented Ken's interests in England. As hotel rooms were at a premium in postwar London, Technicolor helped put up *The River* group at a small charming hotel in Windsor, quite a distance from London. However, I spent many days in London interviewing and making tentative deals with technicians—camera mechanics, gaffers, sound crews, and make-up people—all subject to Jean's final approval. In choosing the technicians, I was advised by Vincent Korda, the art director and technical director of Korda Productions. I could not find a production manager familiar with working conditions in India and left this post for Jean and Ken to fill on their return passage to London. Little did I suspect how much extra work and worry this vacant post would cause me in Calcutta.

After two weeks at the Technicolor plant, Claude returned to Paris, Ram to India, and some days later I was aboard a prop-powered Constellation, taking me to Calcutta.

As I intimated earlier, the enterprise of shooting a film in India was almost tantamount to Marco Polo discovering Mongolia. For me, waking up on the morning of our arrival was indeed like opening a window on a strange, unknown world.

I will often digress here from problems directly connected with the filming of *The River* to speak about general impressions that assailed our senses in this fascinating country. We were confronted by new smells, sounds, colors, and above all, by the warm, trusting eye-to-eye contact with the people around us. These impressions influenced us greatly and were strongly reflected in the film.

Through the open window of the Great-Eastern Hotel came the perennial smell of curry, the pungent smoke of burning cow dung, and the shrill plaintive cries of hovering buzzards. A knock on the door and there they were, the three red-turbaned bearers—servants—bringing a morning glass of tea and biscuits. A large inquisitive crow sat on the windowsill, visibly interested in the biscuits. From this day on the crow became my daily companion for morning tea.

Hari Das Gupta, Jean's future assistant, would join me in the hotel dining room for breakfast. He was an affable young man with degrees from UCLA. Together we planned our scouting trip.

The English family in our film lived in a house that bordered the river.

THE RIVER.

To get a general impression of the river and scout for possible houses for the film, I decided to explore the area by boat. The Hooghly River is a very wide expanse of water with very peculiar behavior. Calcutta is about sixty miles from the sea, but the tides are so powerful in the Bay of Bengal that the strong river current changes direction every six hours. With a thundering noise, the bore—the high tidal wave—reverses direction and the river flows upstream for six hours. I often had the chance to observe this phenomenon when I was building sets. Once I saw the carcass of a dead cow floating downstream, like a strange island crowned with quarreling vultures. Six hours later I recognized the same carcass floating in the opposite direction. This changing direction of the current made river travel difficult for small craft. For our scouting trip we had to hire a powerful steam launch. We took a detailed map with us and marked on it the houses that seemed suitable for the picture. We decided to visit these houses for a closer inspection the next day.

The immensity of the river was impressive and so was the variety of the river traffic: husky steamers towing huge barges laden high with jute; solitary fishermen on crescent-shaped slender boats throwing their butterfly nets in a repeated motion; large rowboats, their twelve to twenty oarsmen rowing standing up with an elegant movement not unlike a dance step; porpoises jumping in and out of the water. Punctuating the riverbanks every so often were temple steps that led down to the water's edge. Bronzed worshippers immersed themselves in the river or gargled the river water to cleanse themselves from sin.

It took many days of careful scouting to visit all the houses we had marked on our map. These houses were called bungalows, but were actually monumental-looking structures, usually built in a neoclassic style with a profusion of columns.

In our scouting I often witnessed signs of racial prejudice, remnants of the English rule. Indian independence was but a young experience, dating from 1947. When we were visiting one of the more opulent residences of an English businessman—the owner of the Scotch whiskey distillery in Calcutta—his wife addressed only me and looked through Hari Das Gupta as if he didn't exist, as if he were absolutely transparent. She was also appalled by the idea that her house would harbor an Indian film crew. "They would all spit the red juice of

Claude Renoir, Jr., on a scouting trip. Looking into the river is Lourie's Indian assistant. The tall man wearing the jacket is Satyajit Ray.

the betel that they are always chewing!" she said. Her house was decorated in the worst possible taste so we left hurriedly. I realized it would be difficult to find a family that would rent us their house.

On their previous visit to Calcutta, Jean and Ken McEldowney had seen one house in Barrackpore, about twenty-five miles from Calcutta. The house was situated on the shore of the Hooghly and had the advantages of being unoccupied; large with an ample garden; and according to Jean, well worth a second look. As with so many of the other houses we visited, this summer bungalow belonging to the Maharaja of Gwalior was a very imposing building.

A circular driveway led up to the house from the main Barrackpore road. There was a garden in front of the house, and in the back, a huge terrace faced the river. However, the river was barely visible, hidden by a heavy growth of green-black mango trees. The lawn was unkempt and overgrown like a jungle.

The state of the overgrown garden and the frighteningly large size of the terrace ruled out this house on our first visit. But we had been obliged to meet and take tea with the old caretaker of the maharaja's house, and after several more days of searching, I decided that the Gwalior house was in fact the most practical solution for our film. The question became how to deal with the elusive caretaker, who lived in a small house on the grounds and whose approach to everything was frustratingly cautious. Working out the conditions for our occupancy, the changes we would need to make, became an arduous enterprise and took many visits, many cups of tea. Each step was a difficult hurdle and at each step, long cables were sent to Ken, who answered with equally long cables.

I had to explain very patiently and most convincingly to the caretaker that our alterations would enhance the beauty of the property since we would be pruning the mango trees and replacing the crumbling brick wall that bordered the garden with an elegant stone balustrade, secured by a strong gate and flanked by two stone benches. Each of these proposals had to be politely presented to his highness the maharaja in Bombay, who with the usual Indian tempo, took weeks for a reply.

The pressing problem was the lawn. First we removed wild brush and mowed the grass. It still did not look like a lawn. I called an expert gardener, a vestige of the colonial days, who wore white jodhpurs and high yellow boots—he looked very much like Trevor Howard. His verdict: the ground had to be plowed and seeded. It had to be done just before the summer monsoon rains and by the fall we would have a gorgeous, lush green lawn, guaranteed. Our only problem was that we had to shoot in two months and be finished shooting *before* the monsoons.

I decided to remove the wild grass and replant the entire area with sod obtainable from the river bank. Then we would water it copiously every day. In spite of the pessimistic prediction of the garden expert, we succeeded—well, partly. A few spots remained yellow and we sprayed them with green paint before shooting.

Usually Indian gardens abound with flowers. Most common are the orange and red kala lilies. Many other colored flowers were also present. They looked beautiful, but what a nuisance these flowers could be, intruding color into the frame composition of the film. At this time Technicolor colors looked screamingly loud, so to retain control of the color composition, I decided to keep the garden entirely green and use hundreds of potted plants as standbys. It would then be a quick and easy operation to place the desired color plants in their proper spots, making it possible for me to compose each frame, almost like painting a picture on canvas. For the time being the twenty garden coolies were kept busy continually watering the transplanted sod.

With the signing of the rental agreement for the Gwalior house, the question of the house and garden set, as well as where we would store our equipment, was all settled. Meanwhile the two heavy electric generators arrived, and we had to find a place to put them. Now I missed the help of a unit manager because I had to make this decision myself. These were wartime German generators, very noisy, and I had to place them near the house to avoid pulling heavy cables. My first idea was to rent the neighboring garden, dig a deep trench, and put the generators underground. But some locals explained that because the Calcutta soil is so wet, as soon as you dig a hole, it fills with water. In fact, many people make primitive swimming pools this way—they just dig out the earth and in two weeks time the hole is filled with water. I did, however, rent the neighboring garden and erected temporary housing for our generators there. Constructed with bamboo frames, these housing walls were made with heavy, jute-filled bags, much like hay-filled mattresses.

Hari introduced me to a young artist, Bansilal Chandra Gupta. He enthusiastically agreed to work with me as my assistant. I also temporarily enlisted the help of Kalyan Gupta, the able Indian production manager. He was later accepted by Ken as a unit manager and became a valuable collaborator.

Jean Renoir remained in Hollywood, but many important locations were still to be found. One of the main settings of the picture was the village street. In the story the father of the English family managed a jute plant situated on the river, and walking home daily from the plant, he passed through the village bazaar. The script called for many scenes in the streets of this Indian village. On our first scouting trip (a party consisting of Hari; Jean's assistant, Kalyan; our unit manager; Bansi, my assistant, and myself), we didn't see a single existing village built near the riverbank. Well, we would try the next best solution.

We soon arrived at a picturesque, seemingly ideal Bengal village. Nestled under gigantic banyan trees, the red-brick, dust-covered earth contrasted strongly with the dark green, almost black, foliage. White saris and dhotis blazed here and there in the strong rays of the sun. The smell of curry was everywhere, mingled with the fragrance of tuberoses and the persistent stench of cow dung and human excrement. Naked children ran around, some with bellies distended from hunger.

Here also was a sacred tree surrounded by a low brick platform. Under this tree were some fruit and flower offerings, three black polished stones, and sitting in the lotus position, a bearded, naked holy man, his forehead marked with white paint, with a little brass bowl for alms at his side. Sitting nearby on the road were bands of monkeys, waiting to grab fruit from an inattentive merchant. A little naked boy sat and carefully peeled a banana. One large monkey detached himself from his friends, ran toward the boy, slapped his face twice, and grabbed the banana. Then he ran away, pursued by his noisy fellow monkeys. The boy cried. We stopped to console him with some candies and proceeded closer to the village to investigate its filmic possibilities. On closer inspection we found that it was far from ideal. The dense foliage created an

Eugene Lourie.

Lourie's assistant, Bansilal Chandra Gupta, called Bansi.

THE RIVER 151

insurmountable lighting problem. We did not have enough amperage to penetrate the deep shadows. There was also the problem of closing the street to its normal activity and compensating the merchants for the money they would lose during the many shooting days. There was also tremendous danger of fire from our arc lamps. Well, Kalyan would estimate the problems from the dollar or rupee point of view. Meanwhile I wanted to investigate the possibility of building our own street set.

With Bansi, we went to the shores of the Hooghly, not far from the Gwalior house. At this point the river was about a mile wide. Long wooden planks over the submerged lowlands led to a landing where ferryboats loaded and unloaded clusters of people crossing the river with their baskets of vegetables, cackling chickens, and baby goats. Fishing boats were moored nearby. Some brazen urchins, amazed by my European coloring, gathered around us and yelled at me mockingly, "Red-faced monkey!"

Higher on the shore under a huge banyan tree was a small shrine to the goddess Kali. A young monk with a shaved head and saffron robe, the guardian of this shrine, invited us for a cup of tea. From him we learned that the lowland shore, now under water from the monsoon floods, would soon be dry. This large piece of land immediately adjacent to the river became in my mind a tempting possibility for building the village set.

Two weeks later we came back. The shores were drying fast. I was pleased with this spot. The land was used only as grazing ground for some goats, and it would be easy to remunerate the few goat owners. It may seem strange to go all the way to India to build a native village. But in viewing the expenses, it became a very practical solution. Besides, I would have the artistic advantage of creating a street to suit the needs of the script. I began projecting the village set. I planned well-placed openings between the stalls to permit a constant view of the river with its incessant activity. We could also organize our own background action on the shore, such as the caulking of the boats or the rolling of the boats to the river as scores of coolies chanted rhythmic songs.

Finally Jean arrived from Hollywood. We reviewed with him the possible solutions to our problem, including building our own village street. This solution pleased him; to shoot the street in controlled conditions would eliminate annoying distractions and the hazards of location shooting. It also appealed to Ken McEldowney since it saved shooting time and cut projected costs.

To build a set of an Indian village in India, we would use the same materials the craftsmen used: bamboo, straw, palm leaves, and the ever-present clay. The problem was how to give these buildings the aged look of an old village. Especially hard was creating the swayback look of sagging roofs. We used the most crooked bamboo we could find for their ridges. Bansi worked furiously, throwing paint, mud, and water to age the walls.

The first building to be erected was the corner teahouse. It was done first for a very selfish reason. As soon as the huge adobe stove was finished and the straw roof covered the airy bamboo frame, we brought tables and benches, and I hired my youngest assistant, an eleven-year-old boy, to have a kettle of boiling water and tea available at all times. We lived under the constant fear of amoebic dysentery, cholera, and other stomach menaces. We didn't drink tap water without boiling it, and we even cleaned our teeth with mineral water. Very soon the shady teahouse became a meeting place for curious visitors, fishermen, boatmen, and the saffron-robed priest of the Kali temple. We shared innumerable cups of tea and smiled at each other, but exchanged few words. Hardly any of our visitors knew two or three English words. But by smiles and gestures we had the friendliest of conversations.

Then every day and all day long, there came scores and scores of children. My candy and cookie budget grew enormously. I remember one deaf-mute child, a pale and slender girl about eleven, who became deeply interested in our activities. For weeks she helped carry bricks and baskets of clay and watched spellbound as the agile workers bound the straw that covered the roofs. Much later when shooting was over, I had to give final orders for the destruction of the set. She was there, looking at us and crying. She understood that this most exciting episode of her life was over and that we would never return. As we were leaving, she ran after our car crying and shouting her incomprehensible sounds. Then she threw herself to the ground, sobbing in despair.

Meanwhile the members of our company arrived in Calcutta. Every morning the bus carried the cast and crew from the Great-Eastern Hotel to Barrackpore and the Gwalior house, our headquarters. As Bansi and I had many errands to do, we had a car and driver assigned to us. The car was an American army surplus car, a dilapidated Plymouth, and the driver was a not-so-dilapidated Sikh, Bachan Singh, who had a luxuriant beard and long hair tucked inside his pink turban. I noticed that almost all of the taxi drivers in Calcutta were Sikhs, the traditional warriors of India. They did not shave their beards, wore turbans, usually carried daggers, and considered taxi driving to be a contest of bravery and skill. The old taxi driver Ram Singh who drove Jean daily to and from Barrackpore also played the part of the English family's gatekeeper. As did all the Calcutta Sikh drivers, he carried a dagger and claimed his right of way by sounding one of his numerous car horns. The taxis usually had four or five. Because I was also taking care of costumes for the film, one day I had to go with Ram Singh to help him select a new turban for his part in the film. There is a street in Calcutta where all the turban dyers operate. While choosing the color for his turban, Ram Singh was surrounded by benevolent color consultants. Because of Ram's age, they all recommended dark maroon or brown. But Ram chose a tender pink; in spite of his old age he was persuaded that his soul was still young. In an hour's time the dyeing was completed and we left with a new pink turban.

The costume designing was quite primitive. I found an English seamstress and we shopped in the labyrinth of the Grand Bazaar for available bolts of material. I decided to dress each of our girls in her own color. That way they would be easily recognizable, even in long shots. Harriet was always dressed in blue, Valerie in golden orange, and Melanie was first seen in a dark school uniform and later changed to red or red and white saris.

The desk in my hotel room became the drafting board for early morning designing. I planned to build a wood-paneled wall to visually shorten the exaggerated length of the terrace at the Gwalior house. I also added a fake stairway for pictorial effect, which would also provide a room underneath the stairway for Harriet's secret hiding place. We acquired a crew of competent carpenters, and they began to build these sets.

With Renoir's concurrence we decided to add secondary background action whenever possible to enrich the texture of the film and to bring in fine details of Indian life. I made a list of possible activities that would be pictorially

Claude Renoir, Jr., Jean Renoir, and coproducer
Kenneth McEldowney (left to right).

Right: *Spectators.*

Far right: *Lourie's youngest
assistant.*

Below, right: *Plasterers working
on the terrace of the private
house.*

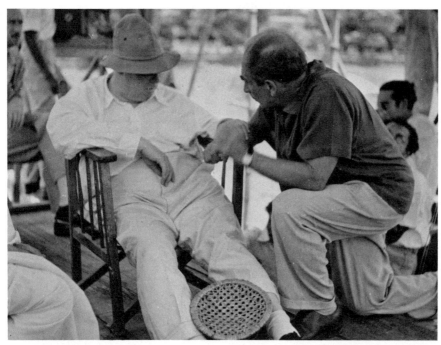

*"We reviewed with him
the possible solutions."*
Renoir and Lourie.

interesting without distracting from the main action. I compared my list with Ram's and Bansi's and conferred with Jean, who made the final decision. To mention but two of the background scenes: the gardeners preparing the marigold garlands while the coffin of little Bogey is brought up the steps and the scene of the monkey man's dancing monkey, which played as counterpoint to the tragic funeral procession.

In the Gwalior garden grew a huge banyan tree. From its upper branches powerful roots dropped down, forming secondary trunks. This single tree was like a green cathedral of entangled trunks, branches, and leaves. Mixed with the banyan leaves were growths of lianas and philodendrons. It would furnish an impressive site for the sequence of Bogey and the cobra.

In the Rumer Godden novel, the tree grew astride the brick wall that bordered the family's garden. Part of the trunk grew inside the garden and part grew outside toward the road. Since this tree, like many large trees in India, was considered a sanctuary for snakes—which were revered as deities—passersby would leave bowls of milk or other donations under the tree as alms. In the film Bogey, playing his wooden pipe enticingly, tries to charm the cobra that lives in the tree with his own bowl of milk.

I was able to build the brick wall with the banyan tree seemingly anchored in it. On the road side of the tree I built a low brick platform for the alms. But I needed to provide for a reverse shot, the view from the tree toward the road. This view was impossible to photograph in the Gwalior garden. There was nothing that looked like a rural road nearby. We shot the necessary reverse shots some ten miles away on a secondary road. For this shot I had to duplicate the foreground brick platform and some hanging banyan roots.

As I mentioned before, the caretaker's house was inside the garden, some distance from the main house. This small bungalow was backed by an entangled banana growth. We decided to use the caretaker's terrace for the exterior of Mr. John's house. In the script the terrace was on the adjoining property and could be reached from the family's garden by climbing a dilapidated brick wall. The bungalow looked right, and it was convenient to shoot the sequence of Melanie's arrival in the old-fashioned buggy and the scenes on the terrace during the siesta sequence without leaving our premises. I had only to build

Left: *Patricia Walters,
Thomas Breen, Adrienne
Corri, Lourie (left to
right), with visitors.*

THE RIVER's *author, Rumer Godden,
with her screenplay collaborator,
Jean Renoir.*

*Lourie instructing local craftsman on
the use of clay construction.*

the old wall that separated the two properties but it had to be easily removable as we used this part of the garden for different sequences. For one important sequence in which Harriet follows Captain John during his wanderings on the riverbank, we found a very interesting brick ruin just above the Ganges. As usual, Renoir was reluctant to shoot the entire sequence on location. The lighting inside the ruin would be difficult and recording the sound, impossible. I later built the set on stage in real brick—staff work being unknown in Calcutta. It was the only solution. For ease of camera movement, I had to have one wild wall, and my ingenious bricklayers built one, ten by eight feet, that moved on wheels.

Many sequences with the children were shot on the lawn, but it was frightfully hot there. I decided to build a convenient place for their games, a summer pavilion, a lacy bamboo structure roofed in thatch. This summerhouse became a favorite place for Nan, the family's Indian nanny, and the children. It also added visual interest to the house.

In the course of building the pavilion, I became acquainted with a breed of craftsmen then unknown to me, the straw-laying artists. One of them, a dark slender fellow, was quite prodigious, finishing the entire roof of the garden pavilion in one day. Later he helped build the village street. One day, arriving at the village set, then in the midst of construction, I noticed that some of my workers were missing. I asked if anyone had seen the straw master. The answer came, "He is sick. He is down with cholera!" I saw him lying on the ground, visibly in pain. Fortunately it turned out not to be cholera, but people's constant fear of the sickness was not unusual. Every day on the front page of the paper appeared a tally of the day's cholera cases. It was as familiar as the weather forecast in the *Los Angeles Times.* In India we learned that the thread separating life and death is a fragile one. In the course of the picture we lost two coolies to the snakebite of a very tiny beautiful green snake that could open its mouth only as wide as to be able to sting the toe or finger of its unlucky victim. Death followed quickly.

I think that Indians developed a certain immunity, a certain familiarity with the idea of death. Once while working on the village set, I saw a group of Indians squatting at the roadside. They had been carrying the body of a friend tied to his string bed, the same bed he had slept in all his life. They probably came from far away, starting their journey in the middle of the night. Now they were tired and hungry. From small bundles of banana leaves they took some cooked rice and ate it, chewing slowly and licking their fingers clean. They sat around the dead man, the same friend they knew in life, his features blank, ashen pale, eyelids closed. The repast finished, four men lifted the corpse on its string bed and resumed their march toward the temple steps of the river. There they would burn the body and throw the ashes in the muddy water. As wood for burning is expensive, some parts of the body, possibly the feet, would remain uncharred. Fish or prawns would feed on them. The ashes carried by the current would be deposited in the rice fields. The men, without their friend, would return to their faraway village, squatting again at the roadside for a rest.

This story and some others I tell may not seem related to the work of a production designer. But in filming this picture, stories like this were important and influenced Renoir's thinking and the rest of us as well. We all worked under the spell of Indian lore and tried to convey our impressions to the future audiences of *The River*.

Another fleeting impression found its way into the picture. In Calcutta some streets are inhabited by craftsmen of the same trade. There is one narrow street, occupied by hundreds of stray chickens, children, cows, and mangy dogs, where in shops open to the street, masters sculpted elegant images of gods in clay. There are many gods in the Indian Hindu pantheon and each god has its memorial date when he or she is worshipped and a festival is celebrated. The sculptors busily prepared the idols of the gods for the dates of their celebrations, called *pujas*. The clay figures, as small as eighteen inches or as tall as five feet, are made in clay on a straw skeleton. They are dried thoroughly in the sun and then colored in the inimitable Indian color combinations. Sometimes they are dressed in silk and shiny jewels. As the date of a particular *puja* approaches, customers arrive. The images are taken away, transported by rickshaw or cart to the places of festivities—schools, shops owned by religious people, or homes of worshipping neighbors. The *puja* is celebrated with fruit and flower offerings, the loud crashing of cymballums, the blowing of noisy conches, and the beating of tablas, Indian drums. The next day the statue of the god is taken to the river and immersed, no longer sanctified since the day of the *puja* had passed. The clay statue dissolves, joining the clay at the bottom of the river.

In our picture the image maker had his shop on the street set. A *puja* was featured during the sequence showing Diwali, the festival of lights, and the Kali statue was seen being immersed in the river. In fact, I had the chance to direct some of these second-unit scenes while Claude was immobilized for some days with typhoid fever and Jean stayed at the hotel to work on the script.

Before shooting started we had our own *puja* organized by the Indian crew. An idol of the goddess of learning and arts—I believe her name was Saraswati, she sat next to a swan—was brought in and decorated with flowers, golden papers, and lights. Alms were brought and the noisy celebration went on for many hours. Next, with not too much ceremony, the statue was immersed in the river opposite the Gwalior house.

The date of the beginning of shooting approached. But the Indian backers of the film insisted on consulting the astrologer for the propitious date. This date was given, but we were not yet ready to start filming. And so to mislead the gods we celebrated a false beginning. The camera was sanctified by a holy man, some flower garlands were hung around the Technicolor camera, and other garlands were hung around the necks of Jean, Claude, myself, and others. Renoir had to shoot some scenes of the film and promise to incorporate them in the release print of the final picture.

The sequence of unloading the jute was more elaborate than anticipated. The jute plants were located in Calcutta, not in the surrounding countryside, as required by the script. And so I had to build wooden wharfs sticking above the water. Technically it was very difficult, sinking and supporting poles in the fast-moving Hooghly River. But human problems were just as difficult. I chose a relatively deserted spot on the shore. However, bricks were fired at a place close by, and in spite of our deal with the landowner, the brickmaker claimed loading rights to the spot. Then another man claimed *his* rights. Each of these claimants came with his agent, and soon the construction site of my set became a gathering place of legal representatives, all dressed in white dhotis—a piece of cotton material that draped around their legs—and all carrying black umbrellas and satchels full of important-looking papers. But I did succeed in con-

Shooting.

structing three slender wharfs that projected far above the river, and we soon
shot the scene of loaded barges pulling in and being unloaded by rows of bronzed
coolies.

In my construction work I had to endure many problems with agents.
When I needed a sewing machine operator to sew canvases for the generator
insulation, I asked Kalyan to send me one. After the man appeared and money
matters were agreed upon, I saw in front of me the agent for the poor tailor
who would come to work the next day but would have to shell over half his
salary to this enterprising individual. When I needed thousands and thousands
of bricks for the construction of the village street, the merchant with whom we
made the deal was not the merchant but a representative who reserved a com-

mission fee for himself. Moreover, he was the one who furnished us with labor, ordered the barges for us, and made a very lucrative occupation out of representing suppliers for the American film company. And as I suspected, when Bansi started to count the bricks delivered to our set, we discovered that one-third of the shipment was missing. I blew up and refused all further dealings with this individual. His revenge proved worthy of any gangster's.

We were shooting a night scene in the village set. Attracted by the cameras, lights, and actors, a crowd of curious bystanders surrounded us. Two policemen tried to keep order. Suddenly our dishonest brick supplier appeared leading a boisterous mob of energetic young hooligans. They tried to incite the crowd by shouting, "The American company is here in India to kidnap young Indian women," and other nonsensical provocations. Stones were thrown and parts of the set were shaken and destroyed.

Protected by the two policemen, the company folded up and departed. The night shooting was canceled. I do not know what arguments or how many rupees it took for Kalyan to quiet the gangster. I do remember that we had to reschedule shooting that scene and come back to the village set days later.

Life for the company was not always peaceful. Bengal and particularly Calcutta were overpopulated, choked by the influx of Hindu refugees from Moslem Pakistan. It was estimated that more than two million refugees camped on the streets, in makeshift camps, or under the roof of the railroad station. Rumors were circulated among these refugees that many remaining Hindus in Pakistan were being murdered, their houses burnt to the ground. In reaction to these rumors, some Muslims were hunted and killed. The newspapers called these incidents a "communal disorder." At night here and there the sky was red from flaming Muslim houses. Driving home from Barrackpore one day, I saw two bodies smeared with blood lying on the ground. McEldowney acquired police protection for our company, and the bus that transported the actors was accompanied by armed guards.

Meanwhile we had to prepare the dangerous scene of Bogey and the cobra. From the snake poison center of the local university, some candidates were brought for the part. The first cobra presented was of the huge desert variety. Jean thought its size was too exaggerated and soon a medium-sized snake was produced. Little Richard Foster, who played Bogey, was brave. Even though the poison was milked from the snake's fangs, the cobra looked terrifying. However, snakes are lazy actors; this particular cobra hid in its basket each moment it could escape from the trainer. The snake reminded me of George Sanders who used to take naps in his trailer between takes.

In Rumer's book Bogey liked to play with lizards and grass snakes; he played army with insects, not toy soldiers. "They are all tin," he said. "I play soldiers with n'insects." He had his own secret life and his only confidant was little Kanu, the Indian boy. In the novel, Kanu was younger than Bogey; but as our Bogey was small and quite childish, finding him a smaller pal who could take direction from Jean was difficult.

In building our village street, I was surrounded all day by children, all eager helpers in our construction and in disposing of our candy supply. One of the boys, the son of a boatman, was unusually bright. I thought he might be good in the part of Kanu. I took him to the Gwalior house to meet Jean, who saw the same qualities in him. But his personality changed the relationship slightly between Bogey and Kanu. Being larger and more mature, it was Kanu (his real name was Nimai) who took the initiative, becoming a bit like Bogey's protector. Their relationship formed a perfect partnership in the film. Soon Kanu became the favorite of the actors and crew. He developed a tremendous appetite and grew heavier each day. I think with sadness of what became of him after our company left Calcutta. No more glory of being in the limelight, no more tasty nourishing meals with the film crew. It was over, and he had to return to the very humble surroundings of a boatman's hut.

The next exterior to prepare was the "Bogey tree," the huge, flamboyant royal poinciana where Bogey climbs a rope to the place where he keeps his lizard and turtle treasures. Tied to the branches of that same tree was the swing Harriet and Valerie used as the place for their eternal quarrels. This exotic tree bloomed every spring and was covered with clusters of bright red flowers. But as I was not sure that the flowers would cover the lower branches, and since the higher branches were out of the camera frame, I ordered scores and scores of paper flower clusters from the Calcutta bazaar. The flamboyant tree looked even more spectacular under its thick red cover of paper flowers.

One of the more important exteriors we had to find was the banana grove where the three lovesick girls play a strange game of hide-and-seek with Captain John. Each of the girls comes with a bouquet of flowers, and two of them finally witness the kiss that Captain John bestows on the blushing Valerie.

This sequence marks the end of an important episode in the lives of the girls. After this scene the film unfolds quickly in a succession of fast-paced sequences: Bogey's tragic death and burial; Harriet's despair and attempted suicide; her reconciliation with Captain John and acceptance of whatever happens; the end of Captain John's visit to India and return to the United States.

The next sequence occurs months later. It is spring. An exuberant profusion of flowers is everywhere. The "Bogey tree" is bright with red blossoms. In the streets noisy crowds celebrate the traditional spring festival of colors, a day during which a person can say to anyone without restraint what he thinks of him. People freely insult each other and throw liquid or powdered colors on anyone's clothes or face without risk of punishment. These colors are difficult to wash off. I saw many poor coolies, who often had but one shirt, wearing multicolored shirts or dhotis—yellow, red, blue, green—for months after the spring festival.

Against the background sounds of noisy merriment, a new baby girl is born to the family, and at the same time, three letters arrive, postmarked from America. The letters are for the three girls, from Captain John. But caught up in their joy at the birth of the baby, the girls ignore the letters, which fall to the ground, discarded and forgotten. The three girls lean on the terrace handrail and look out at the eternally flowing river. The camera zooms in on the river, and Harriet says, "And here is the baby! The baby . . . and us . . . and the big river . . . the whole world . . . and everything!"

This sequence was to be the finale of the picture.

But we had a problem. The house was not close enough to the river for us to shoot the final scene as described. We could approximate the scene by shooting the episode on the terrace; then we would make a reverse shot of the girls' faces and then cut to a shot of the back of their heads to give their point of view. This separate p.o.v. shot would not be done on the terrace but on an independent platform close to the river.

The first kiss. Captain John (Thomas Breen) and Valerie (Adrienne Corri).

"I offered to build a platform on the shore and erect on it a replica of the terrace." Sitting under the umbrella behind the cows is the sound department.

Closer view of the terrace built at the river's edge. Jean Renoir is wearing the hat and stands behind the camera platform. They are shooting a reverse-angle shot.

I thought, however, that this was not the best way of shooting this last scene. I offered to build a platform on the shore and erect on it a replica of the terrace, two columns, and a handrailing. On the replica the three girls would enter the frame and go toward the railing, the camera on a crane following their movement continuously. Then the camera would rise to get the full view of the river. The scene would be shot in one smooth, economical movement.

To achieve this set with an inexperienced construction crew was a challenge. It required all of our forty coolies, with Ken constantly prodding them, to move the heavy crane by hand.

Outdoor shooting proceeded. The idea of placing the artificial flowers in the garden worked fine. Without false modesty I must say that this first Technicolor film shot in India had remarkable colors. One critic even observed that "In this picture Jean Renoir in his color treatment is a worthy son of his father, the great painter." Jokingly, Jean told me about this notice and said, "You see, Gene, you are my 'father' responsible for the color treatment!"

Shooting in color was difficult under the merciless Indian sun. Especially difficult was the contrast between light spots in sunlight and the dark green, almost black, mango leaves that bordered our garden. To help Claude, I sprayed the mango trees in light colors. The traveling shots coming from the shady interior of the teahouse to the brightly lit village street was another tricky problem for Claude. Flooding the interior of the teahouse with all the available reflectors was not sufficient, and these shots required acrobatic precision as Claude and Ram quickly changed the aperture of the lens. Another production problem was that we had to send the exposed negative each day to Technicolor in London. Sometimes Renoir saw rushes weeks later, and Claude was left guessing if his exposures were correct.

In February we were still shooting outdoors; the frangipani trees were brilliantly in bloom and the scent was intoxicating. Mischievious monkeys jumped noisily from one corrugated tin roof to another or sat high in the branches and threw nuts at our actors. One scene is especially memorable. As days were usually warm, Jean left his jacket on a bush while directing a scene in the garden. Suddenly a good-sized monkey approached the bush and grabbed Jean's coat. Dido (Jean's wife) quickly seized the other side of the coat. There they were, the antagonists, each pulling Jean's coat across the bush. The monkey showed his teeth menacingly, but Dido won the contest.

Night scenes after the heat subsided were the most enjoyable for the crew. We shot the Diwali at night, the festival of lights, when thousands of oil lamps festooned garden walls, tree branches, and stairways. We also shot the meeting of Captain John and Valerie on the terrace at night. Inside the house the record player played the haunting "Invitation to the Dance" by Carl Maria von Weber. Night moths, excited by the arc lights, flew around and around in the humid heat finally became entangled in Valerie's hair. It created an enchanting moment in the film.

We still had to find a spot to shoot the purely Indian scenes for the so-called "Tales of Harriet." Scouting was conducted one Sunday so that Claude could join the party. It was a day-long outing toward the small villages surrounded by jungle in the river delta. There were four of us: Claude, Bansi, myself, and Satyajit Ray, at that time a talented designer friend of Bansi's. Whitewashed clay walls, thatch roofs—these peaceful and slow-paced villages were the perfect location for Harriet's fairy tale. We looked at and photographed some interiors of peasant houses and clean whitewashed yards with their round-towered granaries. Later though, Renoir decided to film almost all of Harriet's fairy tale on stage.

Shooting inside the Gwalior house was judged inconvenient, so we decided to build the interiors on a regular stage organized with lights, sound-proofing, and even with dressing rooms. There were numerous film studios in Calcutta. Film production in India was a prolific enterprise, but their mode of production was somewhat different from ours. Their shooting schedules were incredible. Few actors were considered stars; they usually started many pictures simultaneously. When they had finished a sequence of a film, they switched studios and went on shooting another picture. The crews waited patiently for the actors to become available again. As salaries were very low, it did not bother producers too much. On the other hand, they usually worked with very low budgets. I saw studios where the negative was developed, the picture viewed only from the negative, and the first print was made from this same edited negative.

In Calcutta Ken McEldowney found a brand new stage of large dimensions. The cement floors were new, so clean compared with the run-down stages we had visited earlier.

The first order of business was to interview and hire a new crew of construction workers, as our first crew was still busy at the Gwalior house. Kalyan brought me a very impressive head of construction. He looked dignified, like a Roman senator—even more like Barry Goldwater. He was available, but we had to hire him with all his crew. They were all from the same village, too far away for everyday commuting so they had to be housed on the studio grounds. Lodging was no problem once I assigned them a plot in the studio garden. In one day they built a large hut with a floor of clean-washed clay mixed with cow dung. They also built a lean-to for their cooking. The choice of this construction foreman was a happy one; without speaking a word of each other's language, we completely understood each other.

Spending a few hours on the new stage planning the first sets to be built, I noticed some potential trouble. The studio was situated in a quiet neighborhood, but a railroad line passed close by, and I was amazed by the number of trains this railroad operated. Sound takes during shooting would be interrupted about thirty times a day. The other sound problem came from vociferous crows in the trees surrounding the stage. During the production I often witnessed a furious Ken run from the stage to chase away the crows with a slingshot.

The first set built was the living room of the family house where, during the Diwali festival, a dancing party was held, a small affair at which the children danced with their father or with each other. But Captain John's presence and the rivalry among the three girls added dramatic tension to the dancing.

The great majority of floors in Indian homes were in colored cement and thoroughly polished with pumice stone. Often they were also polished with wax. As our stage had a new cement floor, well-finished and absolutely flat, I decided to paint, varnish, and wax it. Little did I know that some chemical in the fresh cement would discolor the paint pigment. The sample test color (the floor was to be red, as in most Indian homes) became absolutely colorless the next day and when repainted was bleached out again. The set was completed, painted, furnished, and the company was ready to start shooting, but my floors remained stubbornly colorless. In desperation, Bansi and I tried every possible gimmick. Finally, one day before shooting, I mixed the supposedly special cement color powder with a floor wax and applied it abundantly to the floor. Miracle—the next day the floor was still red! We were ready for shooting. The only problem—it was dreadfully slippery. In the dancing scenes the actors did not simply move on the floor, they slid. It was like dancing on skates. However, by afternoon, under the heat of the arc lamps, the situation turned normal and we finished the sequence without incident, except for some exaggerated, skatelike, graceful dancing.

The stage was large and I could place the second important set on the same floor. It was the interior of Mr. John's house. The open doors to the front terrace had to be backed by a view of the bamboo growth. Scenic artists as we know them in Hollywood or France or England were unknown in Calcutta. But a friend of Bansi's was a modern abstract painter. He had never painted scenery, but at least he knew how to handle a brush and mix paint. Together with him I undertook to paint all the scenic backdrops. I took this painter to the Gwalior house where we looked from the caretaker's house to the banana growth in the background. We looked by squinting our eyes slightly and saw mostly splashes of dark green or dark red in places of shadow, and light, almost lemon yellow spots in the sunlight. We painted our backdrop the same way, using the largest brushes we could find. The completed backdrop was similar to Claude Monet's impressionist painting of *Water Lilies* (or *Nympheas*). However, in our film, photographed through the open door of the terrace, our banana growth looked more realistic.

I also used the same approach (and the same helper) to paint the very blurred jungle backing behind the set of the ruined temple and the large, landscape backing used for a scene on the river at night. During that night episode, we used a real, sawed-off riverboat for Harriet's scene with Captain John, which occurs after the fishermen rescue her from drowning. I did one thing different, though, for the night landscape backdrop. I used plain blue muslin and on it painted only lantern lights reflected in the river, using soft white pastel chalk.

I learned in this film that loosely painted, impressionistic scenes with blurred images looked more realistic than Hollywood studio backdrops scrupulously painted by professional scenic artists. In fact, in photographs of landscapes the farthest views do look out of focus and blurred.

I designed the Mr. John set as a large room with high ceilings. It was kept completely bare of decoration, conveying the quiet, reflective spirit of Mr. John and the general feeling of simplicity prevalent in Indian interiors.

When it came to the family's dining room, I again opted for plain white walls and minimum furniture—only what was needed for the action.

In all my designing, I followed my conviction that overdressing sets is only confusing. Working on the principle that "less is more," I presumed that in the rapidly changing frames of a film, an audience has no time to absorb all the details and trinkets that often crowd a set. If you want to show a chair, use it. If the chair is useless for action, forget it. When Jean first came to the set, he was surprised by its sparseness. However, he soon accepted my point of view, and I saw him eagerly pointing to a lonely chair or a single sideboard, asking, "Is this piece really necessary?" Soon I found myself saving chairs from being sacrificed.

As I mentioned, the set of the half-ruined temple (for which we shot exteriors on the banks of the Hooghly River) was built of real bricks with a statue of Krishna made by a street sculptor who usually modeled idols for Indian festivals. In the back of this temple was a gaping hole through which could be seen the impressionistic rendering made by myself and the abstract painter.

Finally shooting with the English and American actors came to an end. The only remaining sequence was Harriet's fairy tale. It was to be done in a slightly simplified visual style reminiscent of naive, popular Indian folk images. Only some Indian actors, musicians, and dancers would be used in the shooting, so we relaxed the tempo of our construction. For the barefoot dancing sequence and the festive ornamentation of the ground for the wedding scene, Bansi, Hari, and the dancers and musicians insisted that we make a real Bengal village floor of clay mixed with fresh cow dung. Cow dung in India is supposed to possess very special qualities as a building material. The stage had the strong smell of a cowshed for several days, but we had a smooth floor that was perfect for bare feet.

Jean and the shooting crew were leaving for two days to shoot river scenes

Kenneth McEldowney supervising the movement of the camera crane.

in the pond near a small Bengal village. He left my construction crew to complete the yard and the house for the Indian fairy tale. This set was built on the clay and dung floor.

It was an old Indian tradition to paint an ornamental design on the floor for a wedding. It looked like a painted rug and was usually painted freehand by women using a mixture of rice flour and water. Many of Bansi's friends were artists trained in the folk arts at the University of Rabindranath Tagore, named after the famous Bengal scholar and writer. With their help the floor was painted; and because it looked to typically Indian it was also used as a background for the main title and credits.

We finished shooting Radha's spectacular dancing sequence in Harriet's fairy tale where she is transformed into Lord Krishna's goddess wife. It was done on the stage against a plain, whitewashed wall. The musicians sat on the floor playing the usual accompaniment on tablas, a flute, and cymballums, with the added jingling of the little bells attached to Radha's feet. The plain uncolored background did not detract from the moving silhouette of the dancer.

The composing and recording of the music was a story in itself. Jean needed a song for the beginning of the picture. He wanted to convey the feeling of India in the song of a fisherman as he moves his boat out into the heavy river traffic. In the circle of Hari and Bansi's friends, we found a chorus master, a timid young musician, who rehearsed with singers and improvised songs. He first came to the Gwalior house with his portable harmonium and composed *The River Song,* the song that Renoir used as the film's opening song, as well as its theme song. Some other musical groups improvised and performed other compositions for different scenes in the film, such as the Diwali festival and the spring festival. In fact, when shooting was finished, I remained with Jean to help him record more music and singing. At this time the scoring of the picture was not yet decided, but Jean felt that a native Indian score would be the most appropriate for the film. In this decision he was obviously right. The score from *The River* became a very successful record album as well.

The final decision about scoring the film entirely with Indian music was made later, about a year after we finished shooting. We left India with the Renoirs in May 1950. On my way back to Hollywood I stopped for a few days in Paris. There I was made an offer to design an American production that would be shot in Paris and Nice, starring Errol Flynn, Vincent Price, and Agnes Moorehead. This film kept me in France until November.

Back in Hollywood Jean showed me the newly edited *River.* Only then was I able to see many shots I had missed in Calcutta. In seeing the edited film, I was overwhelmed by the sorcery of this basically simple story. I had the feeling that Jean Renoir, more than in his other pictures, was living compassionately with his characters, not just viewing them from afar.

At this time Renoir decided not to have a musical score composed for the picture. Instead he would use a "collage" of the Indian music we had recorded in Calcutta.

It was obvious that shooting the film in India had added extraordinary visual richness and new moral perspectives to the story. The spirit of India also helped create in the film a deep feeling of magic and enchantment.

The River was premiered at the Venice Film Festival in 1951. It won first prize there, the Golden Lion. *The River* was shown all over the world and was given a loving reception. Some critics thought the story was not significant enough and called it a mixture of a travelog and a sugary concoction of adolescent love. They missed entirely the poetry of the film.

As for their objection to the lack of significance of the film's theme, I think very often the simplest subjects give birth to the truest masterpieces, and *The River* is one of the best examples of this.

After all, three apples on a kitchen table were all that Cézanne needed to produce an immortal painting.

It was one of Renoir's achievements that he created a film as significant and moving as *The River* with such a simple story.

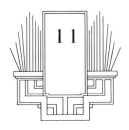

Special Effects Pictures:
THE ADVENTURES OF
CAPTAIN FABIAN and
A CRACK IN THE WORLD

I *was* often asked to design or to direct special effects pictures. These films show actions impossible to photograph in normal conditions, such as volcanic eruptions, tidal waves, collapsing mountains, or dinosaurs in their prehistoric habitat. Some films require sets of unusual size or complexity that would be difficult to build within the normal budget of a motion picture production.

The special demands of these pictures on one's imagination and ingenuity often make them more enjoyable and challenging than designing boring reproductions of hotel rooms and police stations that are frequently the settings of modern films.

From my early connections with motion pictures, I became familiar with various types of "film tricks," or special effects. While designing costumes for the historical film *Le Joueur d'échecs (The Chessplayer)*, I worked in close collaboration with the art director, Jean Perrier. I saw him use a spectacular glass

Painted glass shot (upper half of still) from
LE JOUEUR D'ÉCHECS (1928).

shot where a scene is photographed through a large transparent glass, the upper portion of which was painted over with a large view of the Czar's Winter Palace in St. Petersburg. Through the clear lower portion of the glass was seen the ground of the studio lot, covered with artificial snow and an impressive display of Czarist guards. The combined picture showed a realistic military parade on the snowy ground in front of the palace.

In Paris two of my friends, Minine and Wilke, both Russian art directors, specialized in building miniatures, often combining them with live action. So I became familiar with solving problems of the special effects pictures. I was called on to use my knowledge of miniatures in the film *Les Yeux noirs (Dark Eyes)*, a picture with action set in Czarist Russia, a popular location for films in the thirties. I built an impressively long Russian street in miniature, impossible to photograph on any Parisian location. I made a long traveling shot alongside this street, and we used the shot in the film as the point of view of a troika traversing the imaginary Russian town.

One of my next films was also in a Russian setting, *Nuits de feu (Blazing Nights)*, based on a novel by Tolstoy and directed by Marcel l'Herbier. One of the scenes was to take place in a theater box of the Imperial Opera. The scene was an intimate one between the three protagonists, but l'Herbier wanted the view from the box to contain the entire theater: four rows of balconies, the ballet being performed on stage, and a huge chandelier hanging from an ornate ceiling. The only practical solution that came to mind was using a special effects trick, hanging miniatures. I built the luxurious theater box on a slightly elevated platform because the normal angle of vision from a box plunges down somewhat, below the floor line of the box. I used the largest stage of the Pathé studios, Joinville, which provided ample depth to build the stage with its ornate proscenium and velvet curtains. The distance between our theater box and the stage was about the same as in a real theater. In the space between the box and the stage, a hanging miniature was placed that represented in one-tenth scale the interior of the theater, with its balconies, painted ceiling, and chandelier. In calculating the camera angle, this miniature was placed close to the opening of the box so the miniature proscenium visually blended with the life-size proscenium. It worked perfectly. As I remember, the scene opened as the

Right: *The use of forced perspective from* LES YEUX NOIRS *(1934). The background figure is a child dressed as a man, complete with beard.*

Left: *Hanging miniatures from Marcel L'Herbier's* NUITS DE FEU.

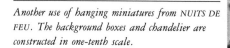

Another use of hanging miniatures from NUITS DE FEU. *The background boxes and chandelier are constructed in one-tenth scale.*

actors took their seats in the box, the chandelier dimmed, the curtain rose, and the ballet, in a life-size setting, began on stage in the background.

The scene was considered successful and one of the scenic attractions of the film. However, the producer, Mr. Luka, wanted to hold a gala reception for exhibitors and foreign theater owners, using a spectacular set from the film, as well as the actors and possibly some of the numerous extras, and he asked me to invent such a scene, even though it did not exist in the script. I came up with an idea—why not show the spectacular stairway of the opera theater and stage the exit of the glittering audience, perhaps including the czar himself. As I had designed the costumes as well as the sets, I knew that we had genuine costumes of the Russian Imperial Guard as well as other full-dress uniforms available for a striking sequence.

I proposed to build only a strict minimum of steps and platforms necessary for the action, and I planned to complete the set with the required arches, columns, chandeliers, and so on in miniature. L'Herbier kindly agreed to my additional scene and even said he found it full of panache. Luka could happily entertain his guests on the film's set and it proved cheaper than the price of champagne at the gala.

I have used miniatures in many films I designed. They can be helpful for many simple or complicated problems, but I know that miniatures are not the miraculous panacea some producers think they are, a cure-all for any difficult problem. In encountering a tricky sequence to shoot, I often heard a producer say, "Gene, let's do it in miniatures." Sometimes I had to answer regretfully that it was not possible.

Basically, here are some situations where miniatures can be used: (1) purely miniature scenes, where everything you see on the screen is miniature, such as views of volcanoes, ships in raging seas, fires, automobile accidents, and battlefields; (2) miniatures combined with live action, shot simultaneously on the same negative. These can be either hanging miniatures or miniature backgrounds; and (3) miniatures optically combined with live action, where the live action is shot separately and combined later through photography. This allows the scenes to be shot in different places and at different times.

Each of these classifications has its own prerequisites. For example, the scale of each miniature has to be guided by practical considerations of construction and shooting. Which scene is easier to build and which is more practical to shoot? As a rule of thumb, large-scale miniatures photograph closer to reality but are more costly to build and require more shooting space.

I personally favor a scale of one-tenth of the actual settings or objects. However, it depends on exactly what the miniature has to represent. If the miniature has to show a vast panorama or an extremely large object, such as a mountain or a skyscraper, it has to be built to a smaller scale. For example, when I made *Krakatoa* at Cinecitta studio in Rome, I had to build an erupting volcano. In reality, the actual volcano was probably more than 1,000 feet high. If the miniature had been built in one-tenth scale, it would have had to be 100 feet tall, almost an impossibility. I chose a more modest size of about thirty feet. I was guided to this choice by the existing sky backing in the Cinecitta studio tank, which was seventy feet high and left sufficient space for the ascending smoke between the top of the volcano and the upper limit of the backing. Also, this size was handy for special effects crews to load the volcano with explosives, smoke, and other effects that would produce an effective eruption.

It is possible to build miniatures in a very small scale, but the construction sometimes will require the skill of a jeweler. Also, much smaller miniatures require considerable acceleration of the camera speed, the speed at which the motion picture is shot. Films are usually shot at twenty-four frames per second. At this speed movements on the screen correspond to movements in life. If the film is shot at double the normal speed, that is, forty-eight frames per second, but is still projected at twenty-four frames per second, all movements on the screen will seem slower.

If moving miniatures, such as a train, are shot at twenty-four frames per second, their movements will seem exaggeratedly fast. For example, when one is shooting a collapsing building, the debris will fall at the same speed as life-size building debris. But the height of a miniature six-story building at one-tenth scale will be only six feet. The debris would fall from supposedly fifty feet in the same time it takes to fall from the six-foot miniature. In other words, the fall of the debris would appear ten times faster. To give the illusion of normal speed of falling, we would have to shoot the motion to appear ten times slower; thus the camera would shoot ten times the normal speed. The theoretical rule is to shoot miniatures at a speed corresponding to the scale; for example, a miniature built one inch per foot should be accelerated twelve times.

However, in practice, slower acceleration of the camera gives a more realistic appearance to the speed of the object on screen. I found that by accelerating the camera four or five times the normal speed (96 to 120 frames per second), I would get a miniature movement that appeared realistic. The slow motion also gives miniatures the appearance of weight, keeping their movement less jerky.

Later in this chapter I describe some problems I had in shooting combined scenes where live action was shot simultaneously with background miniature action.

After successfully handling the foreground (or hanging) miniature of the opera stairway in the L'Herbier picture, I had more occasions to use this ingenious method, so I will speak of two pictures I designed. Both required many special effects sequences, most of them using foreground miniatures.

The first film was *The Adventures of Captain Fabian* with Errol Flynn and Vincent Price, a Franco-American coproduction, shot in Nice and Paris in 1950; the second film was *A Crack in the World*, shot in Spain by an American company in 1963.

Both pictures presented similar problems, the practical and budgetary impossibilities of producing very complicated sets required by the scripts. In the first picture I had to show an 1890s New Orleans waterfront, the set to be erected in Nice, complete with paddlewheel steamers and sailing ships.

In the second picture, *A Crack in the World*, I had to show sets representing an exploding gantry tower, the eruption of a volcano that showered streams of incandescent lava, and a futuristic, underground scientific center as it was destroyed by an earthquake. And more, much more.

For each of these pictures, different solutions could have been adopted, and I will explain my choice of certain procedures.

My work on *Captain Fabian* began in 1950, when I stopped for a few days in Paris on my way back from India, where I had just finished shooting *The River* with Jean Renoir.

It was very pleasant to walk along the Champs Élysées in May. There one day I ran into Robert Florey, the Hollywood director.

"What are you doing in Paris?" he asked.

I told him.

"And you?" I asked in turn.

He told me he was in France to direct a Franco-American coproduction for the producer Bill Marshall. Florey was to direct the French version of the film, then Bill, using the same sets and many of the same actors, would direct the film in English.

"Let's see Bill," he suggested, "I would like to introduce you. He would probably be happy for you to design the production."

That same morning we met Bill Marshall. The script was not earth shattering, but the possibility of picking my own French crew, working with my friend Sacha Kamenka, the production manager, and shooting in Nice and Paris was alluring. Moreover, the picture posed challenging visual problems.

The next morning I was reading the melodramatic script and making a set list.

In the picture a fierce Cajun servant girl decides to marry a society playboy (Vincent Price) from a rich New Orleans shipping family. The girl was played by Micheline Presle, at this time married to Bill Marshall. After some improbable dramatic events and an accidental killing, she is saved from the gallows by a dashing sea captain, Fabian, played by Errol Flynn. She eventually falls in love with him. However, several murders later, she marries the reluctant Vincent Price. And so on. After much treachery, attempted killings, a gang battle on the waterfront, and a final confrontation between Flynn and Price, the picture ends with a spectacular explosion and the burning of Fabian's ship.

In choosing my crew, I first called Max Douy, my talented former assistant in prewar years, now a full-fledged art director. I was very happy about his agreeing to collaborate on this project.

The action of the film was laid in New Orleans, but the setting required by the script did not correspond to the real New Orleans waterfront of 1890. I chose to create a romantic approximation of New Orleans. I also had to create

THE ADVENTURES OF CAPTAIN FABIAN.

Aunt Jesebel (Agnes Moorehead), Captain Fabian (Errol Flynn), Lea Marriotte (Micheline Presle).

an old fortress that would adjoin the wharf and underground passages leading to jail cells.

With an unlimited production budget, the simplest way to realize the scene would be to find an available spot on an existing wharf and there build replicas of paddle steamers, schooners, and other ships of the period. Then we could dress the waterfront with cotton bales and other waterfront props.

But we did not have the necessary budget for this operation, so I decided that we must rely on motion picture trickery.

These tricks are old, consisting of adding nonexisting details to a setting by painting or building. I could build the necessary shooting space on the studio lot and add the paddle steamers, sailing ships, and sea horizon in a post-painted matte shot. Or we could shoot the scene on an actual waterfront and add the missing elements on a painted glass placed in front of the camera, leaving the action of the scene visible through the clear part of the glass.

The problem with these painted shots is they lack movement; even when they are well painted, they look dead or require complicated optical procedures, like smoke rising from the stacks of steamers, to add some live action. The glass shot also presents an additional problem: it has to be painted beforehand when it is difficult to know exactly what the lighting conditions will be on a given day.

That is why I chose the hanging miniature. Here the part of the set impossible to build life-size is built in miniature and placed in front of the camera, between the lens and the actual setting. The miniature is shot at the same time as the action. It also allows movement of sails and ships, rising smoke, and the fluttering of flags in the wind. The set and miniature are lit simultaneously; in our case for *Fabian,* by the same sunlight. The other advantage of this method is that the finished picture can be viewed in the next day's rushes.

The ships in the miniature were placed close together, shielding us from the close view of the surface of the sea. Above the line of the ships, however, we could see the distant sea, a painted cutout decorated with some loose-hanging spangles. Their shimmering gave an illusion of the distant flashing of waves.

Working and living in Nice was pleasant and we had more leisure time than we anticipated. But there were continual contractual problems between

Right: *The hanging miniature.*

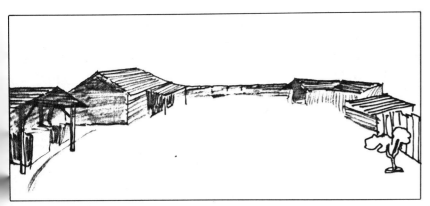

The real set built on the studio lot.

The composite when live set and miniature are merged.

Above: *Placing the hanging miniature.*

Another angle of the miniature.

Left: *The live set and the hanging miniature showing the separation between the two.*

The actual shot.

Dorfman, the French producer, and Bill Marshall and Republic Pictures, the American partners. Other problems occurred between Marshall and Errol Flynn— or rather, between their lawyers. These lawyers were flown from California just to unravel some points in the contracts. The warm Mediterranean sun was not conducive to quick decisions. Errol's beautiful black yacht was moored opposite the Hotel Negresco where Errol resided, while below on the flowery sidewalk terrace, the lawyers discussed as they sipped their cold drinks. Meanwhile, squeezed into his tiny English minicar, Vincent Price and his wife investigated the best-known restaurants in the small towns near Nice.

After all the discussions, it was decided that the picture would be shot only in the American version and that the French would be looped in later. So Florey lost his directorial assignment. He remained on the film as a consultant to Bill Marshall.

We decided to shoot the day and night sequences of the exterior of Fabian's schooner in the Yacht Club harbor of Villefranche, a small, charming marina close to Nice. The explosion and burning of the schooner would be done in miniature in the tank in the Victorine studios. These studios dated from the silent days and had been built by Rex Ingram, the well-known American actor and director. He shot *Mare Nostrum* there, also *The Four Horsemen of the Apocalypse,* and others. Rex, still impressive looking, handsome and moody, kept a bungalow in the very middle of the studio lot. At this time set construction was often done day and night. I often saw Rex Ingram returning to his bungalow at night. I don't know how he could sleep with the hammering of the night construction going on. However, I was amazed at the quiet that reigned in his shaded living room where he offered me, with his urbane hospitality, some Turkish coffee. At home he dressed in Moroccan *djillaba* and sat on low leather cushions, Moroccan style.

Some of the New Orleans exteriors were found in the older sections of Nice and Cagnes. The interior of the old fort and the complicated jail cells with their underground passage were erected on stage at the Victorine studios. On the second stage were Fabian's cabin and the stable where the corpse of Vincent Price's uncle in the film (played by Victor Francen) is buried.

While I stayed with the shooting company in Nice, Max left for Paris to supervise set construction on the stages of the Boulogne studios. Soon I joined him there. We had many sets to build, and they occupied all the available space.

As stock elements of American architecture were not to be found in French studios, we had to build everything from scratch. In quick succession we produced the set for the entrance hall of the rich uncle's estate with its monumental staircase, the adjoining living room set with French windows that opened onto the garden, and the second floor of the estate. We also built the waterfront tavern and Micheline's sleeping quarters.

The large hall of the tribunal required special treatment. To make a long, spectacular shot we decided to show the ceiling of the tribunal with its elaborate chandelier. The rectangular set was crowned by a hanging miniature of the sculptured ceiling and a crystal chandelier. The actual building of the miniatures was simplified, since there was a building enterprise in Paris that specialized in miniature elements. They had an assortment of architectural elements in different miniature scales in stock. There we found complicated carved cornices made of pressed papier-mâché, tiny crystal chandeliers, and all sorts of miniature wagons, furniture, and other props.

The hanging miniature ceiling was relatively simple to achieve. More complicated was the set of the waterfront office. It was supposed to be at a different place on the waterfront from the one we had built in Nice. The waterfront was introduced in a long traveling shot, the camera dollying on Errol Flynn walking, with the usual activity of the seaport in the background. For this set we decided to use background miniatures. In other words, in the foreground we would have a shorewalk on the waterfront that led to the office of the harbormaster. The ships would be seen in the background some distance away. This background view would be done in miniature.

On the very long stage at the Boulogne studio, we built a long shallow tank on a three-foot-high platform. The miniature ships were anchored or moving in this tank. In the foreground was a normal scale set of a shoreline path that led to the office. Between the shorewalk and the miniature waterfront in the rear, I had to place set elements in progressively diminishing scale to make a smooth visual connection between the two. Cotton bales were stored on the

Camera dolly rails in front of miniature waterfront. Lourie, seated left, is looking through director's finder prior to shooting scene.

shore, each row built in smaller scale. There was also a railroad line built in diminishing perspective. Even tiny toy horses were added to complete the transition.

When miniatures have to be shot simultaneously with live action, as in our waterfront scene, shooting in slow motion becomes impossible. To eliminate the speedy, jerky movements of the miniatures, we had to have the sailing ships in the harbor move at deliberately slow speed. We also added cooling chemicals to slow the ascending smoke of the steamer. Shooting this scene was complicated further by the fact that it was a traveling shot. Dollying the camera laterally against the miniature background made this background seem to move with tremendous speed. In other words, the actors in the foreground were moving normally, but the ships in the harbor moved past unusually quickly. To counteract this effect, I had to calculate the dolly shot and compensate the lateral movement of the background by panning the camera backward while traveling. This made the camera remain on the same place of the miniature background for a longer time as it advanced with the forward movement of Errol Flynn. This correction worked.

As we had guessed from reading the script, the picture was an insignificant venture, but I had a great deal of pleasure working on it. Apart from the personal satisfaction of collaborating with old friends and spending time in Nice and Paris, I liked the challenge that *Captain Fabian* offered.

One day in July 1963, while designing a low-budget thriller for Allied Artists called *The Strangler,* Edward Morey, our production manager, called me. He had received a letter from a former Allied Artists producer, Les Sansom, who had asked for my address. I had met Les while I was directing *The Giant Behemoth.* Now he was offering me a chance to design a picture that would be shot in Spain.

I called Madrid the next day. *A Crack in the World* was the projected name for the film. The premise—a scientific team is trying to tap thermal energy from the molten core of the earth. The project goes awry, resulting in a series of earthquakes that threaten the very existence of the earth. The film was a difficult project and had to be executed within a modest budget. The producers felt the work involved more than designing; it required a basic conception of how to create this scientific fantasy. According to Les Sansom, I would work in the dual capacity of art director and director of special effects; in other words, I would wear two hats.

I was intrigued by the challenge. Moreover, the prospect of leaving Los Angeles to work in Madrid was alluring. In a telephone conversation with Phil Yordan, it was decided that I would begin work in Madrid in mid-November.

On November 16 I landed at Barajas Airport in Madrid.

A Crack in the World was the first film for this production company, Security Pictures. Everything had to be started from scratch. From lists of unknown names, I had to find reliable assistants and technicians. I also had to evaluate available studios. But most of my time was occupied with finding ways of realizing the tricky sequences in the film.

*The upper two-thirds of this shot is a hanging miniature,
including the cables attached to the overhead fluorescent
lamps. It took eight hours to make the match.*

There is a feeling of exhilaration in starting a film in a new place, especially in a foreign city. November days in Madrid were sunny and the air crisp with wind blowing from the snowy peaks of the Guadarramas.

In conferring with the producers, it was decided a new script would be necessary, but the basic physical action of the first draft would remain. It was my task to work out the visual aspects of the film. I had to decide which effects were possible and how to realize them. I could also add new effects to bolster the story. I would prepare a technical screenplay of effects that would be incorporated into the final draft, now being written by Julian Halevy.

The main setting of the film was a gigantic scientific center in Africa located deep underground where the molten core of the earth was closest to the earth's surface. The underground structure consisted of an ample central hall with computer banks, communication centers, laboratories, and the living quarters of the scientists. Powerful elevators were the only link between this underground center and the surface of the earth.

The story concerns the following circumstances: After years of successful operation, boring has penetrated deeply toward the molten core. Then work stops as the boring bit encounters a hard belt of basalt. Should the scientists abandon their years of effort, their dream of finding a source of unlimited energy? They had to find a way to liberate the energy imprisoned in the center of the earth. The head of the project proposes using an atomic missile shot down the tube of the bored channel to crush the resisting layer of basalt.

Not all of the scientists agree with this audacious plan. Who knows what incalculable catastrophes could result from this blast? But preliminary work begins. Above the boring hole a slender gantry tower is erected, ready to deliver the missile. However, the final go-ahead must come from the international body of scientists who govern the project. They finally agree.

The missile is fired. There is a tremendous outpouring of dirt, then molten lava. The belt of basalt is penetrated, and at this stage the experiment seems to be an unqualified success.

But soon disquieting news reaches the center. The core of the earth is cracking and this crack is progressing around the globe, bringing volcanic eruptions, earthquakes, and other geological calamities in its wake.

Don't ask me to explain these catastrophic developments or the efforts of our heroes or how a silly stroke of luck saves our planet from destruction. I was not to ask questions, but to make these happenings visually convincing on the screen.

In designing this kind of science fiction film, I had to review my knowledge of special effects techniques. The function of a film production designer is to invent, to visualize the concept of scenes, leaving the technical details of execution to the experts—the special effects technicians.

But a production designer should have a basic knowledge of these techniques. Being aware of which effects are possible is as necessary for the designer as the knowledge of what sounds come from which instruments is necessary for a composer.

I imagined the scientific center built deep in a natural cave, reinforced by buttresses and vaults of concrete to give the impression of a strong, functional structure. The central hall had to be spacious and relatively high. To build the set economically and show the high vaulted ceiling, I decided to use foreground (or hanging) miniatures. I limited the actual height of the built set to twenty feet; the upper part of the set would be added with the hanging miniatures. To obtain the effect of the high ceiling without actually building it, I could use a painted matte, a glass shot, or a foreground miniature. I chose the latter because it allowed us to actually make the rocks shake and fall during the earthquake sequence and to shoot the scene with flickering, changing lights.

As for any trick shots, they had to be calculated from a predetermined camera angle and required a fixed camera position that could not be changed by a last-minute whim. This need of strict directorial discipline was, I suspect, one of the main reasons why this method was seldom used in Hollywood.

The method is not widely known and the mechanics of using a foreground miniature are quite forgotten by most Hollywood art directors. To use it involved a certain amount of showmanship and whimsy on my part. Producing a successful foreground miniature shot was like pulling off a neat magic trick. It would show my fellow Spanish art directors and producers a trick they hadn't heard of yet. My assistants soon learned the know-how of designing, and my building contractor, Francisco Prosper, was eagerly enthusiastic.

Lourie in front of the miniature while making final adjustments.

One of my main concerns was how to create a believable molten lava flow. We projected some early Hollywood films but couldn't find effects comparable to the intense glowing lava flows from newsreels of Hawaiian eruptions. I went through numerous projections of these newsreels, trying to invent a method that would simulate this effect. Then I went to Paris to select some stock shots of volcanic eruptions from the documentary films of Haroun Tadzieff, a well-known French vulcanologist. I also renewed my acquaintance with Henri Assola, one of the best miniature builders I knew, and was able to secure his collaboration on our picture.

Meanwhile in Madrid, Alec Weldon, a fine American special effects master, became available with his well-trained Spanish crew. I enlisted them all in our company.

It was decided that I would shoot the main miniature sequences ahead of the principal photography with actors. I decided to start our miniature shooting with one of the most difficult sequences, depicting the cracks in the earth advancing toward the buildings of the scientific center. It would be a large miniature showing a view of the center, its satellite buildings, and the surrounding hills. The view encompassed quite an area and showed the cracks as they formed in the hills, revealing incandescent lava flowing between the jagged edges of the cracks.

The miniature occupied the entire floor space of one of the largest stages at Bronston studios. To show the large view of the hills, I was forced to use a relatively small scale for my miniature. For the effects of the opening cracks and the fiery lava flows, I decided to use a purely visual trick. The jagged parting of the earth would be done in a complex but mechanically simple way, using set pieces mounted and moved on dolly rails and wheels. The lava flows inside would be moving plastic belts painted in red and orange transparent colors and lit from below with strong lights, directing their beams toward the camera lens. The plastic belts would move on two drums, giving the impression that the "lava" is moving down the hill. When the cracks reached the center, prearranged explosions would shatter the buildings. I drew the contraption and asked Alec to build a test set to see if the effect would work.

Above: *Sketch for scientific center from* A CRACK IN
THE WORLD. *Only the foreground road will be shot
on location. The rest will be a painting.*

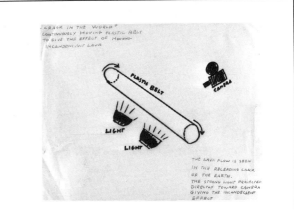

The "lava" on the moving plastic belt gives
the effect of the creeping flow.

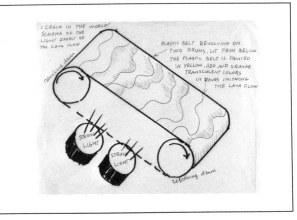

Another view of the lava flow belt.

In the test shot the jagged edges of the crack moved away from each other, opening to the brightly flowing incandescent molten lava. Smoke, steam, and additional avalanches of crumbling stones completed the effect. The results surpassed my expectations. I was pleased to have found a new way to imitate the effect of molten lava, and we decided to go ahead and build the entire miniature set of the sequence using this method. I was to use the same technique some years later for the same producer in the film, *Krakatoa, East of Java.*

Scouting for locations was a pleasure in the crisp, sunny winter of Spain. For a seashore location, we decided to use a deserted beach close to Valencia on the Mediterranean coast. Here I had to create an illusion of an island volcano looming on the horizon. To realize the scene I decided to use a relatively simple optical matte, the so-called split-screen technique. Placing the camera low, the island would appear almost on the horizon line. This line would become the split line; that is, the lower portion of the frame would be the photographic image of the sea. The top of the frame would be the volcano profiled against the sky, a miniature of the smoking, then erupting, volcano, filmed separately and added to the lower half of the frame optically.

On the top of a hill, close to Madrid, a platform was erected, ten feet by ten feet, four feet above the ground. On this platform we built the miniature volcano. The word "miniature" is misleading: our volcano was about eight feet high above the platform. The height of the platform allowed us to place the camera in line with the bottom line of the volcano and to have an unobstructed view of the sky above. The horizontal line of the base of the volcano formed the line where the volcano meets the sea. Miles distant and months later, we shot a view of the sea. Optically combined (it is called "split screen shot"), it became our *composite shot.* On this composite shot I asked the Technicolor lab processing our film to print over the reverse image of the volcano erupting, thus forming the volcano reflection on the water. This reverse image was printed very lightly, not to obscure the movements of the waves.

For the actual shooting of the miniature volcano, we came very early to the hillside location to be ready for the spectacular morning light. We installed our cameras and prepared explosives among peacefully grazing cows. Little did

*Action sketch, which will be matched
in the lab with a shot of the atomic
rig miniature in a traveling matte.
The live action background is blue.*

they suspect that we were preparing a terrific eruption. Shooting seemed jeopardized once when the wind blew volcano smoke into the camera. But as the French saying goes, *"Tout s'arrange."* The wind changed direction, the morning light was still lovely, and we completed the scene with time enough to stop on our way to the next village for a breakfast of crusty bread and sausage and a glass of dark red wine.

After shooting the general view of the advancing crack and the miniature volcano sequence, we came back to the stage and the miniature set of the volcano interior. In the course of the film, a bomb is lowered into the crater of the volcano. Men, dressed in heat-reflecting asbestos suits, guide the bomb down through the crater. One false step can result in a serious accident. One man slips and burns to death in the fiery lava.

The set of the seventy-foot crater, built for the live action, was set up outside against one of the walls of the highest stage of the Bronston studios. But the boiling lava lake at the bottom of the crater was, of course, a miniature set, about twenty by twenty feet, built on the stage.

The lake was a cauldron of boiling lava that steamed and hissed. An articulated puppet was dropped inside, caught fire on contact with the lava, and was instantly consumed in flames. The scene looked quite spectacular. We were shooting ninety-six frames per second and shot the scene twice. The second puppet performed as well, and both takes seemed good. The lava was made of churned oatmeal with silver powder scattered on top and was lit with a red, flickering light. During the action the lava was peppered with sodium and carbide, chemicals that burst into flame and popped on contact with the liquid lava. We also had conduits of steam and smoke, and the overall effect was quite impressive.

Andrew Marton was set to direct the picture. We went over with him all the work we had done; the sets that had been designed and the ones that had to be built. We discussed which special effects we needed and where we would incorporate some spectacular stock shots from Hawaiian newsreels in our picture. It was a pleasure to work with Marton; he was a real professional. Our mutual understanding of problems made collaboration easy and agreeable.

While Marton started to put final touches on the script, I continued to work with my miniature unit. Some art directors have a prejudice against shooting miniatures with an inexperienced cameraman. However, my collaboration with Manuel Berenguer proved very successful. It was the first time he had shot miniatures in all kinds of natural and artificial lighting. Our relationship was very happy and lasted for many years, throughout all my miniature work in Spain and Italy.

Now our schedule called for the launching of the atomic missile, the subsequent explosion, and the eruption of boiling magma. We had to shoot many preliminary scenes for the launching before the spectacular explosion. The dimensions of this miniature set were very large. I chose a plateau on location in the vicinity of Madrid. The plateau was about 500 by 500 feet and surrounded by our miniature mountains. In the center of this plateau were the gantry tower and a service tower; other auxiliary buildings completed the setting. As a final touch, Assola provided a working elevator and moving technicians (actually puppets).

Working with explosives, even for miniature sets, presents some danger. Since our gantry tower was built of metal, the force of the explosion could shat-

ter and project sharp metal parts that might endanger our crew. So I decided
to build two identical towers, one in metal, the other in balsa wood. Well,
almost identical. The balsa wood tower lacked the fine detail of the metal model.
For close shots of the scenes preceding the explosion, we used the metal model.
Then we substituted the wooden one and shot the explosion.

Many scenes around the tower had to be incorporated with live action. For
these combined scenes I took still pictures of the ensemble some days before
shooting. I enlarged these photographs and traced on the enlargements how the
final shots would look with the addition of live action, which would be included later optically by matte addition in the split-screen technique.

To prepare the explosion scenes, Alec and his crew got busy fixing up
high pressure tanks with red colored water, steam conduits, and mortars loaded
with explosives and powdered paint to create the effect of dark smoke when the
explosion occurs. The weather was fine on the day of shooting, and the rocket
was fired from the tail of the missile, plunging it down from the gantry tower.
Three seconds later we witnessed a spectacular exploding fountain of magma
gushing out, bubbling and steaming. Seeded with sodium and carbide particles, it burst into flames. We covered the shooting with three cameras—high
speed, naturally—giving us different angles to choose from in editing the sequence. The next shots showed the entire plain covered with a boiling lava
lake.

Many following scenes of the picture had us shooting earthquakes, collapsing mountains, the destruction of a railroad bridge, and the derailing of a
train.

We worked with a very limited crew, hence very low operational expenses. Sometimes because of weather conditions, we worked only for part of
the day. Or occasionally we would skip a day of shooting to allow the special
effects crew to prepare the next set. This schedule left me with enough time to
go ahead with designing and supervising the set construction.

The CEA studios housed our biggest set, the central hall of the underground center. The foreground miniature hung solidly above our heads. The
camera was installed and Assola worked patiently on the final adjustments,
checking through the camera lens the exact fitting of the miniature details with

Preliminary sketch of atomic rig.

The actual atomic rig miniature.

Sketch and photograph showing split screen of real road and atomic rig miniature.

The miniature rig explosion.

the corresponding details of the life-size sets. The lighting of the set finished, we made photographic tests to verify that all the component parts fit correctly and that no unexpected shaking of the building would cause our miniature to tremble. As a busy street was next door to the stage, I was afraid that when big trucks passed, they might cause our building to shake. Happily they didn't, and many sequences were shot on this set. The foreground miniature performed well. Placing the lens on the nodal point—the lens remained strictly on the axis of the panning camera—we were able to succeed in a difficult shot, panning down until our frame was lower than the miniature line and then traveling forward. When the camera was panned down below the miniature part of the set, we shot action normally in the life-size set and could move freely.

Another difficult scene was at the end of the picture when the earthquake hits the center; rocks and reinforcement pilings cascade down. We had to coordinate exactly the falling of the miniature rocks in the hanging part of the set with the life-size rocks pushed from high platforms by the special effects crew.

Alec, like a field commander, directed the operations. "Attention, señores," he shouted. Then "Basilio!" and Basilio unleashed the miniature rocks. A whistle blew and life-size debris, made of styrofoam, fell from its high platform. Meanwhile everything was shaking on the set and Dana Andrews, one of the scientists, died under the falling iron beams in the best tradition of a melodramatic hero.

The panic scenes in front of the elevators completed our work in the CEA studios. We moved to the other side of Madrid to the Bronston studios where the sets of the underground corridors and the scientists' lodgings were located.

I went to Valencia with my assistants to prepare for the beach scene and to install a strong platform for the steady camera shot of the sea portion of our split-screen volcano sequence.

Next to our beach, in a cove, fishermen were preparing paella from their catch. Little did they care about our volcano, our film, and probably films in general. Their morning catch was plentiful, the sunny day pleasant, and life was wonderful with a plate of paella and a glass of red wine. Afterward, finishing our work, we accepted their invitation, and the paella tasted better than any I had before or since.

Back in Madrid we proceeded to the location where we had shot scenes in the vicinity of the gantry tower. This was the sequence where many scenes were to combine the live action with the miniature gantry set.

Usually combining a live action shot in one place with another action or miniature shot in a different location is achieved by using a background process, traveling matte, or split-screen method. Split screen is technically simpler, but it requires that the action of one component shot not overlap the other. Each action occupies its own territory, its own portion of the finished frame, limited by a dividing line, the so-called split line. Shooting these sequences requires much study and many preliminary sketches. In the case of our gantry tower sequence, I took a still picture of the miniature set, enlarged it, and overlaid the proposed live action.

Preparing the shooting of this sequence, I had to mark on the ground the limits where a person or a car could move without overlapping the area that would be occupied by the miniature setting.

Some other closer shots, depicting different activities in preparation for the missile launching, were made in traveling matte. The foreground action of the preparation was shot on the so-called blue backing, making the matting-out of the action easy to do optically.

The establishing shot of the caravan of cars arriving at the center entrance was done on location, the upper part of the frame completed by a matte painting of the center exterior. The painting was done in postproduction at the London Technicolor lab.

In one scene of the film we had to see the interior walls of the crater where the scientists guide the bomb. The fall of one scientist had already been shot in miniature. But for the purpose of the live action, we built a very high set outside the highest wall of the Chamartin studios showing the interior of the crater. Shooting from below we could look up to the sky and see a helicopter hovering above.

The final sequence where flames destroy the center was made partially on an exterior set built on location and partially on a stage with blue backing, to which we later added a long-shot miniature of the flaming crack and the final explosion of the center.

For the finale of the film we had to see a portion of the earth's crust projected into outer space, surrounded by flames as it forms a fiery satellite. Many effects were tried and tested. Finally a very simple trick succeeded. I sprayed an ordinary floor mop with glue, sprinkled it with spangles, and made it rotate in front of a black velvet backing. The camera traveled and zoomed back. The shot was double printed together with a night sky, and the result looked like a fast-receding satellite, turning and burning, going towards the moon and the stars.

I shared a final dinner with Andrew Marton in mutual congratulation and we promised each other to repeat our pleasant collaboration. We have not had the chance yet. But the result of our efforts was one of the most successful science fiction pictures of the year, all for the astonishingly low budget of $600,000.

LIMELIGHT

In the spring of 1951 I got a phone call. An unknown voice said, "Eugene Lourie? This is Lonnie Dorsay, production manager. We are preparing a film. Are you free?"

"I am."

"Do you know London? Did you work in London?"

"Yes, I know London." I had worked there in 1933 designing and painting scenery for the Ballet Russe de Monte Carlo. And in 1950 I prepared production of Renoir's *The River* there. I loved that fascinating city, and the possibility of doing a film in London flashed into my mind.

It happens often in Hollywood that an offer to work in a film comes unexpectedly from an unknown source. A new film to design is always an interesting challenge, but the idea that the film would probably be made in England was an added incentive.

The next morning I was in Lonnie's car on the way to meet the producer.

"We are going to see Charlie Chaplin!"

Lonnie hadn't told me the name of the producer the day before. I had the greatest admiration for Chaplin's pictures. Charlie Chaplin's "Little Tramp" had become part of the culture of our generation, which was deeply influenced by motion pictures. Chaplin's genius appealed to wide audiences in every country of the world. Simple peasants in India, factory workers in France, Turkish longshoremen, they all accepted Chaplin as their beloved relative and his antics greatly amused them. In past years, I had seen French audiences hilariously happy to see their old, eccentric friend Charlot.

I had found Chaplin's later films to be overly sentimental, with a propensity to easy philosophizing. But this pose didn't diminish my admiration for his flair as a filmmaker.

He was one of the genuine film *auteurs,* a performer, writer, director, and composer of his musical scores. I liked the idea of meeting Charlie Chaplin and possibly working with him.

We found Chaplin's house on a quiet street in Beverly Hills. A servant in a white jacket opened the gate and guided us through the house to a back terrace where Chaplin was having his breakfast. Lamb chops. I was fascinated by the elegant, precise way he cut them. It reminded me of the famous scene in *The Gold Rush,* where he carved a boiled shoe with the same elegance and then sucked the shoelaces with gusto.

The man in the white jacket served us coffee, and Chaplin explained his project, one he had been working on for many years, for which he had written and rewritten the script and composed the music, every measure of the score.

The film was called *Limelight* and was about an accidental meeting between two lonely people and how this meeting changed their lives. Chaplin's part was to be that of the Great Calvero, an aging actor, famous in the heyday of music halls, but now almost destitute and trying to keep his dignity. The part of Terry, a young, unsuccessful but talented ballet dancer, was to be played by Claire Bloom, then at the start of her acting career. The action of *Limelight* would take place in London, but the shooting, Chaplin said, would be done entirely in Hollywood. So it seemed I would not be going to London.

We spoke about London. In Chaplin's view the correct feeling of this town,

Calvero and Terry (Charles Chaplin and Claire Bloom).

its sights, smells, and sounds, was very important in designing the film. He asked me if I would accept a trial period, in which I would read the script and meet with him two weeks later to discuss my ideas about the designing of *Limelight.* I agreed heartily to the trial period and found his request understandable, since the choice of an art director—a close collaborator on the project he had worked on for so many years—was crucial for him. In Hollywood choosing an art director for a picture is often haphazard, and usually the director and his collaborator do not have the chance to exchange ideas before they are thrown together in the adventurous enterprise of making a film.

I don't know what prompted Chaplin to ask for me. I had never worked with him before or met him, although he did know about my work with Renoir. He was adamant about having somebody who knew London. The correct feeling of London was important, not just the architectural details, but also the inner feeling of the city. I learned later that he had interviewed one very well-known art director before speaking to me, but the person was a German, and in speaking with him, Chaplin sensed that he didn't have the knowledge or the inner understanding of London's spirit. Chaplin gave me the script to read, and we fixed the time for our next meeting.

Limelight tells how Calvero, the fading music hall artist, rescues Terry, a young ballet student, from suicide. Through Calvero's efforts to restore Terry's confidence and desire to live, a close relationship builds between them. Later when Terry becomes successful, she tries to help Calvero. But he realizes the situation is impossible and steps out of her life, knowing his place in her heart will be taken in due time by Neville, a composer she had met earlier. As I read the script, the scenes brought to my mind the poetic melancholy of some middle-class districts in London and the dreamy solitude of the Victoria Embankment at night.

When I met Chaplin the second time, we discussed the sets and spoke at length about London and the fading of vaudeville in England. Our collaboration was decided. At the end of our interview he played some tunes from his film score for me on the piano.

The beginning of designing a film is a happy, exciting period of doing research, trying different solutions for sets. You don't know exactly what you

A research photograph eventually used as a photographic background.

"The beginning of designing a film is a happy, exciting period . . . everything seems possible."

will do, but everything seems possible. The art director's preparation can be compared with actors preparing their parts, trying to find their characters. An art director has to try to live in the skins of the characters, immerse himself in the mood, the place, and the period of the script, which in this picture was an ever-present subplot—London at the beginning of the century. While I probed these problems in my mind, I started to scribble possibilities for the floor plan of Calvero's rooms. I always approach the conception of a set by organizing the space where the actors and the cameras will move. For me, the floor plan is the basis for any set. In *Limelight* the biggest part of the action takes place in Calvero's apartment, and I started by designing that set. Chaplin asked me to start building it immediately, because he wanted to rehearse there with Claire Bloom and planned to continue for four weeks, up until the shooting date. This picture was basically a two-person picture, and Claire Bloom was at this time an unknown actress and very young. So Chaplin was mostly concerned about their scenes together and their relationship, and developing these scenes took four weeks of very hard rehearsals. By the way, it is amusing that in all the time we spent on the picture, in spite of our close working relationship, Chaplin always addressed me in a formal British manner as "Mister Lourie" and I called him "Mister Chaplin."

We located our main sets at the old Chaplin studio on the corner of Sunset and La Brea. On the Sunset side of the lot was a large garden and a bungalow where Wheeler Dryden, Chaplin's half-brother, lived. And still remaining in the cement of the studio yard was the imprint of Charlie the tramp's famous big shoe.

The set for Calvero's apartment was built and dressed with carefully chosen, cheap Victorian furniture. Personal touches, props, and photographs would be added later. The back yard, seen from his window, was very important in Chaplin's mind, and he explained the feeling he wanted—a shabby-looking London back yard, typical of low-rent Victorian houses. He planned to play many scenes sitting at the window with a clear view of the yard, and I decided to make the backing for the yard as a three-dimensional reduced-scale building, rather than as a painted backdrop.

Here were the blackened brick walls, chimneys emitting smoke, even miniature garbage cans. Hanging laundry could be changed for different sequences, and windows could be lit for night scenes. Chaplin was highly amused by this miniature back yard and played with it as with a new toy, often changing the direction of sunlight on the walls, then deciding on gray daylight for the back yard.

From ten in the morning till four in the afternoon, Chaplin rehearsed with Claire Bloom. The second day he asked me if possible to add some eighteen inches to a wall. He explained that he rehearsed action like a ballet and missed those eighteen inches for the walk from the door to the kitchen above.

"How long will it take to do those changes?" he asked.

"Mr. Chaplin, you can start rehearsals the usual time tomorrow morning. The changes will be completed," I assured him.

In my discussions with him earlier, I had detected a certain hesitation on his part about the dimensions of the sets, and so I built the walls with three extra feet on each side. In moving the flats we could easily reduce or expand the sets.

The picture opens on a London street, where Calvero, slightly tipsy, tries to open the entrance door of his rooming house. But traveling to England for location shooting was out of the question. At this time, work on location was not being done anyhow, and we had no money for it in the budget. Building a street from scratch was also too expensive, so I concentrated on searching for Hollywood possibilities. Of all the streets built on different studio lots, Paramount's seemed the best for our picture. Their lot had a complex of New York streets, and on the residential section of this set was a long row of uniformly built Victorian houses. This entire setting reminded me very strongly of many London streets. Besides the entrance of Calvero's rooming house, I had to make sets for two different pubs, an exterior of a physician's office, the entrance to the Empire Theater, and some other sets. I found a way to build all of these sets in the New York complex on the Paramount lot.

I first considered building the entrance of the Empire Theater to the height of the marquee, and then add, as a matte painting, the elaborate marquee itself and the façade above it. But Chaplin found this solution too expensive for the one shot he needed.

I remembered well London's Empire Theater in 1933 when it still had its old front. The Ballet Russe de Monte Carlo performed in a theater close by on Leicester Square, and I passed by the Empire every day. To get the feeling of this old theater as seen through the slender trees of Leicester Square, I proposed to Chaplin that we place the theater director's office in a building on the opposite side of the square; thus the front entrance of the Empire Theater could be seen through a large rounded window behind the director's desk. I asked my friend Vincent Korda to dispatch one of the still men from London Films studio to make or find appropriate research photos of the Empire Theater and also for another sequence—an early morning view of the Victoria Embankment. Soon a thick package arrived with glossy eight-by-ten photographs. Included also were measured drawings and detailed photographs of typical lampposts and benches from the Victoria Embankment. These still pictures were used later by our scenic artists and prop makers for our sets.

In the film the old English music hall plays an important part, and it was amusing to recreate its particular ambience, especially the old-fashioned painted backdrops.

The usual practice in the old theaters was to use the same painted backdrops over and over again. There were three or four stock painted drops and every act was played in front of one of them. Vaudeville theaters were already on the decline in Calvero's time, so I tried in these painted backdrops to express the shabbiness of overused painted canvases and the naïveté of the late Victorian style of scenic painting. I was lucky to find some old scenic artists who knew this type of set painting well. In fact, they were happy to paint "like in the good old days."

Later on, for the second part of the film, we constructed a three-dimensional set for a ballet-pantomime, different from the painted backdrop usually used at that time. The action showed a gala spectacle for Terry, now a prima ballerina, and Calvero, glorious at having again found success. The script called for a sequence during the intermission showing the backstage activities: the set being dismantled, the flats being carried away by the hurrying stagehands, the folding ceiling rising up to the flies. All this action had to be performed very quickly, while in the background the painted backdrop of the romantic, moonlit church was being lowered for the second act of the ballet. The action, as usual, was to be accompanied by the emotional score of Charlie Chaplin's music. To make the mechanics of the set understandable and to show its exaggerated theatricality and forced perspective, I constructed a small three-dimensional model of the set from cardboard. Chaplin was very pleased with it, and it was at this time, I think, that I gained his full confidence.

Much later when we were ready to shoot the scene, Chaplin asked if the stagehands could carry away the flats and fly the ceiling in eighteen seconds.

"I know they can do it fast, but I don't know if it will be done in exactly eighteen seconds or nineteen or maybe even sixteen." I answered.

"But it is very important," he said. "The music for this scene is already recorded. Let's rehearse the action for timing!"

"Well I think, Mr. Chaplin, that we should shoot the scene instead of rehearsing it. If we succeed in eighteen seconds, you will have the scene in the can. If not, it will serve as a rehearsal. Moreover, if we have to put back the set, it could take another hour."

Lights, camera, playback . . . The scene was shot exactly in eighteen seconds.

In *Limelight* I was very conscious of the importance of theatrical stage settings. I was also aware of the striking difference between stage settings and everyday life. The theater was the world of Calvero. He lived in its atmosphere, the strange, exciting, naive world of make-believe. It's very easy to exaggerate the style of stage scenarios of that era. In my designs I tried carefully to avoid succumbing to facile caricature. On the other hand, I tried to avoid all theatricality in settings of the everyday, prosaic surroundings where Calvero existed.

Where the script called for interiors of theaters, we decided to scout many actual old theaters in Los Angeles and Pasadena, as well as the theater sets at film studios. It was a common practice to shoot in existing theaters because it was much less expensive than building a theater set. I personally preferred shooting in a set built on a studio stage, since it was so much easier to compose a setting to my own idea than to adapt to an existing, immovable theater. I knew of two theater sets on studio stages: one at Universal studios, built for *The Phantom of the Opera*, still called the "Phantom Stage," and another quite abandoned set in Culver City studio—at this time called RKO/Pathé. We found that the theater set at Universal had a complete stage, backstage, proscenium, working curtains, and a well-appointed auditorium. It was our choice. This set could be easily converted to represent different theaters in the montage sequence of our film, where Terry is shown performing on tour. We could also use the stage with the machinery to fly painted backdrops up or make quick scenery changes as in a real, well-equipped theater.

The set also had audience boxes, orchestra seats, stairs, and the promenade used for intermission scenes where the girls of easy virtue paraded in their plumed hats. We shot all the musical acts of *Limelight* on the "Phantom Stage."

For the two different London pubs I was able to remodel some houses of the New York street at Paramount studios, building a different front for each pub. I was also able to squeeze in the exterior of the doctor's office, the stationery shop, and the pawnshop on this same set. But I built the interiors of these sets at the Chaplin studios.

My previous work for the ballet company in London made me familiar with the problems of designing the ballet-pantomime sequences for *Limelight*. Although the style of my ballet settings had been quite different from the sort used for Victorian vaudeville or pantomimes, my knowledge of stage settings in general helped me tremendously.

It is amusing to note that André Eglevsky, who danced the part of Harlequin in the pantomime, had also danced in *Choreatrium*, the Massine ballet I had designed years before in London. At that time he was very young and traveled with his mother, who like all Russian "ballet" mothers and sisters, was ever present at theater rehearsals. The costume I designed for Eglevsky was golden ochre in color. But when his mother saw the sketch, she became outraged.

"My Alioshinka will never dance in *this* costume. It is the color of shit!" she said. Russian ballet mothers, although possessing Victorian manners, used crude language easily.

It took all the authority of Massine, the choreographer, to quiet her and assure her changes would be made. When the costumes were finally ready, the dancers dressed and came out onto the illuminated stage.

"Now, look at my son," she exclaimed. "He looks positively like a young god. All in gold!!!!"

It was interesting to watch Chaplin and Buster Keaton, who performed as the piano player, rehearse their routine. There was a definite competition between the two, each one trying to upstage the other. I especially recall the scene where Chaplin, in his baggy pants, tries to master his violin at the same time that he tries to subdue Buster Keaton performing at the piano, with his music falling all over the keys. There is no laughter on the soundtrack at this point, but there was uncontrollable laughter backstage from the crew watching each variation of the routine. In a perpetual quest for perfection, the Chaplin–Keaton scenes were shot and reshot many times, each time with new, ingenious changes in the scene. The shooting of this scene went on for days. Then more shooting time was requested for the final moments when Chaplin falls into the orchestra pit and reappears embedded in the drum.

Almost all exterior scenes were shot on the street set on the Paramount lot. But there was an important exterior sequence that takes place at daybreak on the Victoria Embankment, the scene where Calvero and Terry, two lonely people, sit on a bench at the Embankment in the predawn hours. I decided to make this scene indoors on the stage under the controlled conditions of stage lighting—using either a painted or back-projected photographic backing, one based on the photographs I had earlier ordered from London.

To get the right perspective, I had asked that the photographs be taken from a height of five feet—approximately the height at which our motion picture camera would be placed for this scene. To have a choice of lighting moods, I had also asked that the series of stills be taken at intervals, starting from the very dark hours of night, then progressing to clearer and clearer morning sky. These shots were to be taken alongside the embankment looking toward Big Ben in the background. It was the perfection of these stills with their moody lighting that prompted me to back project the photographs rather than use painted scenery. For this sequence the research photos and measurements received from London also helped the prop shop reproduce the bench and the foreground lamppost, both with beautifully sculptured dolphins on them.

Somewhere in the mess of studio storage, there still exists a perfect reproduction of a Victorian bench and lamppost.

From the beginning of our work on *Limelight*, the relationship between Chaplin and me was friendly. On my part there was a kind of shyness and reserve due to my respect and admiration for Chaplin's genius. On his was increasing confidence. He would make a frame with his fingers and ask, "Mr Lourié, could you give me a beautiful composition for this frame?" Backslapping and being buddy-buddy was not his style, but ours was a sincerely cordial friendship.

In directing, Chaplin was highly aware of the timing of scenes. After each take he would turn to the script girl and ask her how long the take was.

"Thirty seconds, Mr Chaplin."

"Well, let's do it again. This time we will try to make it three seconds shorter," he would say.

I think this strict sense of timing came from his work on musical scores and possibly from his days in music halls, where timing is so important.

Once he said to me, "You see, if each scene is only a few seconds too long, it will slow the tempo of the entire picture very much." Usually his remark after a take was "Too long, too long. Let's do it again."

I am sorry that I wasn't able to be present more often at the shooting. However, I could not fail to notice one thing very characteristic of Chaplin, his pursuit of perfection in the minutest detail, especially obvious in the shooting of his own musical numbers. There were many rehearsals, many takes. Each was performed with mathematical precision but each with a variation. His songs were shot many times, and each time the scene was a little different—a change, an improvement. And each repetition made the stage crew laugh uproariously. The changes were in the performances, but the camera work remained the same— deceptively simple. The work was not in shooting the scene but in playing it. In this, Chaplin was very difficult, especially on himself. He would play the number and say, "No, I can do it better" or "No, I can do it differently."

In general, Chaplin avoided taking "artistic" camera angles. He deliberately did not play with the camera as many directors did at this time. Bob Aldrich, Chaplin's assistant on the film, had some ideas for artistic shots. His ideas, which were sometimes interesting, were usually rejected. Probably Chaplin was right, because for his storytelling the filming technique was simple, and you didn't have to think, "Oh-oh, what a wonderful shot!" You were concerned with the content of the scene and the acting.

In writing about Chaplin's early films, some critics have noted that his sets were "shabby" and "unimportant." I personally find that all of Chaplin's early pictures had sets that rightly expressed the style of his comedies. They were "shabby" intentionally. There was a certain power in their impersonality. In remembering Chaplin's comedies, you can hardly dissociate them from their settings. Thinking of Chaplin's pictures in retrospect, I see the vivid images of his sets: a memorable one for *Easy Street* filmed in 1917, the precariously swinging cabin in *Gold Rush*, and others. In general, insignificance can be an achievement. In fact, the best art direction in films is often that which you are not aware of. As a general rule, if you especially notice the sets or admire them, it means that the art direction has surpassed its functions. René Clair said once, "In pictures, you should not be aware of the sets." Or as Lazare Meerson, one of the great motion picture art directors, said about designing sets, "It is an art of self-denial."

There was a preview of the film for the behind-the-camera crew and actors. And then a last dinner at the Chaplins' where we wished them a bon voyage for their forthcoming trip to England. We didn't suspect that this vacation trip would become a long exile, and that the picture would be boycotted and not shown in regular theaters for many years. Meanwhile, ironically, Chaplin's music from *Limelight* was being played all over America.

THE BEAST FROM 20,000 FATHOMS

In many ways work as an art director or production designer prepares you for directing. In designing, you have to visualize the action as well as the settings. I began designing in France a long time ago. We had very tight budgets for films and short schedules, which forced us to make thorough preparations. Very often I had to prepare detailed shooting scripts, breaking down sequences into individual scenes, indicating each change in the camera angle, dolly shots, pan shots, and so on. I usually prepared these shooting scripts with directors.

Sometimes when a director was signed later on in the production, I had to do these scripts alone. Often I used to prepare a floor plan of the set for each day's shooting, with indications of all camera positions and lenses for each shot. All the camera and actors' movements were marked on these plans with numbers corresponding to the place in the script. The prints of these plans were posted every morning on the set, so the technicians knew what shot they had

Preliminary sketch of the dolly shot of the two monsters retreating to the river.

Steps in making composite of step-by-step animation and live action shot.

STEPS IN MAKING COMPOSIT SHOT COMBINING STEP-BY-STEP ANIMATION WITH THE BACKGROUND SHOT I.E. "PLATE"

A — PUPPET PHOTOGRAPHED ON THE PROJECTED BACKGROUND WITH MATTE IN PLACE

A

COUNTER-MATTE IN PLACE: CORNER BUILDING AND LIVE ACTION PHOTOGRAPHED ON THE SAME STRIP OF FILM

B

C — COMPOSITE PICTURE

C

to prepare. This procedure saved a lot of time and was a helpful reminder for the director and technicians. In preparing these detailed plans, I had to mentally direct the film.

As for actual directing, the idea had probably been in the back of my mind, as it must have been in the minds of many other cameramen, editors, and writers. This idea usually emerged when I came up with a particularly interesting idea for a picture; or while looking at finished sequences on a projection screen, I would think of how I would do them differently or better.

In the early spring of 1952, I was called by Hal Chester, one of the producers of Mutual Films. The second partner was Jack Dietz and the third, or associate, producer was Bernie Burton, whom I knew as a film editor. At this time they planned to produce three low-budget films for an independent circuit of regional distributors. Knowing of my work in the "prestige" pictures of Jean Renoir, Charlie Chaplin, and others, and at the same time of my designing cheap pictures for TV at the Hal Roach studios, they asked if I would be interested in doing the art direction for their three pictures. They didn't have scripts, only short outlines. One of the outlines, *The Monster from Beneath the Sea,* was about a prehistoric dinosaur coming alive after being frozen in the Arctic for millions of years. At this time the idea seemed novel and challenging. It was a project with complex production problems, almost insurmountable on a Mutual Films budget. They had allocated $150,000 for each picture.

I was curious to know who they had in mind to direct their pictures. "We don't know yet," was their answer. "If you have difficulties in finding a director for the *Monster* picture, I am ready to tackle it," I said jokingly.

It was not a premeditated remark but came on the spur of the moment. I probably had an inner conviction that I could complete the picture within their tentative twelve-day schedule. Also, the idea of developing this science fiction story was interesting. Anyhow, my reply was thrown to the winds, and I forgot about it and about Mutual Films until three weeks later when Jack Dietz called. Their plans had been changed—no more three pictures, but they would like to go ahead with the dinosaur sci-fi saga. After a pause Jack Dietz asked if I had been serious when I had offered to direct the picture. I answered, "Yes," and the next thing I knew, I had been saddled with the pressing job of finding a writer with whom I could develop the screenplay, along with designing and attending to all the complex production problems. One of the most urgent questions was the method we would use to bring the dinosaur to life. It was, after all, our principal actor.

After a quick review of the different methods at our disposal, we decided that stop animation, also called frame-by-frame animation, was the most practical technique for us—a technique where a three-dimensional puppet is photographed on one frame of the film, then moved a little, photographed again, and so on, one frame at a time, until the action is complete.

I remembered vividly the enchanting sequences from a pre-First World War picture *Stella Maris,* where a poet tells fantastic tales to a young girl. One of these tales was about an orchestra made up entirely of frogs (in silent films they couldn't *tell* stories, they had to *show* them). All musical instruments were expertly handled by frogs; so was the baton by a frog conductor. The true-to-life frogs were in fact animated puppets. The film was realized by the brilliant animator-cameraman W. Starevitch. More recently *King Kong* and *Mighty Joe Young* were also successful examples of this technique. As for myself, I had never used stop animation before. Hal Chester told me that Willis O'Brien, the master animator of *King Kong,* was an expensive technician, but he had contacted a young animator who had assisted O'Brien with *Mighty Joe Young,* and I was to meet him.

I met the animator, Ray Harryhausen, in his workshop—his garage—where he was painstakingly shooting some charming fairy tales, hoping to release them to elementary schools. He drew on his experience with George Pal's Puppetons. Ray showed me some of the footage, a fairy tale about a girl with very long blonde hair, Rapunzel. I liked what I saw: the animated movements were smooth, not jerky, as in many animated films. Ray was a very agreeable person and fully dedicated, immersed in his work. For our picture he suggested that we buy from RKO the special equipment they had built for *King Kong,* a small-scale stop-motion, rear-projection camera. With this camera he could matte out certain portions of live action shots, animate the beast in front of this projection, make contre-mattes, and reproject the formerly matted-out action. He could

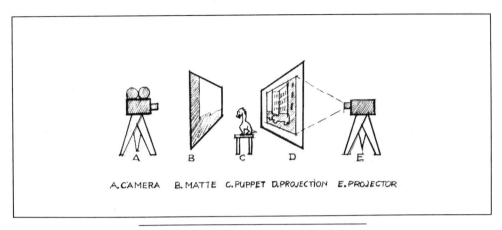

A. CAMERA   B. MATTE   C. PUPPET   D. PROJECTION   E. PROJECTOR

Frame-by-frame, matte rear-projection composite set-up.

do it by himself, and it would not involve the costly, time-consuming operation of the specialized film lab.

I felt that Ray would do a good job and be a valuable partner in our project. We shook hands, and I advised him to obtain the best deal from our "lean cow" producers. I am afraid that, like all of us, he had to work for a pittance. And for Ray that work would be very demanding, since successful stop motion, or frame-by-frame animation, requires a very special person with very special talents. It calls for tremendous patience and unfailing concentration; moreover, it calls for a knowledge of and feeling for animal movements, even their facial expressions. Shooting frame by frame, stopping after each frame, is a time-consuming technique. Sometimes it takes some six to eight hours to animate one minute of film. Think about it. One minute of projection time requires 1,440 frames, which means the camera must stop each time an animated character is moved. For one minute of projection, these movements are often measured in a fraction of a millimeter and have to be performed 1,440 times. The animation takes a tremendous amount of nervous energy and requires in addition to the careful camera work meticulous setting up of each scene and cutting out and placing the exact mattes and the needed miniature props. If there is a false move, the animation becomes jerky and the entire sequence has to be started all over again. As I remember, it took Ray about six months of incessant labor to complete *The Beast from 20,000 Fathoms.*

As I mentioned, *The Monster from Beneath the Sea*—a temporary title—was but a short outline. My task was to get a playable screenplay in the shortest possible time. With a writer friend (who for personal reasons chose not to be named), I started to construct a story line showing live characters and action.

The story begins in the frozen immensities of the Arctic seas. An experimental blast of an atomic device melts huge amounts of ice, freeing and bringing to life a prehistoric dinosaur, which had been embedded in ice in suspended animation for millions of years. Hereditary instinct and sea currents drive the animal south where it meets with the hostile civilized world. I was not trying to preach a gospel to nature lovers or show how our villainous civilization kills innocent animals. I tried to tell the story matter-of-factly, as if it actually happened. I didn't take sides. The animal has to eat a New York policeman, for example, because the policeman was in its way. The men had to shoot the animal because of all the destruction it had caused. I felt that by treating this story with sobriety it could transcend the limits of a simple horror film.

In this kind of science fiction story, I felt, only one fact was deliberately fictitious: the survival of a dinosaur after millions of years. From then on we had to develop the story in very realistic, everyday surroundings.

In literature the master of this kind of story was H. G. Wells. For instance, in his *Food of the Gods,* the incredible phenomena of monstrously gigantic plants and insects took place in a very prosaic milieu of London suburbs.

Meanwhile we ran across a short story by Ray Bradbury, called "The Foghorn." It was a poetic tale of a dinosaur attracted to the wail of a foghorn. Taking the sound for the mating call of another of its species, the dinosaur crawls out of the ocean, destroys the lighthouse, and slithers back to the sea.

Bradbury had a large following in science fiction circles, and Jack Dietz believed it would be advantageous to add his name to the main titles. He acquired the rights to the story, and we incorporated the lighthouse incident into the odyssey of our drifting dinosaur.

We completed the first draft of the screenplay, and I made a tentative breakdown and estimated the probable cost of the picture at $200,000. We got the green light. My producers asked Fred Freiburger and Lou Morheim to polish the script and provide the dialogue. We rented stages at the Motion Picture Center studios on Cahuenga in Hollywood. Ray Harryhausen was busy finishing construction of our main actor, the miniature dinosaur, and preparing his animation studio.

In July 1952 I left for New York with Bernie Burton to shoot process plates and some production scenes on the waterfront and streets of lower Manhattan. These plates were to be used later, together with shots of an animated puppet. As the plate is often used as a background for the frame-by-frame animation, the camera had to be absolutely steady to avoid jerkiness of movement. I took great care to choose every location and note the direction of the light at different times of day in each camera position. It was done for logistics in moving from one shot to another.

I spent two days preparing the detailed shooting schedule. It was like a railroad timetable, allocating fifteen minutes for each scene, including the time needed to move from place to place, to prepare the cameras, and to shoot the scene.

My crew was minimal: one production manager who also functioned as my assistant and script clerk; one very able veteran cameraman and his assistant; and finally, one grip who came as a package with his stationwagon. His car also served as our camera car and a platform for high set-ups. The shooting was to be done on Saturday and Sunday when downtown Manhattan was free from traffic.

We met on Saturday at 7 A.M. in front of the Fulton fish market pier. I had to shoot the plates for the sequence where the beast appears from the East River and climbs ashore, creating havoc among the stevedores.

For this type of film where the animation is concurrent with live action, the shooting usually follows carefully prepared storyboard sketches. However that procedure was useless for this picture, first because I was directing as well as designing, and I alone was responsible for each shot. Only after choosing the New York locations could I decide how and where the beast would be placed in each shot. Sometimes while shooting I would make a quick thumbnail sketch to indicate where in the shot the beast had to be placed. Each time I had to be careful to keep in mind the relative sizes of the beast and cars, people, and surrounding buildings. You always have to think about relative size. In *King Kong* if you look carefully, you can see that the monster changes in size throughout the picture in relation to the set and other objects. Later when we went back to Hollywood, I made photo enlargements of the scenes where the beast would be added. On these enlargements I traced my idea of where to place it. These tracings went to Ray for his evaluation, and he often improved my ideas with his acrobatically clever animations.

This particular Saturday we had scheduled our shooting with a small number of extras. Some of them were to impersonate the Fulton pier stevedores. Unfortunately they looked puny, more like Greenwich Village intellectuals, which is exactly what they were. But I was able to enlist some regular fish market stevedores, not great actors, but they looked right and performed with gusto. They even ran clumsily, like the real stevedores they were. After we finished they asked to have a photo taken with me so that later they could prove to their wives they had really worked in a film instead of spending their Saturday drinking in a bar.

The next day, Sunday, was the only day we were able to shoot in downtown Manhattan without interfering with traffic. Due to our modest budget, we had planned a minimum number of extras for the "panic" scenes. There were to be fifty extras, some furnishing their cars as well.

Early Sunday morning I met my crew and a small group of twenty-five people on a deserted Wall Street. I asked the production manager when the remaining extras would arrive. He replied, "Never. It's Sunday, you see, and they would have had to be paid double, so I had to limit the number."

Discussions were useless at this point, but I decided that the sequences in the street would be as impressive as intended. My idea was to shoot every scene short, keeping the tempo of running crowds undiminished. Quick montages of these short scenes would give the impression of a running multitude. I knew, moreover, that most of the crowd scenes would be shot later in Hollywood where I had been promised 400 extras. My work in New York would serve mostly to place the action in the deep canyons of lower Manhattan and other recognizable

Above: *Director Lourie
with his "real" extras.*

*"Sunday was the only day we
were able to shoot in downtown
Manhattan without interfering
with traffic."*

New York landmarks. This day we made more than forty different set-ups, many with the camera tied down to create a steady image for animation.

The entire New York junket, including our transportation, living expenses, technicians, extras, film, and lab, cost $5,000 dollars. Altogether we got some sixty scenes and numerous stills to use for photographic blow-ups for backings.

We went back to Hollywood to design sets and take care of casting. A short time before I had seen a picture called *The Thief of Venice*, its lead actor an unknown named Paul Christian. He had a slight German accent and an engaging personality. I asked Hal Chester to inquire about him and if possible set up an interview. Christian had quite a reputation in German theater and film and was known there by his real name, Paul Hubschmit. He still performs with success in leading roles in Germany and Switzerland and for many years has played Professor Higgins in *My Fair Lady*.

In the science fiction pictures of the period, actors seldom had striking parts to play. The characters rarely had emotional or personal problems. By being believably real, the humans lend credibility to the beast; however, they have to move the story forward with speed and a feeling of urgency. The rhythm of the film depends on them.

In designing this film, I always had our limited budget in mind but I was determined not to think "small." I knew that by not splurging on useless details, I could build large sets quite inexpensively.

The snow set occupied the entire large stage of the Motion Picture Center. It represented the chaotic agglomeration of large ice blocks remaining after the explosion. In the distance the set blended with misty sky. The entire set was snowed in with crushed ice to a depth of one to three feet, practical for maneuvering the snowmobile.

For Cecil Kellaway, playing the affable paleontologist, I wanted to create an office space adjoining the museum. I remember how impressed I had been by a huge skeleton of a mammoth I had seen in the Museum of Natural History in New York City. As mammoth skeletons are not easily obtained in Hollywood, and manufacturing one was beyond our means, I decided to use a huge photographic blow-up that would occupy the back wall of our set. However, my prop man reminded me of a dinosaur used in *Bringing Up Baby*, an old film by RKO. All those old bones made of papier-mâché were in a dusty warehouse at RKO. It took many days for my assistant and ingenious prop people to find which bones connected with each other. Once mounted, this skeleton towered sixteen feet and became a dominant element of the set.

Many other sets, some requiring rear projection, were erected on the third and fourth stages.

Shooting began in the miniature tank on stage with a scene that showed the cracking and collapsing icebergs. Later the descent of the miniature bathysphere was made on a dry, fogged-in stage, using underwater lighting effects. These scenes were done as preproduction, so our camera and special effects crews could practice techniques to be used later on.

Then one Friday morning we moved to the New York street set at Paramount. We had some 400 extras and a high crane.

The head cameraman was Jack Russell, a no-nonsense technician who created the moody realistic lighting throughout the picture. We shot the panic scenes in the street: people running in terror and the police advancing fearlessly to meet the beast.

We used night shooting for the scenes in the deserted dark streets where, lit by searchlights, the army columns advanced, following the blood puddles left by the wounded beast in its escape toward the sea. Many soldiers followed this path of the beast and became violently ill, stricken by a mysterious virus emanating from the monster's blood. We finished shooting late at night. Our production manager had scheduled this shooting on Friday so that we would have Saturday and Sunday to recuperate.

On Monday we started filming with the actors. The first day was spent on the snow set. It happened that this was the hottest day of the year in Hollywood. The two ice-crushing pumps had to snow in the entire set early in the morning, and as soon as the snow melted, keep on adding new layers of snow. Actors, dressed in heavy snow parkas, suffered from the heat. The falling snow—corn flakes—adhered to their perspiring brows. This snow, however, looked quite realistic on their fur hoods.

Driving in a snowmobile, the scientists stop close to the explosion site.

Animation model of the beast.

Night shooting in the Long Beach amusement park (Coney Island in the film).

They must proceed on foot to check the radiation monitors. The first monitor shows a high amount of radiation, and the scientists hurry to investigate. One of them falls into a crevice and injures his leg. It begins to snow. Suddenly he hears an ominous animal cry and through the blinding snowstorm, he sees the gigantic silhouette of the howling beast. Panicking, he shoots a signal pistol. Professor Nesbitt, Paul Christian, finds his wounded comrade but is unable to hoist him from the crevice. He tries to get help but the snowstorm intensifies. Paul also hears the plaintive cry and sees the monster. He loses his way and hours later is found in the raging snowstorm. The snowmobile drivers take him back to the base, but they are unable to find the other scientist.

As you see, the shooting of this sequence was a complicated enterprise. Sticking to my schedule, we finished shooting on time. I had promised the producers to bring the picture in on budget. I shot according to a well-organized shooting script and tight schedule, and I didn't believe in extra shooting for protection. In fact, I was afraid of giving the editor the opportunity of altering my conceptions of scenes by cutting or intercutting. I remember at the end of the second or third day of shooting Bernie Burton, who edited the picture, worriedly told me, "Gene, you know, you don't give me enough coverage."

"Bernie," I said, "when I am shooting a scene in a continuous traveling shot, I don't want to give you the option of interrupting the scene and intercutting some coverage shots. Moreover, on our budget and schedule, do you think I have the time for unnecessary shots?"

Providing film for coverage shots was not an ironclad rule, and in many of the dialogue scenes between two or more characters, I gave Bernie plenty of coverage—close and medium shots and invariably a comprehensive shot where you see the ensemble of the participants and the setting where the action takes place.

Due to my mode of shooting, the editing of the film was extremely rapid. Bernie confessed that he had never finished a picure so quickly.

Other sets followed quickly one after the other. First were the sets for the polar base and the radar room where the scientists wait for the results from the radiation explosion. The unconscious Nesbitt is brought there before he is airlifted to the hospital in New York. There Nesbitt learns from the colonel that no one else saw the beast, and Nesbitt's vision is diagnosed as a hallucination. Positive that the beast was real, Nesbitt visits Cecil Kellaway, a leading paleontologist at the Museum of Natural History. The huge skeleton of the dinosaur in the background adds reality to Nesbitt's descripion of the beast. Kellaway is sympathetic but doubtful that a monster could be found alive after millions of years of extinction. "So you think I am crazy, too?" asked Nesbitt. Professor Kellaway is still skeptical, but not his pretty young assistant. What science fiction picture at this time could avoid the cliché of an attractive female scientist?

Sometimes four sets were used in a day's shooting. A stone wall collapses on a group of frightened bystanders. The lighthouse keeper is crushed in the iron circular stairway of the shattered lighthouse. The fishing trawler advances through the foggy sea and is attacked and destroyed by the beast. And so on. Altogether we shot some twenty different sets, some of which used rear-projection backing.

The total shooting for the picture was completed in twelve days, nine shooting days on the three stages of the Motion Picture Center, one day of shooting on the Paramount street, and the remaining two days—actually nights— in the amusement area of Long Beach.

We had obtained the exclusive use of the Long Beach amusement area and the roller coaster from 10 P.M. until 3 A.M. We shot there for two consecutive nights. The shooting involved about 300 extras, military vehicles, motorcycles, dolly shots, crane shots, and so on. Jack Russell was a tremendous help, quickly lighting complicated long shots.

While shooting these scenes I met a young actor who moved with the grace of a wildcat. He had to play the very small part of a sharpshooter who must kill the beast without spreading the mysterious virus. "There is only one way to stop the monster," says Professor Nesbitt. "Radioactive isotopes!" Nesbitt hands the isotope gun to the young actor and says, "Ever use one of these?" "Pick my teeth with it," Lee Van Cleef replies. And you believed him too.

During the shooting of the picture, the construction crew built some miniatures that were delivered to Ray Harryhausen for his animation sequences.

Right: *The roller coaster after the beast has smashed it.*

Then, after the principal photography was completed, I had some more miniatures to build and shoot. One of these was the roller coaster, which stood some eight feet high. I worked with Ray, planning and shooting this sequence. I had to precut sections of the miniature, coat them with rubber cement (for effective burning), set them on fire, and then jerk away the precut sections, pulling them with a thin wire, to correspond to Ray's animation of the beast tearing apart the roller coaster. The sequence was very long and required many flaming precut pieces to fly into the air. In the same miniature I had to shoot the crash and final explosion of the runaway roller-coaster car when the speeding car hits the gasoline barrel.

The shooting of the picture proper was finished. Ray continued his painstaking animation work. As soon as he finished a scene, it was incorporated into the edited picture.

I would like to mention here that while the animation was usually performed by a dedicated solitary artist like Ray, who avoided outside interference, there were also some group animation outfits. Soon after completion of the *Beast*, I visited a well-appointed studio in the suburbs of Amsterdam, Holland, which specialized only in three-dimensional animation. There I met Yup Geesing, the jovial director of Dollywood studios, where at this time some ten well-staffed units were busy animating different productions, mostly for publicity. There I was shown the just-completed film for the Phillips Electric Company, an ambitious production depicting the history of artificial illumination from candlelight to the latest uses of electricity. On one of the stages I saw the shooting of a similar commercial for General Electric. The large set represented, in about one-tenth scale, night in a busy modern street, with moving streetcars, automobiles, pedestrians, cross-street signals changing from green to red. Shop windows were illuminated and electric signs blinked in intricate patterns.

The camera had been placed on a dolly track, traveling from a height of twelve feet down to the street level. The tubular rails of the track were marked at millimeter intervals to show the grips how much the camera should move for each frame.

Many crews of animators, each person in charge of a specific group of puppets, rushed after every take to move their assigned puppets according to a predesigned chart.

I didn't ask how many seconds of animation could be achieved during one day of this multiple activity, but it was highly impressive to see these organized efforts by teams of eager young animators.

Directing *The Monster from Beneath the Sea* was a wonderful experience for me. As for my reactions to the finished film, it is difficult to have a fresh impression after seeing shot sequences projected in the cutting room every day.

I felt badly about some scenes, especially the handling of some opticals. But neither Ray nor I had the opportunity to reshoot any scene. Overall, I felt that the picture did not fail us. The action moved forward, the story progressed, the tempo was never lost. I think I caught the feeling of panic in the streets and the loneliness of the beast trapped in the deep walls of Wall Street or caught on the roller coaster. Moreover, I think the picture had a specific tone of its own.

When all the shots were spliced together, the end sequence came as a surprise with the beast dying in the flaming ruins of the roller coaster. It was emotionally strong, like the finale of a tragic opera. The beast dies like an opera tenor.

Seeing the picture in the theater among a strongly reacting audience was satisfying. I took Jean Renoir with me. It was a matinee. Renoir reacted just like the youngsters surrounding us. *"Eh bien, mon vieux,"* he said. "You surely had a wonderful time making this film." I think he was remembering the fun he had while making his early fantasy picture, *The Little Match Girl*.

The strongest and most unexpected reaction came from my daughter, age six. She cried, "You are bad, Daddy, bad. You killed the nice beast."

When *The Monster from Beneath the Sea* was finished and edited, Jack Dietz realized he had a potential success on his hands, a picture far too good for his small regional distributors. He decided to seek a national distributor and offered it to Jack Warner. Warner, however, was not interested in releasing it but in buying it outright. An interesting detail: when Warner projected the picture he asked Tony Wright, his production manager, "How much would we spend to produce this type of picture?"

"I wouldn't touch it for less than a million," said Wright.

The deal was concluded and Jack Dietz agreed to sell for $450,000.

In Jack Warner's hands the picture was retitled and became *The Beast from 20,000 Fathoms.* Warner found our score not rich or commercial enough. A new score was written and recorded with double the number of musicians and an amplified brass section. A useless ballet sequence was added from Warner Brothers stock footage. Otherwise the picture was not altered.

Preceded by a fanfare of publicity and with clever exploitation, the picture quickly became a success, remaining at the top of the national box office for many weeks. At the end of the first year of exhibition, it grossed more than $5 million, a considerable performance for an unpretentious picture that was produced for $210,000. This success later became an albatross around my own neck and drove the original producer, Jack Dietz, to a frenzy of jealousy.

For me, the results of this financial success were felt much later. The picture was released more than a year after we had completed it. The success of *Beast* strongly influenced my career. In the eyes of prospective producers, I became identified with a specialized form of science fiction that dealt with prehistoric monsters. I began to get fan mail, including one letter from a ten-year-old admirer from Kansas City. He wrote that I was his favorite director and asked me to send my photograph and a photo of the beast.

I was getting scripts and offers to direct some sci-fi pictures, all of them unbelievably bad. Meanwhile I got an offer to collaborate in France with Sacha Guitry, a witty writer-direcor. For him I directed some sequences of *Napoleon* and later *Si Paris nous était conté.* Then a producer, Dave Diamond, asked me to direct a modestly budgeted coproduction for Allied Artists and England's Eros Films. It was to deal with another kind of monster; this time not a live creature but a blob of expanding radiation. To complete this deal between AA and the English coproducers, Dave had to present the shooting script. Once again I was caught by the reputation of *Beast.* The English producers insisted that our story had to deal with a visible physical creature, a monster, and they let us understand that it should be a duplication of *The Beast from 20,000 Fathoms.*

The script had to be presented in a very short time and Dave Diamond's writers had difficulty in producing a decent script. I was saddled with the task of rewriting it as quickly as possible. With my friend Daniel Hyatt, we rushed through a rough draft in some ten days. I was plagiarizing myself and reluctantly gave this draft to Dave Diamond with the understanding that this script was a pro forma document to be used only to sign the producers' contract and would be drastically changed and developed in London where we had to start preparations at once. But the rewriting was never done. And so I had to shoot this second edition of the *Beast,* finally called *The Giant Behemoth.* I began to choose the most appropriate landmarks of London to use in this new saga of the perennial dinosaur.

It was, however, not my last involvement with these creatures. In 1958 King Brothers asked me if I had an idea similar to the *Beast.* I again took the tired dinosaur out of retirement and joyfully destroyed the city of London once more, this time in color and with a wonderful display of spectacular photographic effects.

For this picture I invented some novel approaches to the saga of a dinosaur confronting the cruel, civilized world. The story now dealt with two monsters instead of one. They were also strikingly different in size. The first encounter is with a monster of relatively modest dimensions—about thirty feet tall, twice the size of an elephant. Our heroes catch it and imprison it in a zoo. However, in the second part of the film, a gigantic beast appears; in the story it is the mother of the first, coming to the rescue of her "baby." In keeping the promise I had made to my daughter, the monsters were not killed but retreated majestically back to the deep sea. I personally think that this mother-baby relationship in the story positively influenced the King brothers, known for their strong attachment to their mother. Anyhow the project was accepted, and I was commissioned to write the screenplay together with my friend Daniel Hyatt. Our story was entitled *Kuru Island*, and it took place on one of the Pacific islands and in Tokyo, Japan. These locations were chosen because originally King Brothers projected a coproduction with a Japanese company. However, plans changed and instead of Japan, the picture had to be located in England. True to the usual Hollywood practice, the producers commissioned a new team of writers to do a drastic rewrite of the screenplay, changing not only the locale

*Working sketch of monsters returning
through the flames.*

*Miniature set and the "baby"
monster. "See GORGO! 'It's alive!' In
new AUTOMOTION."*

of the story but also adding some violent action and illogical developments. When I asked King Brothers for the reasons for this rewrite, the answer was, "But, Gene, it is to your advantage. As you will direct this film, you will have an enriched screenplay. Believe us—two brains are better than one!" I was committed to direct, and while directing tried my best to bring some logic to the embarrassing developments of the new story.

The actual making of the film was interesting, and I tried to make it as spectacular as possible. Instead of the frame-by-frame animation used in the previous *Beast from 20,000 Fathoms*, I opted for a stunt man wearing the rubber-casted skin of the dinosaur. I also decided that only one miniature beast would be used for both monsters, however different in size. For scenes with the "baby" monster, the action was staged on a miniature set scaled down relative to the monster's size. But scenes with the giant "mother" beast were shot with much smaller miniatures sized proportionally to the beast's size.

It was, however, quite tricky to make two different-sized animals appear in the same frame. In the scene of the two monsters making their way to the waterfront among the burning buildings, the master shot was of the "mother" moving, shot against the smaller-scale miniature set of the waterfront. The "baby" was shot separately on blue backing, reduced, and printed onto the master shot by a traveling matte process. In the same shot we added views of panicky, running people, shot on the studio back lot and fitted exactly into a predetermined place on the frame.

The combined shots demanded thorough planning and presketching. The mastery of Bill Howard, the head of optical effects in the MGM studios in Boreham, England (where *Gorgo* was shot), made my task easier. The film in fact contained a multitude of difficult trick shots made mostly in unusual haste; amazingly, only very few had some technical flaws.

In addition to the miniature dinosaur, we built a life-size head, paws, and tail for the "baby" monster. For scenes where we had to first see the drugged animal on the deck of the ship, then transported on a platform truck from the docks to a special enclosure in the amusement area of Battersea Park, London, we used a subterfuge—the entire body was covered by tarpaulins, with only the head and paws exposed.

hourié

Sketch of monsters breaking
through roller coaster.

Miniature set for *GORGO*,
filmed at MGM's Boreham-
wood studio in England.

Among the spectacular effects involving the gigantic "mother," we shot the beast destroying Tower Bridge, Big Ben, and scores of central London streets—all done with breakaway sets. For these scenes we had built a large tank about three feet deep, occupying an entire stage of MGM studios, in which were replicas of the Tower Bridge and the surrounding shore installations. Here we staged the destruction of the bridge and the beast wading away in the river. Afterward the London port authorities decide to burn the monster to death by opening the valves of a tanker and covering the surface of the river with oil, which is then ignited. The beast, however, escapes through the soaring flames.

Going on location into the city, we shot the cutaway scene on the real steps of the Thames River embankment, where some curious boys approach the water's edge to have a better view of the monster. They are caught by rapidly advancing fire, and engulfed in flames, one of them runs up the steps. On the river we also shot a real tanker, the opening of the valves, and the introductory scenes to the burning.

We obtained benevolent cooperation from the British army and the London police authorities. We were allowed to use army tanks and vehicles and to shoot day and night sequences on the Tower Bridge and many central streets. We later had to combine shots made at night in Piccadilly Circus with shots of panicky crowds, as simultaneously the beast was destroying the luminous signs on the roofs of the surrounding buildings.

From the sheer number of effects, it was a very ambitious enterprise indeed. Despite my misgivings about the screenplay, I enjoyed working with the English technicians and Fred Young, the cameraman; and also with actors Bill Travers, Bill Sylvester, and others. Also the short location shooting in Ireland was a very pleasant experience.

After this picture, my last directorial encounter with dinosaurs, I accepted an assignment to do the design for *Flight from Ashiya*, to be shot in Japan. However, the aura of special effects stuck with me—in *Flight from Ashiya* I was asked to design and direct some of the biggest miniature sequences in my life: a helicopter flying to survey an avalanche in the Alps, a seaplane landing in a stormy sea, an explosion of an army barracks, and other marvels.

FLIGHT FROM ASHIYA

One day in the summer of 1962, I got an unexpected telephone call from my agent: "Gene, a producer wants you to design a picture in Japan. It's urgent. If you accept you have to leave tomorrow." I said that I'd like to go, but I needed one more day to fetch my passport.

Ingo, my agent, didn't know the specifics of the project. The producer, Harold Hecht, was then in Washington with Gil Kurland, the production manager, trying to get some delayed authorizations from the army for use of their planes. The entire company, already in Japan, had been waiting for these authorizations for many weeks. Harold Hecht's production office at Columbia studios didn't have the script, but they had my plane ticket to Tokyo.

On the way to Tokyo, on the stopover in Honolulu, I met Gil Kurland, who was on his way from Washington. We traveled together but we didn't speak about the film—he said he would give me the script when we got to Tokyo.

That same afternoon we were in Tokyo, in the beautiful new Okura Hotel overlooking the city. There I met Michael Anderson, the director, who was interviewing a few Americans for some secondary parts in the picture. I also met the official translator, Markarov, a young Russian—born, raised, and educated in Japan.

The hotel was new, and from my window I saw some thirty or forty gardeners working like busy ants: digging and planting tall trees, then supporting them with bamboo poles; making stone steps and tiny waterfalls. I was impressed by their bringing order out of chaos and thought, "Goodness, if the studio workers are as industrious, it's a good omen."

The picture was being prepared and would be shot almost entirely in Kyoto. The train ride there took us six hours (although the trains are now much faster). In Kyoto I was brought to the hotel, given the script, and the next morning driven in a taxi to the Daiei studio, located outside of town. I was ushered to the production office and offered an office where I could "break down" the script. But I felt that Gil kept postponing presenting me to the Japanese art department. The picture was a coproduction with Daiei Japanese Company and had a Japanese art director assigned. Hecht Company had accepted the arrangement, but when it came to the actual start of production, they decided they needed someone else in addition and hired me without telling Tom Shimogawara, the Japanese art director, that I was coming. As the Japanese are a very proud people, the production manager didn't dare tell him about me, so I spent two days in the production office reading the script, speaking with Michael Anderson, but not meeting the people with whom I would have to work.

The story of *Flight from Ashiya* is complicated, told in so many flashbacks that reading the script I found myself as confused as the characters later were on the screen.

The plot deals with the personal conflicts among three men in the Air Rescue Service (Ashiya), an outfit that helps shipwrecked people, using seaplanes and parachutists. (Ashiya had formerly operated from worldwide bases but now operates from Japan.)

Yul Brynner plays the Japanese-American pararescuer, who remembers his tragic love affair with a Moroccan girl (Danielle Gaubert). Now in Japan, he is being comforted by a Red Cross nurse (Suzy Parker). Richard Widmark, the pilot, is a bitter man who had once fallen in love with an American magazine photographer (Shirley Knight), whom he married while both of them were in the Philippines. They had a child, but both wife and child died in a Japanese prison camp in World War II. Widmark mistrusts all Japanese and particularly resents Brynner for his ancestry.

The third protagonist, George Chakiris, is also a pilot, who once had a serious conflict with Widmark, his commanding officer, while on a rescue mission in the Bavarian Alps. Chakiris is now happily married to a Japanese girl (Eiko Taki). Confusing, isn't it?

The day finally arrived when I met with the art department. They assigned me a translator because nobody spoke anything but Japanese. Tom Shimogawara was told I was there to act as a liaison between the director and the art department. But Tom was a very clever man, and he probably understood what was going on. Eventually I was given the title of production designer, and he kept his title of art director. Together we went over the set list and then to see the facilities at Daiei studios, about which I was concerned because Daiei specialized in samurai pictures. How would they handle the many European sets required by the flashbacks in our script? Or the technical sets on the American Ashiya base?

Visiting the back lot I saw many wonderful Japanese medieval streets, as well as the studio tank. This tank looked very small to me, too small for the scenes we had to do. I told Gil Kurland that the tank was too small and got the usual disbelieving reaction of a production manager to a new unforeseen problem. A very human reaction.

"What do you mean, too small? The studio assured me they use this tank for all their productions," he insisted.

Well, it depended for what kind of shots they used it. Maybe it was large enough for miniatures or close shots, but in our picture we had to use the tank for a complicated sequence involving a raft carrying some twenty survivors of a shipwreck in a raging sea and had to show two parachutists climbing on the wildly moving raft in the waves of this strong storm. We decided with Kurland to examine the tank thoroughly some days later with Michael Anderson and the cameraman who was expected from Hollywood.

Designing for a Japanese crew was a new experience. I usually worked out the floor plans and elevations first, discussed them with the director, then proceeded with working drawings and sometimes sketches or models. Here I was very careful to make measured plans and elevations. I had to translate them into the conventional Japanese measurements. In Japan the sizes of houses are measured by the number of tatamis, or floormats. Each floormat is a definite size—as I remember, six by three feet. All rooms are covered with these mats. The carpenters and assistant art directors didn't use other measurements. They would say, "the room of six tatamis" or "the room of ten tatamis." Moreover, I was amazed to watch the diligent assistants study my floor plans and elevations and make little perspective sketches from them, annotating them with the number of tatamis in every room. Seemingly the carpenters could not read plans and elevations but had to build from the perspective sketches. In my work with the assistant art directors, every explanation I gave had to go through the female translator. Unfortunately, this lady was not familiar with architecture nor with the technical terms I used in set construction. More complications arose because the metric system is used in Japan, and later the difference between feet and meters created a serious misunderstanding between Tom and me.

The collaboration with Michael Anderson was easy and agreeable. On one of the first days we went to Osaka—about an hour's drive—to scout the actual seaplanes at the Osaka Airport. During the preparation of this film, I had to make this trip to Osaka many times. Each time riding in the taxi was a suicidal affair through a kamikaze complex of cars and other taxis.

Constructing the seaplane mock-up was my primary preoccupation. Technically it would have been a very difficult task even in a Hollywood studio. But in the Kyoto Daiei studio, which specialized in samurai films, it was a big problem.

The Osaka manager of the Grauman planes was a big help. I asked him if he could lend us some seats from planes now in repair. He said that we could take an entire plane, as he had some that were beyond repair. I made a deal with him. Using a torch, his workers would cut a plane the way I instructed them. We would have to pay only for the actual working hours spent on this job. I took the blueprints of the seaplane and returned to Kyoto to study them and mark where the plane would be cut for our mock-up.

To maneuver this mock-up on the stage easily and also to imitate the plane moving in the stormy sea, we would usually use a gimbal, a contrivance on which the body of the mock-up is placed. My translator did not understand my explanation. With the help of Tom Shimogawara and Markarov, I confronted the crusty old construction foreman. I showed him a toy airplane, indicated the movements I wanted, and he understood immediately. Smiling and bowing—don't forget, we were in Japan—he said something that means, "You shouldn't worry," a phrase that was worrisome enough by itself. I had heard this answer before, and I was to hear it often in the future. But usually they were right, somehow everything worked out. You were never sure if the smiling prop makers, carpenters, and painters really knew how to solve the problem or if it was a show of Oriental pride—never show that you don't understand or do not know.

The Japanese carpenters were amazing. I saw them arriving in clusters at eight in the morning at the same time I alighted from my taxi. They rushed through the gates, each with a handsaw hanging from his belt. All the carpentry, however complicated, was done with hand tools. The studio had no power tools. But all was made with skill and diligence. All the stages had dirt floors, very handy for Japanese sets where houses were built one or two steps above ground on terraces and surrounded by gardens. For European sets we first had to lay down floor platforms and then build our sets on them. The smell of the stages was striking for a newcomer. As lumber was scarce and expensive, walls of the sets were built on burlap frames, pasted over and over with many layers of papier-mâché. Women laborers, their heads wrapped in voluminous kerchiefs, pasted the multilayered old newspapers. The buckets of glue they used were offensively odorous. The doors for our sets—and European doors were much different than the Japanese sliding panels—were built of the flimsiest plywood.

When the energetic Yul Brynner slammed the door in one scene, the door and the papier-mâché wall vibrated for many seconds. To hang a picture on these unsteady walls was an ordeal.

Outside the stages it was early summer, very hot and humid, and the grass was green. On the way to the art directors' office, I passed by Yul Brynner's huge trailer, air transported from Hollywood. Yul knew how to make himself respected. Not satisfied with this degree of privacy, he ordered a bamboo fence to be erected around his trailer. There gardeners were busy planting chrysanthemums.

Seeing this opulence, Dick Widmark complained of unequal treatment. As a result he and George Chakiris were given multiroomed dressing quarters.

Gil Kurland organized catered hot lunches from the Kyoto Hotel for the American crew. Since we had our daily allowances paid, he charged us the price of these lunches. Small revolt! The warmed-up food was not good, and some of our crew joined me and the art directors in a little Japanese restaurant outside the studio walls. There, shedding our shoes, we sat on the floor in front of very low tables and tried to pick up the rice with our chopsticks. Happily I was able to obtain a fork. Sometimes Dick Widmark escaped the organized hotel lunches and joined us at our tasty, simple Japanese meal.

Sometimes our studio day finished at six o'clock, sometimes later. After the suffocating heat of the day, we rushed for showers in our respective hotels. Most of the American crew stayed in the comfortable, central Kyoto Hotel. But some stars were lodged in splendid desolation at the Miako Hotel, situated in a park. It was usually dark when, refreshed, we emerged from our hotels. The streets were alive with ever-moving, chattering crowds, dressed in a mixture of western jeans and traditional kimonos. All these people seemed to be rushing somewhere; the majority young, gay, and uninhibited. Many carried packages tied in colored kerchiefs, presents people brought when visiting friends. Very often we ate dinner in the friendly grillroom of the Kyoto Hotel. Usually the Miako crowd joined us in the warm atmosphere of our grillroom, abandoning their solemn, isolated hotel.

For a flashback one of our large exterior sets had to represent a Bavarian church half-buried in an Alpine snow avalanche. Only the roof and the clock tower could protrude from the snow. For this set we scouted the outskirts of town and finally decided on a hillside where workers from a brick factory needing earth for the clay had dug out the entire side of a hill. The sharp cut of the hill was about sixty or seventy feet high, rising abruptly from a flat field, the configuration of which could easily pass for the abrupt end of a snow avalanche. When we started to build the set, we covered the entire hillside with chicken wire and then with white muslin, on top of which we put a coat of plaster and whitewash. The entire hill covered with bamboo scaffolding looked like a gigantic anthill alive with women laborers climbing up and down and plasterers in their knee-high leggings laying out plaster. Against this cut-off hill that would represent the avalanche, we built a church roof and bell tower protruding from the snow.

The misunderstanding about feet and meters between Tom and me occurred because of this bell tower. As I mentioned earlier, I usually gave the art assistants measured sketches. The drawing of the tower indicated a top platform only three feet wide. I wanted that platform to be quite narrow. When I visited the set, however, I saw a tower considerably wider. I asked Tom what had happened. I was younger then and blew my top more often. Tom answered that the tower was exactly three meters wide, just as my drawing had indicated. Misunderstanding—meters, not feet. He declared heatedly that rebuilding the tower was out of the question. In fact, I didn't ask for it. Looking at the set more calmly, I came to the conclusion that the width of the platform would be all right as is—so the tower was left as it was originally constructed. But Tom didn't speak to me for a week. Later on though, we became friends— real friends.

Some days later when we were ready to shoot this set, we had another kind of mishap. At six o'clock on the morning we planned to shoot, I approached the site in the car with Kurland and Anderson. On the road we were stopped by a wildly gesturing Tom.

"Don't go down there!" he yelled. "An accident!"

"What happened?"

"All the snow. It's pink!"

"Pink?"

It happened that the snow was made of a kind of plastic foam used for heat insulation in house construction. When it was sprayed it dried to a spongelike surface and looked like snow; you could even walk on it. We had a huge surface to cover, the entire field in front of the church where the helicopter lands. The insulation company had sprayed the field the night before with the wrong solution and the foam had dried pink.

The mistake was repaired quickly. The insulation company sent trucks and trucks with new spray. The shooting proceeded with only a three-hour delay. The helicopter lands in the falling snow, and the imprisoned churchgoers manage to escape by way of the bell tower, thinking that now they would be evacuated. But the helicopter does not have enough room for all of them. This is the point of the drama that causes conflict between compassionate George Chakiris and coldly realistic Dick Widmark. Later on when the helicopter returns to the church during a snowstorm, George witnesses with dismay a new avalanche that buries the remaining survivors.

We had a night street scene to shoot where Yul Brynner and Suzy Parker are running under a driving rain to take refuge in a small Japanese hotel lobby. For this sequence I used the Daiei medieval streets, adding modern signs and neon lights. It looked in fact like a genuine modern street somewhere in Kyoto or Tokyo. To these streets Tom added a wonderfully authentic Japanese hotel lobby.

The sets of German hotels and a beer hall, used in another flashback, were quite an ordeal to build. It was difficult to find authentic European props and German beer mugs in Kyoto. The furnishing of hotel rooms was also a problem. I had some still pictures with me, research photos of the interiors of German hotels. I gave these photographs to Abe-san, our set decorator, to show him what kind of furniture we should have. Three weeks later when I asked him to show me what he had found, he answered, "Not to worry." At this late date I really started to worry. Finally he proudly produced a bed, chest, and wardrobe copied exactly from my photographs but built in such flimsy plywood that they swayed the moment an actor walked on the set.

Meanwhile the matter of the water tank became urgent. We visited the Daiei tank again, and it was obvious we would not be able to film our complicated scenes there. We went to Tokyo but were unable to find an available tank.

"What to do?" Gil asked. "Hollywood, London, or Rome," I said.

I had visited all the European tank facilities three years earlier while scouting for my science fiction picture, *Gorgo*. I gave the tank sizes to Gil. Hollywood and London were out of question for some reason. Moreover, the company had planned location shooting in Morocco or Tunisia, and Rome was closer.

Again the misunderstanding between feet and meters surfaced. We received an answer from the Cinecitta studios in Rome. Gil called me to his office and triumphantly announced that I was wrong. The tank in the Rome studio was only 100 feet long, he said, instead of the 300 feet I had told him. It's amazing how some people are eager to show that they know everything better than you. I had to tell him that in Rome they also measure in meters, not feet, and 100 meters represents about 300 feet.

There were many trips to Osaka to follow the work of cutting the Grauman seaplane. Finally the cut body of the plane was delivered to Daiei studio. The construction foreman produced a huge wooden beam. I had never seen even telegraph poles of such proportion. The body of the plane was placed on top of the beam. The beam was put on top of the new gimbal that the proud foreman presented as a surprise. With the help of some twenty men, the plane could be inclined and pivoted in all directions, imitating the most violent movement in the strongest storm. It was sufficient to make many of our actors seasick.

The Daiei studio had a well-organized special effects unit. Directors, builders, and cameramen were all available for shooting miniatures. They were a wonderfully efficient crew and after they showed me how successfully we had shot the first miniature, I had to invite the entire crew to a chicken dinner in a charming Japanese restaurant that overlooked the river. But more of that later.

For the time being I made a clay model of the complex miniature set we had to build. There was to be a mountain and the church buried under the avalanche. The miniature was to occupy the entire stage, some 100 to 150 feet long. The model, made of modeling clay, was cut in six-inch sections, each representing ten feet of the actual set. We had a regular production meeting—the miniature builders, the camera and grip crew, the director, and myself.

Together we sat round this model and went over each shot. The last words were, "You shouldn't worry." Familiar sounds. Coming some days later on the stage where this miniature was being erected, I was amazed by the ingenuity and artistic ability of each individual worker as he created a difficult set of realistic mountains with touches of lichen and snow in crevices. At the same time there appeared a specialist in miniature helicopter construction from Tokyo. We needed two sizes of helicopters for our shooting. In my previous visit to Tokyo, I had left our expert drawings and photographs, and now he brought us the very finest miniature helicopters. The miniature scenes were being shot concurrently with the main production unit, and I was unable to assist with all of the laborious takes of this shooting. After the first sequence made by the miniature unit was shot, the entire miniature unit staff invaded the projection room. As usual we all took off our shoes and sat down to watch the rushes. The difficult sequence showed a helicopter flying close to the sheer mountain rocks, then plunging under high-tension lines and hovering above the half-buried church. It was perfect. Lighting, effects, everything. Hence chicken dinner for the entire crew.

We got the same perfection later when we were shooting the avalanche descending the mountain and burying the remains of the church. The shot was done from a moving crane, the point of view of the helicopter pilot. Again timing and precision couldn't have been better.

Then came the difficult shot of the miniature seaplane landing in the raging sea. Here we could use the small Daiei tank, although just barely. The miniature plane was about ten feet wide from wing tip to wing tip. The nylon threads guiding the plane were invisible in the turmoil of the storm.

As my departure for Rome approached, Tom and I went over the designs for the remaining sets, including the Widmark set in the Philippines. We scouted and also found an impressive location outside Kyoto for the destroyed wooden bridge where the hungry people walk from their ruined villages. And we built the prisoners' camp, exterior and interior, in a schoolyard, empty now because it was vacation time. Finally I had to leave. At six in the morning I left in a taxi for Osaka, caught a plane to Tokyo, and a direct flight to Rome. I was sorry not to be able to stop in Hong Kong, but I was expected in Rome the same day. I landed in Rome at about 2 A.M. An assistant to the Italian unit manager met me and we drove to the hotel. Some six hours later the car waited to take me to the Cinecitta studios. There I met Bruno Avesani, an assistant art director, who was assigned to the picture by the Roman unit manager. Bruno helped me organize my work in Rome. Then I met Alberto, the young and kind chief of construction at the studio. He helped me a lot later on. After Japanese the Italian language was easier to understand, and with Bruno I could speak French.

The tank at Cinecitta had been built some years earlier by MGM, I think for *Ben Hur*. It was roughly 300 feet long and 400 feet wide with an imposing 70-foot-high sky backing. Cinecitta had antiquated wave machines and no dump tanks, which we needed for filming our storm at sea. These tanks containing some 2,000 gallons of water are mounted on towers thirty or forty feet high. During filming—and this can be done for both life-size objects and miniatures—water is dumped down slanted chutes, creating waves on the surface of the pool of water. So new dump tanks and their towers had to be erected. Also, the hard-wall backing at Cinecitta had to be covered by stretching a new canvas, which would then have to be painted as a dark, stormy sky.

As no special effects men were available for me yet, we had to design all these contraptions with Bruno. The drawings and photos of the raft built in Japan served to duplicate the same raft in Rome. Basically I was in Rome to prepare the tank sequence. The company was expected in Rome some two or three weeks later, and after completing the storm sequence, would proceed to Morocco for the North African sequence of the script, which required a plaza in a Moroccan town, a native café, and a bus stop. There we would see the usual activity of a town and units of the American army, at this time engaged in fighting Germans. I had to wait for Gil Kurland and then go with him to Morocco to scout locations. However, in my opinion the logistics of shooting scenes in Moroccan towns, reproducing the war years, would be very difficult. It would be much easier to build a Moroccan set in Rome and shoot these complicated sequences there. In looking around the remnants of Roman Empire sets on the huge lot, the Via Veneto reproduced for Fellini's 8½, and so many other disparate sets, I discovered a partly destroyed set of an Algerian Casbah next to a large empty lot. What a place to build a Moroccan town, using the Casbah walls as a possible backing. Remembering the streets and the Casbah in Morocco from my two months' stay there, I could easily imagine this set on the Cinecitta lot. I made some quick thumbnail sketches and asked Alfredo to give me an approximate estimate on building the set. The policy of Cinecitta was to build sets on a contract basis for a fixed price, and Alfredo told me he would build it for $12,000 exactly. I kept this figure in mind.

Working in Italy, living in Rome, was a welcome change from the mistrust, suspicions, and mistaken translations of Kyoto. I felt freer with friendly Italians and did not have to check and doublecheck all my decisions with my production manager and then with the Japanese management. Even without speaking Italian, I understood them better. And Alfredo understood some French; Bruno, my assistant, spoke it fluently; and so did Giorgio, my set dresser. Finally, for everyday meals I frankly preferred Italian cooking to the Japanese cuisine of the Hotel Kyoto. The terrace in the Cinecitta commissary was charming and we spent some happy moments there drinking cups and cups of cappucino and discussing sets.

Soon, Dock Merman, the former head of the Fox production department, appeared in Rome. Gil Kurland, still busy in Kyoto, had asked him to prepare the North African location. He was on his way back from Morocco. Shooting there was out of the question because the Moroccans wouldn't give authorization for a film containing a scene where a Moroccan girl sunbathed and flirted with an American soldier. Dock planned to leave the next morning for Tunisia where Moslem rules of behavior were not as strictly enforced. I told him my idea of shooting the sequence in Rome.

"How much?" he asked.

I told him it would be $12,000.

"If they told you $12,000, it will be $36,000. I know, I made *Cleopatra* here." (*Cleopatra* was known for its cost overruns.) Merman said that anyhow he had to go to Tunisia because all the arrangements were made.

In the middle of the night I got a telephone call. It was Dock Merman. "Gene, when you spoke about possible set construction in Rome, were you serious?"

"I said yes, I was serious.

"I'm coming back. Shooting this picture in Tunisia is impossible. It would be very difficult to reproduce wartime street conditions, to get enough vintage vehicles and everything else we need. We would have to spend a fortune. Tomorrow morning I'll be back in Rome."

The next morning I showed him what I planned to build. He telephoned Harold Hecht in Hollywood to get his okay. The same day I began my drawings and we started building.

This set was quite complex. It represented a busy plaza in a Moroccan town, a corner sidewalk café, some shops, a fountain, and the bus stop. For the background I built a big city gate and beyond the city walls—for depth—a slender minaret tower in miniature scale. I also had to provide some narrow Moroccan streets where sunlight and shadows throw intricate patterns on cobblestone alleys. In these narrow alleys, Yul Brynner tries to find the house where the beautiful girl he met at the beach (Danielle Gaubert) lives. I built the interior of her Moroccan house on stage, duplicating the window with its complicated latticework through which Danielle watches Yul look for her house.

The Cinecitta studios had a well-appointed stage for blue backing shots; the backing was painted an intense ultramarine blue, and blue reflectors were set up to light it. It was a permanent installation for shooting the foregrounds for traveling matte sequences. There we shot the helicoptor and plane interiors. Meanwhile we were ready for the storm sequence, our original reason for shooting in Rome. We built our dump tanks containing 2,000 gallons of water each. A tubing company built for us thirty-foot-high towers and chutes three feet wide, slanting in forty-five degree angles toward the water of the studio pool. The waves produced by these tanks were so strong that I was afraid Yul Brynner might actually drown fighting against the powerful waves. But Yul jumped successfully with his parachute and reached the storm-tossed raft with its motley crew of shipwrecked passengers.

The sequence of the raft took many days to shoot; then we went to our Moroccan street. In the final scenes of the Moroccan sequence, the American army units abandon town because of the German approach. Leaving town they decide to blow up the small bridge leading to the city gates. Trying to see the departing Yul Brynner once more, desperate Danielle runs toward the gates, unaware that Yul and his companions are preparing the explosives under the bridge. They see her approach, running, but it is too late to stop the explosion. It blows up and she disappears. It was a spectacular explosion and a heartbreaking scene.

In the script there was another scene where the army unit drives out of their barracks, and as they depart, the barracks blow up behind them. Michael Anderson asked me how I would do this scene.

One of the exterior walls of the Cinecitta studios was a plain wall with high iron gates that could easily pass for a barracks wall in any town of North Africa. For this scene I prepared the camera outside the studio wall for a long shot of departing trucks and jeeps. I left enough distance above the top of the wall in the frame to accommodate the view of upper floors of the barracks appearing above and beyond it. The miniature barracks would be built separately in Japan and exploded; then the shot of this miniature would be married to the shot made in Rome of the departing army unit. It would be done in the split-screen technique; the top of the Cinecitta wall would become a split line where the scene shot on location joins the miniature explosion scene, shot much later in Kyoto. After the location shot was made, Gil Kurland said, "Gene, you will probably have to travel back to Japan to make the miniature shot. But now go back to Hollywood, prepare the working drawings, and then we will organize the Japanese shooting."

The Roman shooting was at an end. I reluctantly parted with my Italian crew and Bruno, with whom I would work later in preparing and shooting miniatures in Rome for the film *Krakatoa.*

However, I never got back to Japan. The Japanese special crew was so efficient that Kurland decided they could successfully do the shot with my working drawings. So I am sorry to say I missed Kyoto in October when the maples leaves are red.

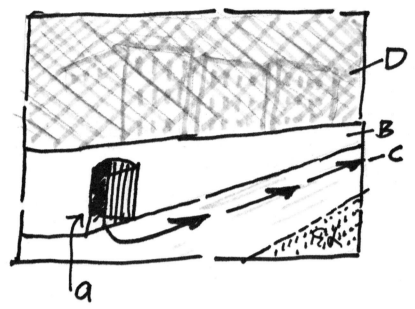

A — STUDIO GATE

B — STUDIO SIDE WALL

C — DIRECTION OF DEPARTING ARMY UNITS

D — AREA MATTE OUT WHERE LATER BARRACKS AND EXPLOSIONS WOULD BE ADDED /IN MINIATURE/

Explosion scene as diagramed for director at Cinecitta.

BATTLE OF THE BULGE

The German offensive in the wooded plateau of the Ardennes, Belgium, in December 1944 became known as the Battle of the Bulge. In a sudden surge German tanks surrounded the "bulging" American and British positions. This dramatic episode from World War II was the theme of a projected film, to be called *Battle of the Bulge*. By the nature and scope of the events to be portrayed, it had to be a very big production, which would entail many production problems.

The action involved the massive movements of American and German tanks and troops. Battles were fought in the bitter cold of snow-covered forests. The logistics of this production were complex and challenging.

At the start of the project, there was as usual only a vague and grandiose vision of the picture and the amount of money it would cost to make. It would be up to the production designer to provide visual shape for the film and find practical ways to achieve it.

I started preparations in November 1964. My first job was to gather information: the types of armaments used by the Germans and Americans and the locations of cities and hamlets where the action took place. The writers and producers had the names of places and the types of tanks used, but I had to do the visual research and at the same time gather practical information about shooting facilities in Spain and other European countries. At this time production plans were fluid and every possibility had to be considered. From Hollywood, Paris, and London I soon received scores of photos and old issues of *Life* and London and Paris illustrated magazines.

However, the search for armaments for our production was unavailing. In this offensive the Germans had used their large new Tiger tanks. These tanks were practically nonexistent some twenty years after the war. A few of them were kept as museum pieces or as monuments in public places, but they were not in working condition. We would have to find our own solution to this tank problem.

Of all the countries contacted about army cooperation, only the Spanish army seemed promising. Their army used two models of tanks, both American made. The smaller tanks were almost identical to the U.S. M-4 Sherman tanks, the ones used by the American army in the Battle of the Bulge; the others were more modern and larger and could possibly be used as the German tanks.

At this time we also acquired German and American military advisors. Together with the producers and writers, these advisors discussed the ways we could camouflage the large Spanish tanks to look like Tigers. I studied the possibilities and concluded that no camouflage could withstand the violent movements and beatings the tanks would get in action. Any sort of plastic overstructure would jeopardize movement, and the unavoidable repairs would be costly and time consuming.

I ordered two photographic enlargements: one a profile of the German Tiger tank and the other, from the Spanish Army, a profile of the available American tank. Compared side by side, the difference between the two could hardly be detected. You would have to be a specialist or superimpose one photo directly above the other to detect which tank was which. And so we made the wise decision not to attempt phony camouflage but to use the existing tanks

One of the miniature Sherman tanks with Lourie.

and mark them with German black crosses and typical lettering. We went ahead with drawing, measuring, and photographing these tanks so that we could build our miniature replicas. At this step of preparation, it was decided that I would use miniatures for all the explosions and destructions. After all, we couldn't burn the property of the Spanish army.

After studying the possible shooting locations, we soon realized it would be impossible to shoot on the actual locations, as in the Ardennes. We couldn't move Spanish tanks to Belgium. We couldn't stage any explosions, fires, or destructions in the town of Amblève or any other town that had been rebuilt after the war. While eager Sapnish location managers scouted to find a Belgian-looking town in Spain, I easily convinced producer Phil Yordan that the most practical way to solve this problem was to work in a controlled condition and build our set right there, as close to the studio as possible.

The largest part of the battle had to be shot in a snow-covered forest. Close to Madrid, about an hour and a half drive, were mountains and some ten to fifteen miles of forested hills that descended toward the plains and the town of Segovia. There was even a half-ruined village that later became part of the set for the outskirts of Amblève. When we scouted this area in early December 1964, it was covered with heavy snow. It was an ideal location for the picture. Also close by was the charming town of Segovia with a sufficient number of hotels where we could lodge our company.

Meanwhile I received the first draft of the script. There was no director as yet, but I proceeded with my work. Although the script required two different Belgian towns, analyzing the dramatic needs of the picture, I saw that the action could be confined to only one town, Amblève. Notwithstanding historical truth, it would not change the dramatic flow of the action. In my opinion this unity of place would make the actions of the American commander and his defense of the town even more understandable. At any rate it would present an appreciable savings in production costs.

Our production company rented the facilities of the Sevilla studios in Madrid. There was a large back lot that measured some 400 by 400 feet. It was large enough to hold the big set of the Belgian town. But not two of them! To build a second town would mean finding and renting a vacant property, probably at a great distance from the city. Transporting workers and then the company, feeding everyone, parking the numerous vehicles—the usual caravan surrounding the shooting company, the loss of time—all would be incredibly expensive. I proposed the solution of telescoping the action into one town to our producer-writer team, Phil Yordan and Milton Sperling. After hesitating for some days—it is hard to convince writers to make changes in their scripts—they finally agreed.

The script also required a sequence where the German tank commander (played by Robert Shaw) is driven through a destroyed German town on his way to a fortified underground bunker, the headquarters of the German tank division. The town is destroyed and deserted. An idea came to me that instead of building a life-size set of this town, I could build it in miniature. I proposed to do a traveling shot alongside the miniature ruined streets as if seen from a passing car and then in the foreground print in Robert Shaw in his car.

Plaza and streets of Amblève constructed in Madrid, Spain, on the back lot of the Sevilla studio.

To complete the sequence I would have to build the life-size entrance to the underground bunker, which is protected by sandbags and guarded by Nazi soldiers. As the commander exits the car, he looks back to the destroyed town. His point of view would be a cut to a long shot of the miniature.

By this decison I would save the cost and avoid the problems of building and shooting the set of the destroyed town. Instead of a set requiring at least 300 feet of depth, I would build a thirty-foot-long miniature and shoot it with my reduced camera unit.

In going over the research of bombed-out towns in Germany and Britain, I noticed that the architectural differences between the buildings were obliterated. They all looked alike: uniform ruins, empty shells of houses with gaping holes in place of windows. In some places there were only hips of collapsed masonry with chimneys left standing.

This similarity among ruins gave me an idea of how to simplify construction. As I planned to build the miniature in one-tenth scale—the usual height of a four-story house being about forty feet—the miniature replica would be four feet.

I decided to design only four prototypes for front walls, each with differ-

ent fenestration. I presumed this would give enough variety among the houses. I would cast many similar walls in plaster, each about four by six feet. In cutting the walls to different heights and widths and breaking them differently, I would have a variety of ruined house fronts. Moreover, I painted these fronts in different colors and blackened some as if in the aftermath of fires and explosions. With these precast walls the entire thirty-foot-long miniature set of three streets was erected in less than one day.

As our schedule called for an early start, I had to continue designing and construction before the director was assigned. I worked with four assistants—in Hollywood they would be called set designers. Assola, who had worked with me on *Crack in the World*, came from Paris again and began work building the prototype of the miniature tanks in a one-to-ten ratio. Alec Weldon and his crew were busy preparing the special effects props. I had to import a vacuum-forming plastic machine from Italy and we started to manufacture false gasoline drums and other props. Prosper, the head of construction, had under his command some 100 carpenters, plasterers, painters, and metal workers. We also had a well-known abstract painter, Mampasso, who was a talented illustrator as well, and together with him, we prepared sketches for the sets and the main scenes. The plaza of Amblève was completely designed and partly built and the miniature model of the set completed.

It was at this stage of preparation that Ken Annakin was finally assigned as the director of the film. It is always a touchy situation when you meet the director so late in the preparation stage, especially after you have gone ahead alone with the designing and decision making that normally should be discussed with the director. Oh yes, it has happened in my career that I have had to design a production ahead of the director's assignment. It even happened twice that I completed the building and dressing of the sets and met the director only on the first day of shooting. It is, however, not a usual practice and should not occur at all; at least, not in motion pictures of this scope and complexity.

Working with Ken proved to be an easy and happy experience. There were no modifications to be made on any decisions that I had made. I took him to the back lot where the construction of Amblève was already underway and showed

Cardboard model of the miniature set for a bombed-out town with its creator.

Several views of the miniature set of Amblève.

him the miniature model of the set we had prepared. I also told him of my plan to build one of the town buildings in real bricks to be crushed in the scene by an advancing German tank. He agreed to the shooting of the destroyed town in miniature, later to be combined with the traveling matte of Robert Shaw.

We had taken still pictures on our earlier scouting trip through the snowy Guadarrama Mountains north of Madrid. However, when we returned there in January with Ken, the snow was gone. The decision was made to use this location no matter what, and if the natural snow did not appear in time for our shooting, we would use artificial snow blown by wind machines. Nature played into our hands. When the actual shooting started in early March, we had to use snowplows to clear the roads.

Meanwhile preparations and set construction were proceeding full speed. The very complex set of Amblève was growing. To give the illusion of depth, I built the upstage portion of the streets in forced perspective. Bricklayers were busy laying bricks for the house that was destined to be demolished. The houses were built with complete roofs and I built several furnished interiors in some of the houses so that when they were destroyed, you would be able to see these interiors. In the foreground was the plaza with its three-storied city hall, used as the temporary headquarters of the American army. On the opposite side of the plaza was a church, a terrace built in packed earth to withstand the weight of the advancing tanks. In the center of the plaza was a stone-carved replica of a fountain, now under a blanket of artificial snow.

In designing the interior sets, I met with a delicate problem. The entire picture was conceived very realistically. This type of war picture should have the feeling of a newsreel. Without copying any specific town exactly, we made it utterly believable. But in describing the German underground operations center, the writers became very theatrical. The set they described would have been proper for a James Bond science fiction melodrama. The producers and writers probably didn't feel this discord in style as sharply as I did. Anyhow, they did not budge from their theatrical conception and I had to try to bring this conception within the limits of reality.

In one of my trips to London, I had the chance to see the World War II underground command post where Churchill spent many sleepless nights fol-

Sketches from various sets used in BATTLE OF THE BULGE.

lowing the progress of the Battle of Britain on the map. This underground center was very simple and functional.

I decided to follow the description in our script, but I would tone down the extravagance of the writers' conception and give the set a feeling of authenticity by using realistic structural and technical details. Following the script and the research, I designed a platform that overlooked the center. Looking down from this platform, the commanding officers could observe the large—twenty foot square—table map of the front lines. Soldiers were placed around this table with long sticks to move the miniature tanks decorated with German or American emblems on the map. These movements showed the advancing Nazi Panzer units or the positions of the Allied tanks. From their high iron platform, the commanding general and his staff officers could observe the fluctuating positions of the armies. On the same platform was a bank of complicated communication gadgets. There was also a gigantic wall map where illuminated arrows showed the movement of German columns. At the point where their tanks met Allied resistance, the light arrows stopped. Direct telephone communications with commanders on the field, a countdown clock, loudspeakers reverberating under the vaulted ceiling of the operation center completed the set, lending verisimilitude to the action.

Other sets were built simultaneously on other stages of the Sevilla studios.

Meanwhile I was dispatched to direct the second-unit shooting of the German soldiers parachuting behind American lines. Dressed in American uniforms with military police insignia, they were assigned to disrupt American communications, change Belgian road markings, and cut telephone lines. We had to shoot the parachuting scene early in preproduction to allow us to prepare a matching set on the stage for close shots of the parachutists hitting the ground.

March 1965. Snow was falling on our location in the Guadarramas. The Spanish army moved their tanks to the temporary barracks in Segovia.

A convertible Mercedes carrying a German general rushes down a deserted snowy road. Suddenly an American observation plane appears in the sky. It passes very low above the car, buzzing it. Panicking, the German driver brakes, throwing the car into a ditch. So began the first scene shot for *Battle of the Bulge.*

The second scene had some forty German tanks, camouflaged under stately pines, ready for attack. Camera, lights, everything was in place. The action was carefully explained to the tank drivers. A wrong movement would mean a big loss of time. Ken Annakin patiently repeated commands. As the noise of the tanks would be deafening, the commands would be transmitted by radio communication to each tank commander. Also, visual signals would be used. Robert Shaw, the commanding officer, gave a short signal from the turret of his tank. Suddenly everything came alive; the noise of the motors and the terrifying clatter of the metallic armada. The tanks moved ahead in a rising whirlwind of snow and smoke.

In the noisy confusion of the moving tanks, it was difficult to see if the scene was done correctly. And so, second take, please. The tanks began a difficult maneuver to retreat to their starting positions. Fresh snow had to be blown in by wind machines to obliterate the tracks.

In spite of the military discipline and promptness of command, it was difficult to make the officers realize that each scene, however complex the action, had to be performed in a very short time, usually seconds. From the first days of shooting, they had to accustom themselves to the precise timing required by film.

In our dealing with the officers of the Spanish army, I observed signs of empathy between men of the same military caste that transcended national frontiers. A high-ranking German ex-general was our military advisor. A ramrod-straight Prussian, he reminded me strongly of Erich von Stroheim in *Grand Illusion*. In reviewing the tanks with a suite of Spanish officers, I was amazed by the respectful attention paid to his every word by all the Spanish officers. This also reminded me of the idea expressed in *Grand Illusion* that the officers of opposing armies are closer to each other than to other classes of their own nations.

Taking advantage of the abundant snow in our forested mountains, we plowed ahead, fighting the Battle of the Bulge. We were working in cold and difficult conditions. We had to break the ice to move our equipment on the roads, and our cumbersome production machinery had the same difficulties as the tanks moving through ice and snow. Cameras had to be warmed under electric

"The tanks moved ahead in a rising whirlwind of snow and smoke."

blankets. Bonfires were burning constantly to warm the freezing fingers of the cast and crew.

Day after day the German tanks progressed relentlessly, overrunning isolated American positions. Finally the tanks surrounded the city of Amblève. On location we built the outskirts of the town around the ruins of the Spanish village. The fierce battles were staged between the entrenched Americans and the advancing Germans, the crushing of the last resistance.

One episode of this war was difficult to realize. It was the crossing of the bridge by German tanks and the pushing of a disabled American tank in the river to clear the way. First we had to find a suitable stone bridge, secure permission from difficult authorities—and so many of them—and then carefully remove a portion of the stone balustrade to substitute it with a dummy one, to be restored when the shooting was completed. In building a replica of a disabled tank—a miniature would not work for this complicated sequence—we had to make it realistic and heavy enough to make a believable splash when pushed in the river. We also had to build an underwater contraption, a submerged platform to prevent the tank from going too deep so we could hoist it back up with a crane.

We shot many scenes on the freezing roads and snowed-in forest, with tanks and without them.

To build the impressive set of the fuel depot, we had to find thousands of empty gasoline drums. I think we bought every available drum from every town in Spain. Daily processions of trucks brought these drums over the icy roads. Our sign painters, with freezing fingers, tried to finish the multiple signs needed for this set. At the same time I had to continually reassure our nervous producers, assistants, and the permanently anxious production people that we would deliver our set on schedule.

Germans dressed in American uniforms occupied this important fuel depot. In their turn, they were dislodged by an American outfit. Unsuspecting German tanks approached the depot, believing it was still occupied by their own troops. The column of heavy Tiger tanks clattered up the ascending mountain road. However, they were met by gasoline drums rolling down toward them, ripped open and then ignited by exploding hand grenades. This scene was done on the set on location with water substituting for the escaping gasoline and nervous special effects men trying hard to guide the rolling drums against the advancing tanks. The actual explosions, fire, and destruction were realized later by my miniature unit, except for the climax of the sequence, which was again shot on location, where Robert Shaw escapes from his burning tank and falls, consumed by flames.

The location shooting was coming to an end as the snow was melting. The Spanish army tanks moved from Segovia to their barracks and military grounds close to Madrid where we would stage the big battles. The company also moved back to the studio.

We prepared the sequences in the streets of Ambleve. The set was realistically "snowed in" with Epsom salts. The problem with Epsom salts was that horses liked to lick it and Epsom salts are known to be a strong laxative. But the snow looked quite realistic, even in close shots. The streets were full of retreating army units and civilian refugees. The sound of guns could be heard. The American headquarters began to evacuate but then the commanding general, Robert Ryan, decided to stay and defend the town until the end. At least it would slow the German advance.

The long-shot point of view from the German tanks, the shelling of Ambleve, and the subsequent fire were shot on stage in a large miniature of the town.

The shelling of the streets was done in our set on the back lot. As the last refugees leave town, shells explode and some walls and roofs are blown from their foundations. It was a spectacular display of explosions by the special effects crew. Then the tanks advanced, destroying everything in their path.

For that purpose we built one house in real bricks, with real wooden rafters and roof shingles. The cameras were set low to give the most effective shots of the tank breaking through the middle of falling bricks, collapsing rafters, and shingles. The shots were spectacular, but in spite of the slow motion we used, the movement came too fast as a tank seemed to appear quickly from a collapsing wall. It was an unexpected happening, and so I decided on shooting an added dolly shot from the top of the tank as it approached and actually broke through the wall of the house. It would help create a moment of sus-

"It was a spectacular display of explosions."

"The set was realistically 'snowed in' with Epsom salts."

pense. We built a breakaway house for this shot, put the camera on top of a reinforced camera platform protected by plastic shields, and actually broke through the wall of the house.

The second sequence of the town of Amblève was shot in the same set, but as seen after the battle. Houses were in ruins and the city hall was gutted by fire.

Now to the stages and the sets of the underground bunker complex, the corridors, the luxurious general headquarters, and the spectacular scene where the young German tank operators are inspected by their new commander. The set was all gray; cement walls, iron doors, and the tank operators' uniforms were all black. Their war chorus was memorable.

I had an idea that would, in my opinion, effectively counterpoint the severe color scheme. I put large red banners with Nazi slogans on the wall to have the contrast of gray and black with bright red.

The next set was the forementioned command post with iron platforms dominating the lower floor and a gigantic map of the Ardennes where diligent German soldiers moved miniature tanks showing the breakthrough and advance of the Panzer units.

The large interiors of the American headquarters lodged in the city hall was our next set. Then the temporary new headquarters in a ruined chateau, the dream set for any art director. Then the interior of the mountain fort and the humble stairs and room where Telly Savalas kept his black-market merchandise. And there were many other sets as well.

Ken Annakin and the first unit moved to the tank battlegrounds in the military terrain close to Madrid.

My miniature unit occupied the partly cleared back lot of the Amblève set. While Ken was staging the master shots of the tank battles, he daily relayed his requirements for detailed shots of these encounters. I projected his shots and prepared matching landscapes in miniature. Tanks would advance, shoot the ambushed enemy point-blank, and explode the trapped tank. Sometimes our American tanks were caught, shot at, and burned. My miniature tanks were about three feet long with two-horsepower motors, and had numerous electric commands to advance, retreat, turn the turret, and shoot the guns. They had realistic recoiling guns and were perfect reproductions of real tanks, down to the smallest detail. All the scenes that were difficult or impossible to achieve with real tanks were performed by miniatures.

The road leading to the fuel depot and the rolling gasoline tanks, the fiery end of the Panzer column, even the close-ups of the burning command tank, all were done in miniature. So was the general view of the fuel depot from the observation plane as seen by Henry Fonda. It was shot on the stage from a dollying crane.

On the other stage at Roma studios, I reproduced the close view of the terrain where the German parachutists landed on a foggy day. One empty stage with a gray backing was reserved for the shots of the miniature of the observation plane flying through the dense fog.

We accomplished this with a familiar trick of the trade. Miniature planes are very difficult to move smoothly in the air because they are hung on threads and you cannot move these threads easily. I discovered—as I think others did independently—that it is much easier to move the camera against the movement of the plane. We were lucky; we didn't have to have sky, only gray fog. So to create movement we had to blow wind and fog against the forward movement of the plane, and by tracking back with the camera and moving forward with the wind, we created the illusion of a flying airplane.

On August 14, 1965 the production was finished as far as the shooting was concerned. After all those battles I was happy to take a two-week swimming vacation in Mallorca with my family.

Back to Madrid. In viewing the rough cut of the picture, the producers had decided on some added scenes. An entire new sequence had to be shot. "To relieve the besieged Amblève, the American command sends two large-caliber guns there." The sequence involved a passing train carrying two giant guns—dummies of course—loaded on open platforms. Passing through numerous tunnels, the train is spied on by Germans plotting an ambush. Finally, while exiting one of the tunnels, the train is shot point-blank by a waiting German tank. I went to shoot this sequence on a spectacular railroad line in the mountains behind Málaga. Our train with the dummy guns was loaded on a freight platform as we crossed the awesome precipices and tunnels.

William Conrad was dispatched by Jack Warner to help Annakin direct some second-unit shots. Conrad went back to Hollywood and told Jack that we were making some wonderful miniature sequences. When the picture was finally edited, Jack Warner came to Madrid to see the projection of the first print.

In the comfortable projection room, drinks were served. Jack, in high spirits, told us about Conrad's comment and said he was eager to see the miniature shots for himself. And they were numerous. At the end of the projection when the lights went on in the theater, Jack puzzled, announced that he hadn't seen *any* miniature shots in the picture. That was the best compliment he could have given us.

September 11. The end of production. The making of this film, which I described so briefly, was actually quite complex. Physical difficulties sometimes seemed overwhelming. Building sets and shooting in the bitter weather of the Guadarramas was especially painful.

In all it took almost eleven months of incessant labor to prepare and shoot this *Battle of the Bulge.* And I assure you, we did not spare our efforts.

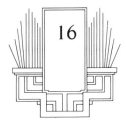

16

KRAKATOA, EAST OF JAVA

One of my special effects pictures was *Krakatoa, East of Java*, filmed in Spain from 1965 to 1966. I presume that my successful handling of the special effects sequences in *A Crack in the World* gave my producer the idea of doing a film spectacular. The new project was prompted by something Philip Yordan had read in a book about volcanos: The eruption of Krakatoa was the strongest volcanic eruption ever recorded in the history of mankind. Coming on the heels of successful box office prospects for the newly completed *Battle of the Bulge*, it was enough to get the multimillion-dollar production rolling for Cinerama Productions.

In early October 1965 I began work on this ambitious project. At this time there was no story at all, only the title and a sketchy catalog of special effects. There were many different ideas on how to handle the script; as a somber tragedy based on the disaster, a travel adventure à la Jules Verne, or a musical comedy.

The castastrophic eruption of this island volcano happened in 1883. Reading the descriptions of this event, I was appalled. The tremendous explosion literally blew the island apart. The sound was heard thousands of miles away. Thick clouds of volcanic ash obscured the sun, plunging the neighboring islands of Java and Sumatra into a pitch-black night for four days. Titanic tidal waves destroyed villages, ships, and many thousands of lives. No one was left alive within hundreds of miles of the island.

In all of the prospective scripts, the heroes survived the catastrophe, although it was clear from my research that no one could have done so. Phil Yordan, the producer, decided that if the events did not fit the story, he would change the events. And so the writers changed the timing of the eruption, inventing a preliminary eruption that would create suspense and allow the possibility of escape.

While the writers were busy laboring on the script, I was busy with research and the practical preparations for production. I went to Paris to view the magnificent documentaries of various eruptions around the world shot by vulcanologist Haroun Tadzieff.

Practically, one of the most urgent tasks was to find a suitable steamship that we could alter into a combination steam and sailing ship, now required by the current version of the script. No shipping companies in Madrid had anything that approached our requirements. I would have to investigate seaports around Spain for a ship, as well as for a seaport suitable for our "Singapore" location.

So one of my assistants and our production manager left with me, driving first to Bilbao in northern Spain and then south to explore some ports along the Atlantic coast. We reached Bilbao in misty rain. The busy port stretched for miles on both sides of the river. We followed the wharf and the succession of loading and unloading ships. Almost at the end of the line, we saw a steamer unloading coal on the rainy wharf. It had the shape of a former passenger ship and seemed of the right vintage and size for our picture. We learned from the friendly skipper that she had been built in England around 1880 and was formerly a mixed passenger and cargo ship. Now she was a tramp steamer carrying occasional loads of potatoes or coal between Spain and Morocco. We visited

The miniature Indonesian village built in Spain.

some other ships but none was as suitable as the first. I don't remember the name of this ship, but for us she was to become the *Batavia Queen*.

The next morning we drove east along the winding road. This trip gave me a kaleidoscope of impressions: twisting roads opening suddenly to quaint small fishing ports, sturdy stone breakwaters, fishing boats huddled in protective basins, huge loads of seaweed gathered in low tides, and friendly drinks in waterfront bars. In the darkness, approaching the port of Gijón, I saw a fiery display of incandescent slag dumped down the shoot of a Gijón steel mill. It gave me an idea of how to use this slag in the miniature sequence as the red-hot lava flows down the slopes of Krakatoa, destroying coconut groves and villagers' huts.

In planning this picture it became clear that we would need an adequate tank to shoot our miniatures, but there was none in Madrid or Barcelona. As I wanted to base all of our production in Spain, I decided to study the possible use of the large salt lagoons off Valencia and the inland sea, Mar Menor, near Cartagena. I also had to scout seaports of the Mediterranean for our location of "Singapore." None of the ports on the Atlantic was suitable because of the big, changing tides. Continuous changing of the levels of water can complicate the shooting enormously. For one scene a ship is high above the pier and for the next take she is on a different level. Once I was shooting a science fiction film on the beach in Cornwall, England. In the scene a man overcome by a mysterious ailment was convulsing on the beach. As the tide changed rapidly, for each next take we had to move the convulsing man and the camera. It was a problem to keep the right continuity of shots. We finished the scene marooned by the mounting waves. We wouldn't have this problem now; the Mediterranean tides were significantly smaller in places.

We started in Valencia and proceeded south. The salt lagoons in Sóllana were impressive, but the cost of installing shooting facilities would be prohibitive. The same objections held for Mar Menor—an interior sea. Several Spanish productions had staged their sea battles there. However, shooting requirements for *Krakatoa* were demanding. To create an island volcano in the sea, to stage the eruptions and storms, meant we would have to build new wave machines. To dump thousands of gallons of water from a height of thirty feet, we would need to build towers and huge "dump" tanks, used to store water to create the waves. Moreover, the complex electrical equipment and provisions for numerous technicians would all be impossible to provide at Mar Menor. We would need facilities at a well-equipped studio. For the "Singapore" location, however, I found the port of Denia ideal. It had a very wide basin, permanent stone wharfs, and some large old-fashioned warehouses.

Finally we arrived in Málaga and found the tropical gardens we were looking for, rain forest gardens unique in this dry, barren countryside. I was sorry to learn on my return from this scouting trip that the tropical forest was no longer needed in the latest version of the script.

In Málaga we also lined up the shipyard where we would later remodel our ship. By this time the ship was contracted and thoroughly photographed and measured by Fernando Gonzáles, my assistant. I decided on the scale of the miniature replica of the ship. As a rule, the larger the scale of a miniature ship,

The S.S. BATAVIA QUEEN.

the more natural her movements will appear on the water in relationship to the sizes of the waves we can create in a studio tank. However, the very large miniature ships are difficult to maneuver and more expensive to build. I decided that the *Batavia Queen* would be built in a one-to-ten ratio, the scale that I had used most often for miniatures in my previous films. Since I needed some very long shots of the ship when she approached the island of Krakatoa, I also built one miniature ship in a one-to-twenty scale. But after I shot a test with this very small miniature ship, I decided not to use it. The small *Batavia Queen* looked like a toy duck in a bathtub, her movements too jerky. Designing proceeded quickly for the remodeling of the actual freighter and the eighteen-foot miniature ship. For the real ship we had to build a new bowsprit and a wood-carved figurehead, make the smokestack higher, and provide taller masts with new yards and a set of practical sails. All these alterations would have to pass strict maritime inspection, a complicated and laborious procedure.

In the new script material there appeared a very important new element, a hot air balloon. After some inquiry I decided to rent an existing balloon from Charles Dreyfuss in Paris, and ordered two miniature replicas from a Belgian manufacturer.

The question of the water tank was not yet resolved. Our next scouting trip was to Malta and Rome. Malta was oppressively hot and the tank there impressively large. The horizon line of the tank blended well with the horizon line of the open sea. Powerful pumps filled the tank with unusual speed. Later on I learned that they also pumped in the contents of the Maltese sewers. As our picture required a continual smoke-filled horizon, I was dubious that we would be able to cover the vast expanse of the sea and sky with smoke. The tests conducted with the English navy's camouflage smokes could not achieve it, and the wind blew the smoke away. Other doubts concerning the Maltese tank were the necessity of importing lights and technicians from England or Italy and building new dump tanks and wave machines. I am speaking of conditions as they were in 1965. I heard all this was changed for the shooting of *Raise the Titanic*.

I had used the tanks at Cinecittà in Rome for *Flight from Ashiya* and planned to use them again for this project. I stopped there to ascertain the state of the sky backing, the tank facilities, and the studio availability. However, without a definite shooting schedule, we couldn't make final arrangements.

Back in Madrid preparations were going ahead. A set list was made according to the latest edition of the changing script. We began with designing and prepared for construction. The tentative schedule called for principal photography to begin in the early spring of 1966; shooting of miniatures would follow in the summer or fall of the same year. However, the producers did not foresee the complications of getting the script finished. As a result the actual production time kept being postponed.

I may have mentioned before that I don't believe in the need for complete storyboard sketching. It is different, however, when you have to deal with sequences that combine miniatures and live action or added matte paintings or any multiple manipulations of final images. In this case the preliminary planning and sketching could be of tremendous help. For *Krakatoa* I started sketching with the help of Mampasso, a talented painter and illustrator. I decided to make these sketches in color to help the color coordination between the live and miniature scenes.

The designing of the *Batavia Queen* completed I left for Málaga to complete the deal with the shipyard that would make the alterations on the steamer. Meanwhile in Madrid we started to build the miniature replica of the *Queen*. The construction of a miniature ship is a complex affair and has to be done as exactly as the building of a real ship, from the keel up, the profiles of each rib calculated perfectly.

Our production contracted two studios: the Bronston studios and some large stages of the Sevilla studios. As the large Bronston stage had a cement floor, I decided to build there the sets that required the use of water hoses and dump tanks for the storm sequence. On a large platform about sixty feet long mounted on hydraulics, we built the set of the deck with its superstructure. We could incline this set in all directions and subject it to the concentrated fury of four-ton-capacity dump tanks, wind machines, and fire hoses.

On the same stage we built another hydraulic platform, planning to erect many other sets there: the captain's bridge, the furnace room, the companionway among them.

Pages from Lourie's KRAKATOA *script. The illustrations are by Mampasso.*

KRAKATOA - LOURIE'S SCREENPLAY   <u>Page 4F</u>
May 23, 1966.

<u>EXT. BRIDGE, SET ON ROCKER. (MADRID)</u>   339

BRINK, coming from the bridge, grabs the railing, looks
with alarm at the forward mast.

<u>EXT. FORWARD MAST, MINIATURE (ROME OR MADRID)</u>   339A

The howling wind has filled the sail - the mast is
cracking under the tremendous pressure.

<u>EXT. DECK. STAGE (MADRID)</u>   339B

BRINK rushes down the steps, gives orders to the sailors.

<u>EXT. DECK. STAGE (MADRID) AT THE MAST</u>   340

BRINK, grabbing an axe from one of the crew and beckoning
the men to come with him, slowly fights his way toward
the mast.

<u>EXT. DECK. STAGE. (MADRID)</u>   341

ANOTHER ANGLE AT BASE OF MAST. Reaching as high as
he can, BRINK chops away at the lashings so as to free
the sail and save the mast. (See technical advisor as
to what ropes to cut.)

<u>TO BE WRITTEN OR OMITTED</u>   342, 343

<u>EXT. FORWARD MAST, MINIATURE (ROME OR MADRID)</u>   344

With a crack, the mast snaps and crashes down.

<u>EXT. DECK. STAGE (MADRID)</u>   345

BRINK works feverishly with his axe at cutting the ropes
that are holding the broken mast attached to the ship.
The broken mast lies at a crazy angle, dragging in the
sea, dangerously imperilling the ship.

EXT. SHIP. MINIATURE (ROME)   346

The mast, attached by many ropes to the ship, is dragged
in the stormy sea, alongside the ship.

EXT. DECK. STAGE (MADRID)   347

Near the railing, a young sailor is cutting the entangled
ropes (which hold the broken mast). A huge wave hits
the deck. The young sailor loses his footing. BRINK
rushes to his aid but the youngster is washed away.

EXT. RAILING AND THE BROKEN MAST. TANK (ROME)   348

BRINK, trying to grab the youngster, falls in or jumps
into the turbulent sea after him.

EXT. DECK. STUDIO (MADRID)   348A

REVERSE. Reaction of crew and or ERIKA.

EXT. MAST IN WATER. TANK (ROME)   349

Helping the youngster, BRINK grabs some ropes, inches
his way toward the mast; they are mercilessly beaten
by the storm and waves.

EXT. DECK. STAGE (MADRID)   350

REVERSE, with broken mast in f.g. Reactions of sailors.

EXT. MAST IN WATER. TANK (ROME)   351

BRINK and the YOUNGSTER are inching their way up the
broken mast.

EXT. DECK. STAGE (MADRID)   351A

BRINK and the YOUNG SAILOR reach the deck. BRINK'S
body, almost naked, is welted and bleeding. On hands
and knees, ERIKA and FRIEDA crawl up to him to see if
he's all right.

The second stage at Bronston studios was for the ship's bar, salon, companionway, and some other cabins. The large stage of the Sevilla studio was reserved for the blue-backing shots and some other matte shots of the same sort that had been done for *Captain Fabian*, *Colossus of New York*, and other movies. As you will recall, blue-backing shots are traveling matte shots where the action is photographed on a backing of an intense blue color. By optical means the blue background is eliminated (matted *out*) and the action is superimposed (matted *in*) on a background shot (called also a "plate"). This plate shot is usually made at a different time, in a different place, often on location or in a miniature setting. By this method two different actions could be reunited; thus an actor could be seen driving a convertible car, shot on a blue-backing stage, in a street of a faraway city, shot on location.

The script at this point required many scenes on rubber plantations in Java, exteriors of Indonesian beaches, fishing villages, and palm growths. For these scenes we planned extensive second-unit work in the tropics. I left to scout in southern Malaysia with Irving Lerner, who was to manage the second unit. We stepped from the Quantas plane into the humid heat of Kuala Lumpur. The ultramodern architecture of the airport and the rich residental district set in luxurious greenery contrasted sharply with the usual Oriental turmoil of downtown, dominated by a red mosque done in an exuberant Turkish-Victorian style. Irving had connections with some former students from the motion picture department of UCLA. They helped us to organize scouting and informed us of the available local help, which was almost nil.

Rubber plantations extended for miles and miles: row after row, planted in regular patterns, each tree bleeding white liquid from incisions in its bark, dripping into small crockery pots. Usually the work was performed by Indians. The only interesting light for photographing this plantation came in the early morning, when the slender trees cast shadows in lacy regular patterns and the white turbans of the Indians caught the morning light.

We went to the seashore off Malacca and visited fishing villages where the tall coconut palms came down to the edge of the sea and gaily painted boats sat on the white sand. These beaches gave me an idea for a spectacular shot for the tidal wave sequence. Shooting from a helicopter, I imagined frightened crowds running to higher ground, pursued by the ominous shadow of the advancing tidal flow. The shadow of the wave could be painted in later in the lab as an easily done traveling split shot.

In a small chartered plane we scouted possible locations for fishing villages. We flew low above the seashore and around small islands where we saw villages built on stilts above palm-fringed lagoons and Chinese junks swaying lazily among the moored fishing boats.

In the steaming markets of Kuala Lumpur, I bought hundreds of yards of printed material, some authentic batik. Later Laure de Zárate, our costume designer, organized a workshop in Spain to manufacture the native costumes. With the cheap Malaysian cotton and the cheap Spanish labor, the finished costumes cost the production about $12 per costume.

Irving remained in Malaysia to iron out relations with authorities. We got permission for the second-unit shooting, but as the screenplay was changed again, we didn't have to go to Malaysia after all. I was sorry to have lost the pictorial possibilities of these exotic landscapes. I boarded the plane to fly back to Rome and make the final arrangements with Cinecitta studios.

Back in Madrid I felt a change of atmosphere. The set building was progressing well, but Phil Yordan, who later left the production, had some misgivings about the script and the casting of the picture. Robert Shaw, for example, did not like his part and refused the picture. Phil offered him another picture, an old pet idea of his about General Custer and his last stand. We would start preparation at once, scheduling this picture immediately after *Krakatoa*. Robert Siodmak, an old friend of mine, came to prepare and direct *Custer of the West*.

Meanwhile Phil Yordan left for the United States with the script of *Krakatoa* to organize casting and to find a director. A few days later he phoned from New York. He was having difficulties with the casting and distribution and would have to do major rewrites and postpone the principal photography, pushing forward the shooting of *Custer*. However, he asked me if I could possibly shoot the miniature sequences of *Krakatoa* ahead of the principal photography.

"I don't see why not," I replied.

"Gene, I know you wanted to shoot at the tank in Cinecitta, so go to Rome and organize the miniature shooting," Yordan concluded.

We had many sets for *Krakatoa* already built on the Bronston stages; I decided to keep them there, reserving the stages for later use. And I reserved the Sevilla studios for *Custer*. We left for Málaga to arrange the docking facilities for the now-completed *Batavia Queen*. Georgio, our production manager, would have to make a deal with the shipping agent for the much-prolonged rental of the ship. I think we eventually rented the ship for two years.

The preparation of miniatures was now scheduled to start at Cinecitta in May and the shooting in July. Meanwhile in Madrid, Robert Siodmak and I scouted for *Custer*. My efforts were now divided between *Custer* and *Krakatoa*. Soon I would have to leave for Rome to direct the miniature sequences, so I had to find an art director who could follow the set construction I had designed for *Custer*. Sometime earlier Siodmak had worked in France with Jean D'Aubonne, a friend of mine and a very competent art director who was later to work with Max Ophuls, designing *La Ronde* and *Lola Montez*. He was available and agreed to continue my work.

It was hectic—following construction in Madrid, conferring with Siodmak and D'Aubonne, reassuring Phil Yordan that the arrangement would work, and making repeated trips to Rome to organize the designing and building of miniatures there. In Rome my unit manager was Giorgio Oddi; Saverio De Eugenio became my art director; and we had three Italian set designers as well. We shipped the miniature ship from Madrid to Rome. It was twenty feet long, quite a huge affair. The red tape at customs was considerable.

Assola, who came from France to help build the miniature ship, would join the Italian technicians to finish the ship and build numerous junks to be used in constructing sets for wharfs, houses, and bridges for the miniatures. Alec Weldon would come later with his Spanish crew of special effects people to prepare mechanical effects and build dump tanks.

I decided to work with my Spanish cameraman, Manuel Berenguer. He agreed to come with me to Rome where he would be working with an Italian crew.

The large tank was now emptied of water and construction began on the set of Krakatoa Island. In the second, smaller tank, we built the port of Batavia and its canals.

Leaving Siodmak with D'Aubonne and all the problems of *Custer* behind in Madrid, I moved to Rome. The largest stage at Cinecitta was 265 by 118 feet, the largest part of which was now occupied by our miniature of the mountainous jungle on Krakatoa Island. The most common difficulty in miniatures of green sets are miniature trees that seldom look real. But here in Rome I worked with an exceptionally talented greensman, an artist, whose tiny palms were perfect. This miniature jungle was used for many different sequences. The most spectacular shot was a lateral dolly, traveling through blazing palm trees and cascading fiery lava. Smoke exploding, burning huts, confusion; all these gave the shot an unusual three-dimensional quality with the camera moving across successive planes of burning palms and collapsing trees.

The miniature village before the tidal wave.

Since we were shooting miniatures, we were cranking the cameras at higher speeds to reduce the jerkiness so harmful in many miniature shots. But we were shooting with three Panavision seventy-millimeter cameras, not the usual production cameras on which rapid acceleration of shooting speed is mechanically possible. Owing to the width of the film, we could not crank faster than three times the normal speed (seventy-two frames per second), and long-lasting takes were impossible because the cameras became too hot to handle. Nightly one or two of our cameras had to be repaired.

On that same large stage we also had the set of the fiery bowels of the volcano, into which the brave Italian balloonist (played by Rossano Brazzi) throws his motor and propeller to avoid being sucked inside.

Krakatoa was my second encounter with the problems of designing volcanos and craters. My first had been *A Crack in the World*—also filmed in Spain with Phil Yordan a few years earlier.

While researching material for *A Crack in the World*, I watched documentary films on volcanic eruptions and had been amazed by the intense glow of their lava flow. Then as you will recall, to render this intensity in the film, I placed a strong light beneath moving, painted, transparent plastic belts, with the light projected upward from below. For the crater bottom we had built a miniature tank and filled it with an oatmeallike liquid. We had then used a strong light on the churning liquid, enhancing the liquid's reflectivity by covering the surface with silver powder and pelting the powder during takes with chemicals that popped and flamed upon contact. By adding some steam conduits and using appropriate noises, we had created a convincing impression of glowing, churning lava. This effect worked so successfully in *A Crack in the World* that I repeated it for *Krakatoa*.

This miniature crater was used for many production shots as well as for background plates for process traveling matte shots, where the balloonist team in the foreground looks into the crater. Rosanno Brazzi and Sal Mineo appear in real jeopardy as they fall lower and lower into the flaming inferno.

In the smaller tank of Cinecittà the miniature set of the port of Batavia was built in progressively diminishing scale to give more depth to the set. Five dump tanks, each with a 2,600 gallon capacity were mounted on thirty-five-foot-high towers. They lined one side of the tank.

"Is everybody ready?" That meant our Italian, Spanish, and French crew. Alec shouted, "*Listo señores*! Camera. Speed. Action!" Within a few seconds, each tank was emptied, precipitating some 13,000 gallons of water down the chutes in a furious waterfall. In the turbulence of the last frames, a thatched roof rapidly crossed the screen and disappeared in the violent fury of bubbling water. Shaken by the waves, one camera fell into the water. The other two still functioned. We looked at each other. Was the shot good? We would see the results in the next day's rushes.

In the vicinity of the Cinecitta studios, the city of Rome was building an extension of the subway. The excavated dirt was dumped on the huge back lot of the studio, forming a mound some seventy feet high. Its shape was similar to that of a volcano. The idea came to me that I could use this mound as a foundation of my miniature volcano. Seventy feet high could hardly be called miniature, but it would correspond to the scale of our miniature balloon. By digging, forming lava flows, and spraying the entire mound with liquid tar, we got a very impressive-looking miniature image of a volcano. Slow smoke drifted from the crater.

The best light for shooting this sequence came in the first sunshine of morning. The crew assembled before dawn and a light wind blew in the right direction. The balloon was guided by an invisible nylon thread and the puppets in the basket were guided by Assola's contraption. The oblique sun rays hit the ground. We had to shoot. The balloon flew above the crater, lost height, and was sucked inside and disappeared from view. We had started the shooting so early and it took such a short time that we had to wait in the studio commissary until the morning coffee was ready.

Sometimes to create the dense smoky ambience that surrounded the volcanic eruption, we had to work for days in the suffocating black smoke of burning tires. I remember one particular scene where we had to see the sun faintly through the passing black smoke, then disappear into total darkness. We were shooting from a hole in the ground. The wind shifted often, chasing the smoke away. To get the shot right we had to do it many times. The crew came out of the hole, blacker than chimney sweeps and looking like performers in a minstrel show.

The Cinecitta lot presented me with another solution for shooting the balloon as it lost its buoyancy and fell into the crater. Years ago they had built a half-buried fort for which they dug out an impressive depression in the ground, some thirty feet deep. By digging some more, I could shape a very believable crater where I could film the fall of the doomed balloon. I used this set for many different set-ups: the miniature balloon descending, the balloonists' point of view as plates for traveling matte shots, and finally the balloon expelled rapidly from the crater, catching fire on its way up.

There was also a scene from above where Cezare Allione, our brave cameraman, was lowered from a seventy-foot construction crane into the smoking crater surrounded by projecting fiery stones.

Meanwhile the small tank was ready with the set of the fishermen's village built on stilts. Falling incandescent debris from the eruption starts a fire in the straw huts. Then the blazing village is engulfed by the tidal wave. Later on this scene was successfully married with a foreground of escaping fishermen in a traveling matte: the escaping fishermen running on a slender bridge were photographed on blue backing, and this shot was optically superimposed on the shot of the burning village as it was destroyed by the tidal wave. In the finished scene it looked as if the fishermen perished in the raging wave.

The big tank at Cinecitta was roughly 300 by 400 feet. The sky backing was seventy feet high and our set of the island volcano rose to forty feet. The interior of the volcano was now stuffed with multiple mortars, receptacles for explosives, colored smokes, water tanks with floating dynamite charges, and gasoline bombs. It was the complicated domain of Alec Weldon, who busily wired this menacing arsenal.

Our shooting progressed nicely, in spite of the continual breakdown of cameras overheated by the rapid acceleration and the delays caused by our fighting the constant wind changes that diverted our smoke in the wrong direction. As we had to have smoke covering the sky in almost all the shots, we placed

Above: *"The balloon flew above the crater, lost height, and was sucked inside and disappeared from view."* Filmed at Cinecitta outside Rome.

Preparing to film the real balloon. Lourie is in the white cap.

three strong smoke generators on each side of the backing. If the wind changed, the smoke would come from another side.

After the opening shots of the island when the volcano is peaceful, we started eruptions that grew progressively stronger. The smoke cast ominous shadows over the mountain. Finally came the explosions: fiery stones were projected high in the air, lava flowed down the slope, and hissing steam rose from the sea.

The director of Cinecitta and a score of secretaries rushed in, attracted by the sound and fury of our spectacle.

The eruption sequences completed, the set of the island volcano was hauled away and the prefab rock moved in for the change of sets. Meanwhile in the small tank we shot the tidal wave destroying the lighthouse.

For me, there is a strange fascination in shooting at night on location. The strong lights were reflected a thousandfold in the turbulent waters of the tank. Grotesquely lit, special effects men moved on their platforms, readying the rocks that would be thrown. Each puff of smoke was etched against the black sky. We shot the sequence where the *Batavia Queen* carefully threads her way through the dangerous narrow passage, pelted by flaming rocks. As our miniature ship visibly lacked any live crew, I tried to envelop her in gusts of smoke to camouflage this absence. Smoke and fire. And so the night passed.

The day arrived when we were almost through with our Roman shooting schedule. The cutting room overflowed with thousands of feet of exposed film. Derek Parson, our editor at that time, was busy cutting off the useless ends of the takes. The only important sequence left was the final storm. All our dump tanks were in place. A sturdy platform for the cameras was ready, cantilevered above the water.

I called Phil Yordan in Madrid to tell him what had been accomplished and my plans for adding some live action shots, taking advantage of the installation already in place for the storm action. It would take only two additional days. But Phil informed me that the *Krakatoa* project had been canceled. He asked me to finish the storm sequence with the miniature ship and then send the miniature back to Madrid. I could keep Parson, who would then travel back to Madrid and proceed with the temporary editing. This abrupt cancel-

Mampasso's magnificent illustrations. The originals are in vivid color.

lation of *Krakatoa* was surely a blow, but working a long time in film productions made me immune to sudden changes of fortune.

I did not tell this news to my collaborators as we were all ready to proceed with the storm sequence. Seeing how our miniature ship would withstand the battering of the powerful dump tanks would be a severe test.

To achieve the proper buoyancy we loaded her with additional ballast. In earlier sequences we had pulled her with a submerged rope, but now it was impossible to move her against the strong waves. We improvised a crew of strong, dedicated frogmen to guide the ship. They were hidden from the camera on the other side of the ship. For each take we unleashed all our dump tanks. The power of the water was unbelievable, and after each take we anxiously checked to make sure that none of the frogmen had drowned.

Wave machines, wind machines, dump tanks, powerful fire hoses, shooting from the shaky camera platform, we withstood this onslaught for three days of shooting. I comforted the drenched Assola with a glass of brandy.

Finally came the end of the Roman shooting. Parting with the crew is always sad. This one was particularly so. We had worked together in a most friendly atmosphere for the last two months with this group of competent, dedicated technicians. I was sorry to leave Rome—outdoor dining in the warm nights, cups of cappucino on the terrace café on Piazza del Popolo, the open-air opera in the ancient ruins of Caracalla's Baths, and so much more.

Back to Madrid. I projected the footage of our Roman shooting with pleasure. Altogether we had forty-five minutes of usable film. Phil Yordan informed me that up to now, including preparations and the Roman shooting, we had spent some $350,000 for the film. Derek Parson found some temporary sound effects, and with the roar of the storm and the hissing and explosions of the volcano, the miniature shots were highly impressive.

Meanwhile the rough editing of *Custer of the West* had been finished. Bill Forman, the head of Cinerama, and many theater directors from London, Paris, Rome, and Tokyo came to Madrid to view this film and map out exhibition plans. After the viewing their reaction was rather negative. Feeling the cool reception in the projection room, Yordan decided to show the miniature footage from *Krakatoa.* "I would like to show you some preproduction reels from our next picture." The reception was enthusiastic. "When will you have *Krakatoa* ready?" they wanted to know. They were eager to establish playing dates.

This reaction prompted a change in the producer's attitude. Instead of being canceled, *Krakatoa* became a viable project. Producer Bill Forman took the print of our footage with him to the United States. Phil Yordan showed it to distributors and to prospective actors, writers, and directors to appraise their reactions, to try to find a concept for a new script that would utilize the special effects sequences. It was a strange quest, like trying to squeeze a new body into a suit made for a different person.

When he came back to Madrid, Phil Yordan asked me to go ahead with more special effects scenes I had in mind to add to *Krakatoa*. While waiting for the future script, I planned some sequences to shoot. Berenguer's camera crew, Weldon's special effects commandos, and my former designing assistants joined me.

We traveled first to Gijón where the iron smelter periodically unloaded the incandescent slag, taking the prepared miniature huts and palm trees with us. Every thirty minutes the white liquid metal, like a melted lava stream, flowed down, setting the native village and palm groves on fire. With each take the meandering and blazing liquid took new and unexpected shapes. Shots were spectacular. Our only problem was that we lacked a narrow-angle lens and the slag made it too hot to shoot closer.

The new script of *Krakatoa* finally arrived. Well, rather the rough idea of a script. In style the new story was similar to the original, a whimsical adventure caper. But in the rewriting, it lost itself and became a sentimental mishmash of scenes.

The script began with a treasure hunt and became concentrated on the search for Diane Baker's missing son. The rest of the cast had equally uncertain parts to play: Maximilian Schell as the kindhearted captain; ever-coughing Brian Keith, dying of TB; improbable balloonists, Rossano Brazzi and his son, Sal Mineo; and a ragmuffin gang of villains.

Three writers came to write the script; Bernie Kowalski, the director, his secretary, his brother, and all their families came to enjoy the Spanish climate. The cast began to arrive. No one had read the script, but each had been promised "the best part of your life." To try to assemble order in the crowd, Phil Yordan delegated Les Sansom, the associate producer, to take charge.

Laure de Zárate, the costume designer, fought bravely with the incredible Madrid costume establishment to manufacture costumes. She organized our own workshop to make native costumes from the material I had brought back from Malaysia.

Chinese are rare in Spain. Our production had to import some fifty Chinese from England. They became an albatross around the production's neck. The script changed daily, the shooting schedule more often than that, and the Chinese participation was required for more and more days, then weeks, then months. Every week, threatening blackmail, they asked for a raise in pay.

But this situation was to appear later. For the time being I was occupied with building the "Singapore" set, testing the *Batavia Queen*, learning how to operate this tricky combination of steam and sails with the crew, and organizing the underwater and helicopter units I would have to direct.

For the live-action sequences, I decided to forego the use of the full-size balloon. The unpredictable wind on the beach and rocks close to the shore could mean long delays or even the loss of the expensive balloon. In redesigning the sequence, I saw that we could successfully use the miniature balloon for all long shots. The closer shots with actors in the balloon gondola could be maneuvered with a helicopter or crane.

The waterfront of Denia was being transformed into the port of Singapore. The roofs of the low warehouses were covered with thatch. Large signs in English or Chinese letters were placed above these warehouses to provide characteristic dressing and useful camouflage for the high-rise buildings in the village of Denia. On the far side of the docks, the view of other high-rises was screened by the set of a Chinese junk surrounded by bamboo scaffoldings.

We restored an old narrow-gauge railroad line on the waterfront. My assistants located the antique locomotive in hidden storage, as well as the antique engineer.

Finally one morning the *Batavia Queen* arrived and was moored at the dock. With her bowsprit and carved figurehead high above the pier, her sails unfurled to dry out in the morning sun, she was an impressive sight indeed.

Our set gave a new exotic life of Oriental adventure to the small, sleepy Spanish port. Hordes of actors, technicians, extras, laborers, and drivers swooped down on Denia and the neighboring hotels, motels, and villas.

With all this crowd miraculously organized, dressed, and made up, the shooting of *Krakatoa*'s live action began. Bales of jute were loaded, street merchants peddled their Oriental sweets, the tiny locomotive puffed, smoked, and steamed its way thorugh the crowd. Led by British policemen, a group of chained prisoners approached the majestic hull of the *Batavia Queen* and claimed passage on the ship, to the indignant dismay of the captain. Thus started the ill-fated trip to Krakatoa, the tiny island in the Sunda Strait between Java and Sumatra.

Shooting continued in Denia and on board the ship. The script was being rewritten daily by the writers. Each of them had worked on a different sequence, which often didn't match with another sequence and had to be revised. The Chinese extras were the beneficiaries of this rewriting; switched from a junk to an open rowboat, they had to wait long weeks for their shooting date.

I left the company in Denia and went to prepare the next location for the company and my helicopter unit.

The village of Sóller is a quiet fishing port on the east coast of Mallorca. This place would become our base of operations. Some thirty miles north were deep canyons and on the coast, a wild cove, inaccessible by road. Claude, the French pilot, appeared in his helicopter and we flew with him to survey the canyons and the cove. The script called for the hectic flight of the disabled balloon, driven by air currents toward the volcano. The deep narrow canyons with vertical walls wandered inland. A lively brook disappeared in the canyon shadows.

Flying quickly above the rocky walls, then suddenly heading up above the surging rocks, was utterly impressive. In the same canyon we also shot the erratic flight of the miniature balloon. The miniature was not that small—some ten feet across.

Meanwhile the company had finished shooting in Denia and had arrived on the *Batavia Queen* to continue shooting in Mallorca.

The helicopter was parked on the local soccer field next to a church. Flying in the morning to our location, the church looked like part of a toy Spanish village. In fifteen minutes we landed at the hidden cove. The crew arrived by boat forty-five minutes later. We had to shoot the start of the balloon flight, supposedly taking place on a deserted beach on Krakatoa. The basket of the balloon was hung on a very long line from the helicopter that hovered above. Rossano Brazzi and Sal Mineo arrived, costumed and made up. I explained the action to them. They would have to climb into the basket, give a signal to the sailors, and hold tight to the basket as the helicopter lifted them up smoothly, the camera following their flight. Rossano objected. "I am not a stunt man," he said.

I had to explain to him that because the shot starts close, I couldn't use doubles. To prove the action was not dangerous, I climbed into the basket, gave the signal, and went soaring up into the air. The helicopter deposited me gently on the exact spot of departure.

"You see," I said, "it's as simple as taking an elevator."

Reluctantly Rossano agreed. "Yes, but only one take." Mineo looked yellow but said nothing. The wind from the helicopter was ferocious. Rossano almost lost his hat. We rehearsed the timing. The camera was ready. "Action . . ." Everything happened as we had rehearsed, but Claude took his helicopter much higher and farther than in my demonstration flight. I saw the basket high in the sky above the ocean. On their return I jokingly told Rossano we would have to retake the shot.

"Oh, no," he said. "Only one take!" We laughed and I offered them lunch with the crew. The local fishermen often came to this cove with tourists and today they made us a wonderful paella. Sitting on the rocks, inhaling the smoky odor of the paella, we celebrated the first action shot of the intrepid balloon with a bottle of wine.

Some days later I had another action scene to do with Rossano and Sal. This time, after they supposedly jump from the burning balloon, they must be picked up by a lifeboat sent for their rescue. It was cold in the morning and the sea was choppy. My camera was in the lifeboat. Shooting from behind the rowing sailors, I would see the boat approach the swimmers. The sea became more choppy. Suddenly Rossano, full of fatherly concern, said to Sal, "Don't you think the sea is too heavy for you? It's really windy and choppy, you see.

It will be difficult for you to swim against the wind!" Sal meekly agreed. Our shooting was postponed until a later date.

One day I had the full use of the ship for the miniature unit shooting. With actors in the foreground it was difficult to place the balloon in the right position in the frame. We had to tow the balloon from a rowboat with a long nylon thread. Sudden gusts of wind often played unexpected tricks. From the helicopter we shot the balloon's point of view toward the *Batavia Queen* and also the p.o.v. of the surface of the sea on which I would print over a faint view of the sunken ship.

We also had to shoot a sequence of the miniature balloon with the burning basket falling toward the sea. I decided to use the high mast of the *Batavia Queen* as the point from where to start the balloon's fall. We carefully added ballast to the basket until the balloon was falling gently by its own weight. We rehearsed the descent for the camera and the fall was perfect. Then we hoisted the balloon to the top of the mast. The descent started perfectly. Suddenly a strong gust of wind lifted the balloon and it flew away from us, farther and farther. We had only one balloon in reserve and I was reluctant to lose it as well. It was a strange chase. The *Batavia Queen*, all 200 feet of her, in pursuit of a miniature balloon playfully flying away as if she were teasing us. Two hours later, with the help of some local fishermen, the balloon was recaptured from a rocky lagoon.

Location shooting was at an end. Claude flew back to Paris with his helicopter. Actors took their last sunbath at the pool of the El Molino Hotel. The Chinese extras in London were counting their pesetas. I returned to Madrid to prepare the shooting on stage.

To expedite the overextended schedule I was assigned to direct the action scenes requiring effects: storms, fire, hydraulic moving of the sets. Meanwhile Bernie Kowalski would direct dramatic sequences on the set of the ship's salon.

The set of the upper deck was sixty feet long, built on a hydraulic platform that could be slanted in every direction, as if the ship were tossed by heavy seas. For the storm sequence I had two dump tanks unleashing thousands of gallons of water, three strong wind machines, and five fire hoses. The power and violence of our storm was such that the stuntmen were washed away, their shirts torn to shreds. There were many days of fire and water, shot from moving cranes on tilting sets. But finally the shooting was coming to an end. Brian Keith had to leave in a few days. It suddenly occurred to me that we were missing an important episode of the story. Somehow with all the different writers working on the script, a sequence had been omitted. In the picture a group of our passengers decide to land in the port moments before the destruction by the tidal wave. We had seen them last landing from a rowboat in the midst of the smoke and tumult of the eruption. Then we never saw them again. I thought it was important to actually see Brian Keith and Barbara Werle perish, crushed by the raging wave. I alerted Bernie Kowalski, the director, and Phil Yordan about this oversight and offered to improvise the shooting of the sequence.

The shot was to be as follows: among the maddened crowd, Barbara and Brian try to escape to higher ground and are overtaken by the roaring wave. For this scene I improvised the set of some corners of native huts, the only visible part of the street photographed from a moving crane shooting down, following the stampeding crowd. Barbara and Brian stop and instinctively seek protection against the wall of a hut. Then we shot a close-up of them and the surge of water from the dump tanks that drowned them quite believably.

I left again for Java where the building of the set for the underwater sequence was progressing. October was warm and I was staying at the charming Java Yacht Club. From my balcony I could follow the construction of the set of a cabin and the part of the companionway of a presumably sunken ship. The set was built on a raft and moored beneath my windows. Later on we would sink the platform with the set to photograph it underwater. With Gil Voxhold, our underwater cameraman, I snorkeled, looking for the most appropriate location for the sunken set. The water was muddy inside the port so we decided to haul the raft beyond the pier. The raft floated on six large drums. When the drums were filled with water, the raft sank. We anchored it in water about thirty to forty feet deep.

Scuba divers usually perform all the repair work in modern ports. But our story required old-fashioned divers in their diving suits and heavy brass headgear. It was difficult to find these old-fashioned suits and even more difficult to find men who could perform this kind of diving. However, two ancient, wrinkled Spaniards arrived with their unwieldy gear. Incredibly they were supposed to portray the parts of Maximilian Schell and Brian Keith. It was their first meeting with motion picture cameras. I explained to them the rather complicated action they would have to perform. We rehearsed briefly and they were amazingly good.

Unfortunately Voxhold did not find the water clear enough. Floating particles would spoil the shot. Overruling his objections, I decided to shoot the scene anyway. If conditions improved we could shoot the scene again the next day. It proved to be the right decision. The same night a sudden turbulence destroyed our underwater set. Parts of it were seen floating in the open sea.

The actors left Madrid. On the large stage at Sevilla studios we shot scenes on blue backing for traveling mattes of the port of Batavia, the burning village, and the escape of natives through the flaming jungle set.

In the story a search for the sunken ship is conducted by Rossano Brazzi from the flying balloon. When he suddenly sees the hazy outline of the sunken ship, he drops a buoy in the sea to mark the spot. Then the captain (Maximilian Schell) and the diver (Brian Keith), dressed in their heavy diving suits, are lowered to the bottom of the sea and approach the sunken ship.

To shoot this sequence I built on the stage a large set of the sea bottom. The haziness of the water was achieved by smoking in the stage; the flickering sunlight was obtained by lighting the set with reflecting broken mirrors in pans of water. The ship is seen in the distance, and I used a miniaturized shape of a steamer. The shot was made through an aquarium with floating sea plants that effectively created the foreground of smoothly floating seaweed.

Some time earlier Jack Willoughby, the Hollywood cameraman, had gone to Hawaii to shoot the huge wave on the north side of Oahu Island. I had given him the sketch and explained how he should shoot this: camera low, the wave head on, at four times the normal speed; in this way I could use the shot as a miniature tidal wave approaching the town. The Willoughby shots arrived and they were impressive. I designed and built a miniature silhouette of an Indonesian town. Optically printed together, it looked as if the gigantic tidal wave were looming above the town, advancing menacingly.

I spent the next few weeks in London supervising the optical work at the

Technicolor lab. Part work and part vacation. I saw the rough cut of *Krakatoa* in Feburary 1968.

Reflecting on this adventurous film, with the long delays in script preparation, the tremendous loss of time due to changes in the shooting schedule, I can see that *Krakatoa* is a good example of how a film should *not* be made. However, it was a success at the box office.

Lourie's acting debut.

THE ROYAL HUNT
OF THE SUN

Royal Hunt *of the Sun,* a successful play by Peter Shaffer, is about the conquest of Peru by a band of Spanish adventurers led by Francisco Pizarro. This tale of adventure, betrayal, and tormented conscience was set in Spain and Peru in the 1530s. The making of this film was an adventurous enterprise. It was also challenging work for a production designer, made more difficult by the modest budget.

I began preparations in 1968.

Here is an outline of the story. Francisco Pizarro, the illegitimate son of an obscure Castillian nobleman, finds himself stranded in Panama, Central America, after his failure to conquer Peru, the unknown land of fabled treasure. Unable to organize another expedition, Pizarro's only hope is to get help from the Spanish crown.

Pizarro is graciously received by the king, who is interested in the tales of Pizarro's strange adventures on sea and land. But most alluring are the shimmering treasures and the possible conquest of this empire for the benefit of the crown.

After a year of deliberations, in 1559 Pizarro obtains powers and privileges in the as-yet-to-be-conquered land of Peru. However he is obliged to raise a force of 250 men.

But he leaves Spain hurriedly with a smaller group of men. Despite the hardship and suffering of his men, the painful crossing of steaming marshes and snowy mountains, all is accomplished as a result of Pizzaro's incessant energy and sheer animal drive.

After crossing the formidable Andes, they are close to the encampment of the great Inca ruler, Atahualpa, who sends emissaries to Pizarro and assigns them as their residence the city-fortress of Caxamalca, now emptied of its inhabitants.

But taking Atahualpa prisoner is Pizarro's secret purpose. Hypocritically he sends a message to the Inca, saying he would be received by Pizarro as a "friend and brother." With hundreds of attendants sweeping the path, the Inca Atahualpa advances, born in an open litter surrounded by dignitaries and guards. On a signal from Pizarro, Spanish guns are fired. Springing from their hiding places, Spaniards on horse and foot rush into the plaza for a bloody massacre. The Indians panic, stunned by the thunder of artillery and muskets. They are trampled down by horses, killed by flashing swords, and Atahualpa is taken prisoner. Ten thousand Indians perish; not a single Spaniard is lost. But as a prisoner, Atahualpa is treated with respect. Soon he discovers his conquerors' lust for gold, and to obtain his freedom, he makes an offer to fill the cell with gold "as high as a man can reach." To Pizzaro this offer represents a fast way to obtain the gold.

The gold comes slowly, despite Atahualpa's repeated messages to his provincial chieftains to deliver all their gold to the Spanish camp. Meanwhile in everyday contact with his prisoner, Pizarro falls under the spell of Atahualpa's personality.

When the chamber is filled with gold, Pizarro's companions insist the Inca be murdered, and after a mock trial, Atahualpa is garroted. Thus begins the conquest of Peru.

The miniature bridge with the articulated cutout figures of Pizarro's conquistadores.

The early sequences of the film were set in sixteenth-century Spain. Scouting locations for these sequences was easy and pleasant. Guided by my Spanish assistants, I discovered a miraculously preserved village, San Juste de Pedraza, not far from Madrid. It had a quaint plaza surrounded by arched colonnades and passages, where we could shoot the scene in which Pizarro, accompanied by a drummer, attempts to recruit warriors, promising adventure and treasure.

I felt this film demanded a certain theatricality in the set conception. In choosing the location of the Spanish village, I was guided by the dramatic, pictorial effect of Pedraza and the surrounding countryside. I staged the scene where the departing army is blessed in an empty, windblown field where I erected a huge stone crucifix that dominated the action. I used that windblown field and the huge silhouette of the crucifix deliberately for theatrical effect; otherwise we could have shot the scene inside any church. The same quest for definite dramatic effects guided me in my design of the Peruvian sequences where, for the Spaniards, their adventures were almost like a fantasy or a strange dream.

Keeping this guiding idea in mind, I tried to underline the dramatic expression of the sets, but still kept them essentially realistic.

The real substance of my work, though, was to create the Peruvian sequences: the dangerous mountain crossing and the Inca town-fortress of Caxamalca where the largest part of the action took place.

A research trip to Peru was out of the question, and I had to gather photographic research in the libraries and museums of Madrid and London. I did not find any pictures of the town of Caxamalca, nor do I know if any ruins of this town still remain. It was, however, not important to me because in this film, I did not try for an archeological reproduction but a realistic visual surrounding that would serve the dramatic action.

In the same way that Peter Shaffer interpreted historical facts to create his dramatic play, I recomposed elements of reality to create a frame for the drama.

From my research I found that in Peru many Inca buildings still remain intact, their construction striking. The walls do not rise vertically but are slanted, and the openings of doorways and windows are trapezoid shaped. The Incas' mastery of stone cutting made it possible to build monumental walls of unbelievably large stones. These stones were irregular in shape but fit very tightly together without visible slits, no mortar joining them.

The sets representing these stone walls were difficult to build because the shapes of the stones were never repeated and formed ever-changing patterns. We had to find ways to cast them in staff without being able to detect repetitions. It sounds simple, but it was not. The cutting of individually cast stones was made possible by the craftsmanship of my Spanish plasterers.

To check our ability to reproduce these Inca walls, I ordered Pascal, our reliable construction supervisor, to make a sample wall of about ten feet by ten feet. For proof of "authenticity" I sent photographs of our sample wall to the archeological museum in Lima. They were sure that our photographs were taken from an authentic Inca ruin.

The surface of many Inca stone walls was often carved in relief images. I added an extra assistant to my art department whose sole occupation was to carve these innumerable reliefs.

"The cutting of individually cast stones was made possible by the craftsmanship of my Spanish plasterers."

"*The museum in Lima was sure our photographs were taken from an authentic Inca ruin.*"

The action in the city of Caxamalca was mostly concentrated in the large plaza. The few existing descriptions of this place tell of a town on a high plateau surrounded by snowcapped mountains. Irving Lerner, who directed the film, asked me if by any chance I contemplated building the plaza on location close to the mountains. My answer was a definite "No! In a set what is important is what we see on the screen," I said. Shooting on location in the mountains would not add anything to the set except cost and practical difficulties. Moreover, it would be foolish to use real snowcapped mountains for the setting. In shooting a scene for many days, snow can melt and the view of bare mountains would not match previous backgrounds.

I decided to use the ample terrain on the back lot of the Sevilla studios for this set. We had had good luck there while building the town of Amblève for *Battle of the Bulge* and the western fort for *Custer of the West.*

The plaza of the fortress had to be surrounded by ramparts, about forty feet high, which would shield us from the view of some tall apartment buildings adjacent to the studio lot. As for the snowcapped mountains that would be visible from the plaza, I planned to erect miniature mountain backings seen above and beyond the soaring walls, to create the feeling that Caxamalca was next to the towering Andes. To heighten the effect I built a three-dimensional miniature silhouette of the snowy mountains above the rampart walls, slightly in retreat. Usually flat painted cutouts are used for backings in motion picture sets, but I decided on more expensive, three-dimensional silhouettes because in shooting outdoors, the direction of sunlight changes and creates ever-changing shadows on the mountain reliefs.

The plaza itself was roughly square in shape. On one side massive wooden gates opened onto the outside landscape—in our set, a scenic painted backing. These gates were the only entrance and exit to the town. On the opposite side of the plaza, stately steps led up to Atahualpa's throne and palace. Toward the back of the square another set of steps led up to a sun temple with a stone archway in front of it. The fourth side was partly free of sets, reserved for the main camera position, and partly occupied by the foreground set of Pizarro's watchtower, the scene of his night vigil before the ambush. All around the

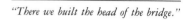

plaza were low stone warehouses used for storing maize. Now empty, they were used as hiding places for the ambushing warriors.

In the center of the plaza I placed a protruding granite rock with a carved sacrificial stone. It was solidly built in cement to withstand the trampling of horses. I would like to mention here that without the incomparable mastery of the Spanish plasterers and painters working with me, I would not have been able to realize this set as perfectly or inexpensively. They had kept their old-world craftsman's skills and had real artistic talent, with a fine sense of proportion and color.

There were few interior sets. The most imposing one was the throne room of Atahualpa with its intricately carved stone pillars. And then there was the Inca cell, a room of twenty by fourteen feet, that Atahualpa promises to fill with gold.

An unexpectedly laborious job was to sculpt and cast the hundreds of gold objects to fill this cell.

For the exteriors of the snowy Andes, we scouted and successfully found mountains in southern Spain, close to Granada, where snow remains year-round and shooting was convenient and easy next to the highway.

In the sequence of the difficult passage through the mountains, the Spaniards come to a halt in front of a precipice. To advance they will have to cross the deep gorge by way of a rope bridge, secured on either bank to a heavy stone buttress. The bridge swings precariously above the precipice, dangerously fragile, and the Spaniards hesitate to venture across it. Finally, prodded by Pizarro and preceded by a priest with his crucifix, they cross, almost losing a horse that makes a false step.

To build a practical hanging bridge above a precipice and to ask actors and horses to cross it was impractical, if not impossible. I had to find a solution. The sequence was short, but vital to the story. I analyzed the scene and broke it into separate components:

(1) The first part is the approach to the bridge by a difficult mountain path. The Spaniards stop in front of the bridge, hesitant to cross.

(2) At the edge of the precipice, they see the hanging bridge swaying above the deep gorge. It looks dangerous.

(3) Pizarro orders the crossing, asking the priests to set an example by going first.

About an hour's drive from Madrid, the mountains look wild, the ravines and huge boulders look dangerous, but they are actually quite accessible. Alongside a ravine we found a narrow, treacherous-looking path. There we built the head of the bridge, two heavy stone pillars with thick osier ropes anchored to them, a believable point of departure for the rope bridge. From these ropes the actual bridge hung but five feet from the ground and was about thirty feet long. Here we could shoot medium-close shots of the Spaniards looking at the bridge.

The miniature of the mountain gorge had to be of a height unusual for any miniature, involving the added expertise of constructing extra scaffolding. In this case I was concerned about keeping within the limits of the budget, so reversing the usual practice of building scaffoldings to support the set, I decided to use the scaffoldings of a previously built set to support the new miniature set. Accordingly I chose the empty space behind the set of the Inca city of Caxamalca to build the gorge. The walls of the city were about thirty feet high, propped, as was commonly done in Spain, by tubular scaffoldings. I used the backs of these scaffoldings to support the rocky surface of the mountain gorge. Excavating more earth to prepare the bottom surface of the gorge, I got a forty-foot drop to the gorge. Calculating the scale, one to ten, it represented an equivalent of a 400-foot-drop, but taking into consideration the diminishing perspective, it actually represented much more height.

At the bottom I prepared a meandering stream, providing abrupt drops in level and rocks planted here and there to create obstacles in the way of the flowing water, which made the stream cascade and foam like rapids.

The next scene would show the Spaniards hesitating at the head of the bridge and Pizarro giving the orders for the priests to advance. The crossing begins.

I planned the crossing itself to be shot in close and medium-close shots of the soldiers and horses advancing cautiously over the swaying bridge. For this scene I built a portion of the suspended bridge about forty feet long ten to fifteen feet above the ground on the back lot of the studio. I planned to shoot upward, the action profiled against the sky.

The sequence was shot as planned. Pizarro's men crossed the bridge, which swayed dangerously. The crossing looked difficult, the sequence was visually convincing, but Phil Yordan, my producer, jokingly voiced his regret at missing the miniature view of the long shot of Spaniards crossing the bridge. I had a possible solution and I offered him a trial shot.

"We wouldn't risk too much in trying," I said. "However, without any guarantee of success . . ."

"It's a bet!" Phil answered.

Among my Spanish collaborators was a clever scenic artist. I explained my idea, and he cut out small silhouettes of Spanish men and horses made in zinc and painted realistically. They were made in one-tenth scale—each soldier was about six inches tall, its joints loosely articulated. We fixed these cutouts on rollers and placed them on a miniature rail crossing the bridge. Pulling them across the bridge with a string gave them a very believable motion. We couldn't see the rail and I placed the camera low and we were shooting upward. The scene looked convincingly natural and was incorporated in the sequence. I won the bet from Phil.

I used the skills of the same scenic artist for another tricky scene in the picture. In the early sequence of *Royal Hunt*, we see three Spanish caravellas anchored offshore and the disembarked Spaniards encamped on the beach. The scene did not require recognizable actors and was shot as postproduction on the sandy shore off Almería on the Mediterranean coast. For our shot we placed the camera on a dune, slightly inland. The silhouettes of the three caravellas, in appropriate miniature sizes, painted and cut out of zinc, were placed close to the camera on supports of transparent plexiglass. They were profiled against the sea and seemed to be floating some distance from the shore.

We had very few available costumes and extras for this postproduction shooting, so groups of encamping warriors and tethered horses were also painted and cut out in zinc. They were placed close to the camera, profiled against the sandy shore. It looked like an encampment on the beach. To give some life to our "cutout" party, I placed some twenty extras and six horsemen on the beach close to the sea. Our cutout miniatures were close to the camera, the sea beach far away, but seen through the lens, they were on the same plane, and my real Spaniards and their horses seemed to circulate among the encamped cutout groups. Camera and cutouts were adjusted, but we couldn't make a shot this day. It was windy and sand blew against our plexiglass supports. And so back to our warm hotel, a drink, and dinner in the company of a visiting French crew, shooting a "desert" location in Almería.

Shooting was finished by the end of 1968. The entire production was marred by an atmosphere of hesitant decisions and uncertain direction. It was almost as if, impressed by the beautiful prose of the stage play, the director and producer believed the film would direct itself.

Most of the time that didn't happen. The first part of the picture did not progress. Instead of telling the story, it became a collection of disconnected vignettes. In the final editing of the film, which I saw again recently, the first part of the film is incomprehensible. In this film actors, probably impressed by the play, acted accordingly as if they were on a stage. Some beautiful scenes between Pizarro and his young page became empty declamations. I seldom saw such an absence of direction in any other picture I worked on.

Each actor composed his own character or adopted mannerisms unrelated to his partners. I vividly remember meeting Irving outside the set where Christopher Plummer was rehearsing a scene. Irving shrugged his shoulders, perplexed. "I don't understand what Christopher is doing. He has invented his own strange way of acting. It's interesting, but quite puzzling."

I was also unhappy with the photography. I carefully prepared my visual compositions, but often they were lost in flat lighting.

Finally I became interested only in the purely technical performances of my sets. I knew, without false modesty, that our plaza of Caxamalca with its monumental carved stone walls was very successful and the gimmick of miniature snowcapped mountains very convincing.

For me, the most satisfying set was the miniature of the precipice with its hanging bridge. No one would ever have guessed that the impressive view of the wild running stream at the bottom of the precipice had been shot in a miniature set. Also highly satisfying was our use of the articulated cutout puppets for the long shot of the Spaniards and horses crossing the bridge.

But designing victories is not satisfying by itself if they are not part of a film you are proud of. *Royal Hunt of the Sun* is in many ways a very interesting film; the story it tells is significant, poetic, and often attains the pathos of a Greek tragedy. Christopher Plummer's performance was stunning; but as a whole, the actors did not live their parts, they declaimed them. Some changes in the flow of the picture remain incomprehensible. Thus the highly dramatic scene of Atahualpa's garroting is followed by a choreographed chorus line of black-fringed Inca priests, which utterly destroys the somber tension created by the previous scenes. Or take the final scene of the dead Atahualpa seated on his throne, face covered by a golden mask. It can only be explained as a desire to shock.

Altogether, this picture in my opinion is a film in search of its own style.

AN ENEMY OF THE PEOPLE

I *read* in the *Reporter* that George Schaefer was preparing a production of Ibsen's classic play *An Enemy of the People*. I knew the play and had seen it many times. I was greatly intrigued by the idea of a Hollywood production of it—it could be an audacious project and an interesting, challenging task for a production designer.

I tried vainly to contact the producer and director, George Schaefer. Time passed and I filed this project among other films I had unsuccessfully attempted to design. Then came an unexpected telephone call from Phil Parslow asking if I was available. I learned it was about *The Enemy of the People*. Phil Parslow, the associate producer, already had the list of my credits in front of him.

"George Schaefer will probably be happy to work with you, but first go and see him. If we have his okay we could start immediately."

I greatly admired George's television films, but we had never met before.

Our meeting was pleasant, and the next day I was reading the Arthur Miller version of Ibsen's play. The script was still being written.

The plot of this play has often been plagiarized. In the original, Dr. Stockmann, director of a flourishing spa in a small Norwegian town, discovers the water dispensed at the spa is polluted and presents a public danger. His efforts to make this discovery public are thwarted by his brother, the town mayor. Remedying the pollution would necessitate extensive renovations, which would close the spa for two years and deprive the town of its prosperity. Prevented from publishing his findings, Dr. Stockmann decides to call a public meeting to expose the truth. He is refused the town's meeting hall and is forced to accept the use of a large room in the home of one of his friends, a sea captain.

In the play this dramatic confrontation between Stockmann and the irate town citizens takes place in a living room.

In motion pictures we are not confined by the limitations of a theater stage, and I felt that playing this highly emotional scene in yet another living room was not visually dramatic and would not help the scene's mood. I imagined the sequence acted in a kind of large, dimly lit place, maybe a workshop . . . why not a workshop where the captain builds sailboats as a hobby. I imagined a half-open place adjoining a snowed-in back yard, with a view of the port and some schooners. In my opinion this kind of setting would help to dramatically express the scene. I spoke to George about my new conception for the setting and got immediate approval.

Working with research materials I often find that without personal knowledge of the country where the action takes place, you miss the key to understanding; you miss the subtle meaning that governs placing the right details in the right places.

I told George I wanted to take a trip to Norway, which would help me create the proper atmosphere. He gave me a wholehearted okay, offering me a rare opportunity to conduct research as it should be done for any motion picture, and his office helped greatly in organizing the trip.

The SAS flight landed under a gray sky on the fifth of June. From the taxiing plane I was already reminded of typical Scandinavian colors, blue-gray and the muted red of the wooden houses.

In Oslo I was met by Lennard Lagerwall who would become my guide. Lennard was in public relations for the Norwegian National Theater and his help made it possible for me to gather much research in the limited time I had to spend in Norway. The next morning in drizzling rain, we went in his little Volkswagen to the old section of Oslo. There we found old wooden houses, as in a small provincial town, and the smell of lilacs everywhere. From there we went to the Norsk folkemuseum where blocks of period buildings, their interiors and furnishings intact, compose the out-of-doors collection. Among them we saw the interior of Henrik Ibsen's study. The same day we visited Guy Krohg, a well-known painter and stage designer. Also present were two other painters who were working as art directors for the Norwegian National Television. Later we drove forty miles to the old town of Dröbak, where it was still light since darkness falls late in the Norwegian summer.

The next day we drove more than 120 miles to Skien, Ibsen's hometown, which was probably the model for the town in *An Enemy of the People*. Closed for many years, the mineral waters establishment was still standing. We heard that these waters had been polluted by industries just as in the play. We visited the imposing Ibsen Museum and we saw his well-preserved house.

On June 8 I visited the studios of Norwegian National Television with its efficient modern architecture, huge research library, and clean, spacious restaurant for studio workers. My new friends, the studio art directors, organized for me a screening of their *Enemy of the People*, done the previous year, which had been filmed faithful to the stage play. In the studio was a well-organized prop shop where I was able to purchase a lightweight plastic reproduction of a characteristically Norwegian cast-iron stove. The same day I went to Oslo University to look through illustrated magazines from the 1880s and ordered some xeroxes of old photographs.

We revisited the period interiors of the Norsk folkemuseum. Then we went to the National Gallery to photograph genre paintings of domestic life during Ibsen's period. I visited some antique shops and junk dealers to buy interesting props and books on domestic architecture in Norway.

Then we flew to spend a day in the port city of Bergen. With Lennard and a representative of Bergen's National Theater, we visited Bergen's open-air museum, a well-preserved old town district complete with streets, alleys, and a marketplace. There was also the interior of a printing office, a pharmacy, and some other shops, all in an amazing state of preservation. Then we were off to Bergen's University Library to see the invaluable collection of photographs of interiors and scenes from domestic life in the nineteenth century. I ordered reprints of more than 100 of them. Before our flight back to Oslo, we had time to visit several seventeenth-century wooden warehouses on the old wharf and the house of Edvard Grieg.

On the last day in Oslo I organized the packing and forwardings of props, including the plastic stove, to send back to Hollywood. I also obtained some additional photographs from the Museum of Applied Arts. We had lunch in the old restaurant of the Grand Hotel where an entire wall is a painted mural, dating from 1880, with well-known literary and artistic personalities of the time seated at their usual tables on the restaurant's terrace. Later we visited the imposing, very modern city hall and the incomparable museum of Edvard Munch, the tortured genius of Norwegian painting.

I left on the early morning flight to Copenhagen–Los Angeles with regrets that I had made such a short visit.

The trip took only five days, yet much was accomplished and the research was invaluable for the film. In my designing I didn't aim to reproduce an interior with utter fidelity but rather to create an inner reality, an atmosphere, a surrounding where Ibsen's characters could live. This short trip, the paintings in museums, the small towns I visited, the people I met, streets and interiors, all gave me the feeling and the understanding of the milieu of the Ibsen drama.

Back in Hollywood the actual designing started, the visualizations of settings in which Ibsen's characters would live and the camera would have to move— sets that would show clearly the fundamental differences between designing for the stage and for motion pictures. In the theater when the curtain opens, you see the entire set at once. You are oriented. In early motion pictures as a carry-over from stage design, directors used a comprehensive long shot, called the establishing shot, at the start of a sequence. This practice, however, has been abandoned in favor of a surprise revelation of the setting as the action unfolds. You progress inside the set, discovering little by little the surroundings as you go along. You are a participant in the action instead of being an outside observer. In a similar way motion pictures can also reveal important clues or mood by close shots of certain details or props in a set.

For *An Enemey of the People*, George told me his method of shooting would involve very fluid movement of the camera, following or preceding the actors as they moved around. Thus the setting would be disclosed as the action progressed. Practically it meant that in the design, I had to provide easy passages for the dollying camera and plan the rooms so that one room could clearly be seen from another. The sequence of the rooms had to be clear to the audience and easily observed.

To achieve this vista I designed wide doors or used open archways between rooms, a common practice in Scandinavian homes. It took many sketches, meetings with George, and making tentative models of sets till we got, I think, a clearly readable floor plan—which I usually take special care in designing because it is the basis for choreographing all actors' movements. An exact floor plan was also very important for George's method of working, and we studied it very carefully and discussed many possible variations till we came to satisfactory solutions.

Meanwhile the props I bought in Oslo, including the famous replica of the iron stove, arrived, as well as many research books. Steve McQueen, who coproduced the film, fell in love with the photograph of a rugged house from the far north of Norway, which was quite similar to our log cabins. McQueen began to visualize Dr. Stockmann's house made from logs. It was impossible for me to imagine this type of rugged house in the middle-class town where Ibsen placed his action. With George's suggestion we found a solution; in fact, a solution confirmed by my research. In the process of remodeling, some Norwegian houses had rooms built much earlier than the rest of the house. And so in our set, Stockmann's study with its old corner fireplace and the entire kitchen wing, was built in a log construction from an earlier style. In fact, it blended perfectly with the rest of the house and added a special flavor.

We now proceeded with the final drafting and building of the miniature three-dimensional model of Stockmann's house. Building three-dimensional scale models of sets, popular in earlier days, was later abandoned. Right or wrong,

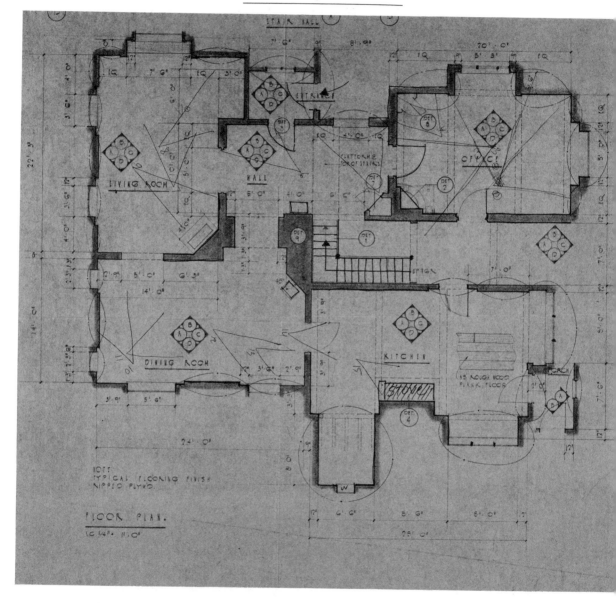

it was assumed that it takes more time and money to build models than it does to do sketches. Time permitting, I favor the use of miniature versions of sets. They can be very useful for the director, cameraman, set decorator, construction crew, and myself.

Tony Mondello, our set decorator, started prospecting for suitable furniture and props with me. The camera is inquisitive: it moves, it reveals every corner of the set and demands utter care for details, minute attention to decoration. As I've mentioned, the furniture and props of a set are for me an integral part of the set conception.

Victorian furniture is often ornate and seems exaggerated to our modern eye. We had to find the right kind, true to the period but with simple lines to give the feeling of an unpretentious family, not poor but definitely not wealthy. The main pieces of furniture were chosen, so I could now visualize the finished sets. Joe Hurley, a sensitive illustrator, began the sketching of our sets with me.

The set of Dr. Stockmann's house was built on a very large stage. I was able to reserve a large area for backings, an area usually sacrificed for lack of space. No actual filming takes place in the front yard of the house, but you see it constantly from many windows. Moreover, a significant scene takes place there when the "bad" boys cross the stone wall (seen from the Stockmann living room) and throw stones, breaking the windows of the "enemy of the people."

For this purpose I made the front yard some forty feet deep, bordered by a low stone wall. The trees in the yard and the stones of the wall were life size, but the low wall became the dividing line between the life scale and the reduced scales of the background. In back of this low wall I placed houses built in miniaturized half-scale; behind these I placed a row of even smaller houses—in one-third scale—and at the very back I placed a painted backdrop of a distant fjord and moored schooners, painted as very soft, almost out-of-focus, foggy landscape. I like to use three-dimensional backings whenever possible. They allow for variation in lighting and use of effects, such as wind or snow. The danger of purely painted backings in my opinion is their dead appearance.

For me, this three-dimensional background was very important. In this film as never before, I tried to recreate on stage the ambience of the outdoors:

Left: *Production illustration.*

Right: *The finished set with miniature buildings and sailing ship.*

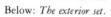

Below: *The exterior set.*

the cool northern light, the misty fjords, all reminiscent of old German Christmas cards or medieval miniatures in manuscripts. To do this was possible only in the film medium—creating a realistic picture where you feel the depth of the distant landscape—and impossible to achieve on the stage of a theater.

To emphasize the aerial perspective that makes backgrounds appear much softer, I sometimes use a gauze curtain in front of the backing. However, in our set the painting was very soft and placed so far back that it was by itself slightly out of focus. Moreover, the huge seamless piece of gauze we would need was difficult to find and extremely expensive. My use of three-dimensional backing in this film had the wholehearted support of George who was himself mistrustful of painted backings. Behind each window I also placed some small trees and used wind to add movement in the branches.

Finally the set building was finished, and we were ready to decorate the rooms. In the Stockmann house we were trying to get the feeling of a lived-in interior and family warmth. So we had to place the furniture exactly, find the right spot for the faded old sofa and cast-iron stove, place framed photographs of the Stockmann family and their personal bric-a-brac on the carved wood shelves. In the dining room I fitted the children's corner with their own work table, shelves with toys, a blackboard, and children's drawings on the wall. In the kitchen I felt compelled to copy the old Norwegian kitchen stove I had seen in the Oslo museum. And in Stockmann's study I tried to create the organized chaos of an absentminded doctor. Here in addition to the stone corner fireplace, a narrow stencil-painted frieze gave the finishing Scandinavian touch to the walls. We thoroughly frosted the windows of the study, but we could see through them to the cool exterior, where plastic snow and salt snowed in the back yard, the roofs, and the trees.

Meanwhile George rehearsed with the actors, first in the rehearsal hall and then during the last week on stage in the finished set. The last week of rehearsals also involved the lighting cameraman, operator, grips, and sound crew. Camera movements, lighting, the last adjustment of props—everything was rehearsed and tested. This procedure reduced the usual loss of time on the shooting stage to a minimum. Above all it created the concertlike performance so admirable in this film. The only other time I remember participating in this kind of rehearsal was with Charlie Chaplin in *Limelight.*

The next set designed and built was for the sequence I changed from a living room to the captain's workshop. It was a bleak setting of dark wooden beams, flapping wet canvas awnings, and dull red backyard walls, which gave a strong color accent to the background of misty gray houses and the faraway silhouette of a schooner. On this set for the final confrontation between Stockmann and the townspeople, I visualized the menacing people like a flock of blackbirds converging on their prey, almost ready to kill Stockmann, who now was their enemy.

The problem in building this set was the size of the stage. I didn't have the desirable depth for my elaborate backing, so I had to squeeze the distance between the yard of the workshop and the miniature houses of the background. I used forced perspective in reducing the farthest buildings and had to place the painted cutout of the schooner very close behind. It left a very short distance for actors to move between the set of the workshop and the miniature houses of the background. Paul Loman, our cameraman, expressed serious doubts that this small space could work. He was sure that the closeness of the miniatures would show. But I was sure that it would work; I had extensively used miniature backings in similar conditions. In the flat, two-dimensional photography we use for filming, the distance between planes in depth are not perceived; it is the lighting and the degree of diffusion that creates the illusion of distance between different planes. To help create this diffusion, I placed a tight gauze curtain in front of the miniature buildings. This gauze effectively separated the acting area from background miniatures. The scene and the lighting worked as intended: it is almost evening and the snow is slowly falling; the smoke rises slowly from chimneys of the miniature houses; the light dims as Steve McQueen, being hissed at by the irate citizens, slowly walks out with his sons.

The last set I designed was the printing office of the local paper. Added to the screenplay was a scene in a neighboring bar, which can be seen from the side window of the printer's office. To make the visual connection between the two sets, I imagined them built in the same building, separated only by a nar-

row alley. Windows in the bar and the corresponding window of the office allow us to see dimly from one to another. The low-ceilinged bar also has a front
window and an entrance door with a view of the opposite side of the street.

To realize this view I could have used a painted view of the street. But by
now we were partial to the three-dimensional miniature backings. We had used
them so successfully in the previous sets. Moreover, it was cheaper to build
them than to paint backdrops of the size needed.

For this set the space of the stage was also a problem. As I didn't have
available the normal width of the street to back up the entrance doors of the
printing office and the bar, I had to build the opposite side of the street in
reduced scale, about two-thirds of life size. I could have a passing horse and
sleds very close to the entrance, but to give life to the opposite façades, I asked
the costume designer to dress some small children as grown-up persons. They
were perfect against the reduced house fronts.

I am in no position to understand the reasons that prompted the producing company to withhold this film from general distribution. For the time being
it is shown on pay TV and in some art theaters. I hope eventually it will find
its place on large screens to do justice to its integrated perfection. At any rate
designing this film was a rare and stimulating pleasure. I rarely have partici-
pated in a film performed with such enthusiasm, where everything fit together
like the well-rehearsed performance of a symphony.

For me, it was an inspiring experience and in a way an artistic achievement. I took extreme care, and I hope I succeeded, in creating the inner feeling
of the small Norwegian town where Ibsen's action takes place. I tried to transcend external niceties and "cute" details of Victorian decor in order to make
people understand the way of life of a profoundly human family, the Stock-
manns, and its relation to a provincial Norwegian town.

Moreover, in this picture we didn't shoot any location; everything was accomplished on studio stages. Designing and treating the backgrounds as an essential part of the sets, I brought the feeling of the surrounding town into the
settings. The outdoors became an integral part of the life of the Norwegian
household.

In the beginning of the production, there was a tentative idea of shooting

An artist's rendering of the alley.

The alley as actually constructed with miniature houses and ships' masts in background.

some real Norwegian exteriors, even if they were to be used only as backgrounds for the main titles. When the picture was completed, however, the idea of real location was dropped, because George Schaefer and Steve McQueen felt that the intrusion of real location shots could destroy the poetic reality of the picture. This decision to omit real exteriors was for me the strongest compliment they could have made to the visual style of the picture.

19

Two Films for Television:
KUNG FU TV *Series and*
CAROLA

The difference between designing TV movies and feature films is very slight. In TV, you have a shorter time for preparation and there is usually much less money for the sets. And since the shooting schedules are short, you have to allow for rapid set changes.

I must say, in some cases these stringent requirements force designers to use more ingenuity, and the challenge is often a welcome incentive to creativity.

TV programs today overwhelmingly require very realistic settings. The general trend is for so-called factual stories—"docudrama" is the fashionable word. These pictures are often shot on real locations or interiors. If the sets have to be built, they must blend with everyday reality. Of course, for the art director it can be challenging and interesting to imitate the textures and details of real locations on stage. But frankly, after you have built innumerable prosaic police stations or prison cells or provided the settings for spectacular car chases time and time again, you can get fed up. Myself, I prefer pictures that offer more personal creative involvement.

In November 1971 I was given such a chance. At this time I was finishing the pilot for *The Delphi Bureau* at Warners. Jerry Thorp, who was a producer on the Warners lot, asked me to design the art for *Kung Fu*, an ABC Movie of the Week, which later became the pilot for the *Kung Fu* series. I think that *Kung Fu* was written originally as a screenplay for a feature film, but had been considered too expensive to produce and was shelved. Later Jerry Thorp saw the filming possibilities of the subject and had the courage to undertake it on a reduced budget for TV.

I read the screenplay. The story was interesting, the surroundings were unusual, and the entire project challenged me. The construction of the story was especially intriguing as the action moved back and forth from the western sequences to the hero's memory of his Chinese past—the hard training in the Chaolin discipline and the silent movements of the barefoot Chaolin monks. I thought it would be interesting to bring out the dreamy quality of the Chinese sequences, then contrast that dreaminess with the harsh reality of the wild west in the last century.

At this time Jerry Thorp was preoccupied with the practical possibility of bringing this project to life; so I assumed he was prepared to compromise matters of style, and for this show, was counting mostly on the physical action of kung fu and the violence of the western sequences.

Anyhow we didn't waste time with profound aesthetic discussions and started our work by visiting the set we hoped to use, a set from the *Camelot* production that still remained on the Warners back lot.

It was a huge set, unused for years. I do believe that the Warners production office, with a gambler's hope that perhaps, someday, some producer would use it for a sequel to another medieval saga, left it standing because the cost of demolishing it was prohibitive.

The set was strange indeed. A large flagstone-paved yard was flanked on one side by a high crenellated wall, on the other side by a cloisterlike colonnade, and on the third side by high rocks. The roughly U-shaped set was open on the fourth side, probably for the best long-shot camera angle. The set had many terraces and stairs, and this multileveled construction was fitted for the spectacular stagings. I understood Jerry's directorial instincts and how he could choreograph the many kung fu training sequences there—in addition to being the producer, he also directed the pilot and many subsequent episodes.

The architectural style of the *Camelot* castle was nonspecific. The talented designer who had created it didn't follow conventional pre-Gothic detailing and invented some fantastical elements that couldn't be categorized. This indefinite style played into my hands. I saw the possibility of modifying it and giving it a Chinese look—well, a Chinese look for our Western eyes—within the dreamy context of the film. I could design some additions of characteristic Chinese roofs, make some changes for the needs of the script, and add an important front wall with a massive, wood-carved entrance door, brick walls with ceramic-grilled windows, and other elements to suggest the monastery of the Chaolin monks.

Thus the first visit to the old set helped us see a practical solution for at least one very important set.

The second important question to solve was the interior of the big central nave of the monastery. A common procedure when working with a reduced budget is to show only a portion of the set. It can sometimes be effective. You show perhaps an oversized column of, let's say, an Egyptian temple. By the size and style of the column, the viewers will imagine and recreate in their minds the huge temple and so complete the set. This trick works often.

In solving the *Kung Fu* set problem, though, I tried to think of ways to actually show the big set. The action was going to be too complex to cheat on the size.

You may have noticed that when you walk into a Gothic cathedral, you seldom see the side walls. You see the columns or pillars that divide the nave from the side wings, and you usually see the altar at the far end of the church and the multitude of flickering candle flames. These are the main impressions.

I firmly believe that in designing a set, it is important to convey the strongest impression and suppress useless details. With this principle in mind I explained to Jerry Thorp how I planned to solve the set problem. Imagine, I said, a large empty stage. I would put two rows of large columns, say six on each side, and on the back wall, a large dimly lit Buddhist religious mural with a simple row of candles in front of it. I would fill the spaces between the columns with multileveled wooden candleholders and burning candles. I would use a constant haze and project strong rays of light as if coming through high church windows.

Jerry was quick to understand the visual conception and the strong economy of this solution. It saved us from building the long and high stone walls of the temple.

When we actually started set construction, instead of an empty stage the studio offered us a large stage, on which was a standing set of the big hall from *Camelot*. The walls of this large set were unusually high. In building our set inside this shell of medieval walls, I was presented with an additional advantage. If we had to use the side wings of the temple, we could see the ready-made stone walls, perfect for a Chaolin temple. I subsequently used the walls in some further episodes of *Kung Fu*.

The geometrically shaped candleholders became very effective. Jerry Thorp often used the multitude of flickering flames, and these shots were very successful. In fact, staging action in front of the flickering candles or behind them became a signature for the *Kung Fu* series.

The other difficult problem was finding a location for the building of the railroad line by the Chinese laborers. We had to choose a location close to Hollywood. We drove to the spectacular Vasquez Rocks, an area well known to Hollywood picture makers. Jerry's first tentative idea was to build a certain length of track, then make the track turn in a curve, which would "conceal" the remainder of the track behind a rock or growth of trees. However, it was difficult to make the actual construction look realistic, and the sharp turning of the rails, impossible. To my eye, the entire set-up was not believable, especially the continuation of rails behind such an obvious masking piece.

Instead of miraculously hiding the disappearing track, I offered to build quite a length of it in diminishing perspective. In this way we added considerable depth to the set. I remember that building the track and the labor camp was unusually difficult due to the bitter cold and strong wind at the Vasquez Rocks.

So the three costly production problems were solved: the exterior of the temple, the interior of the temple, and the railroad construction. They were solved in budgetary terms and in visual terms as well. They satisfied the production department, Jerry Thorp, and myself. We had a go-ahead from the production department and from there on it was clear sailing. In each scene I tried to find an interesting visual approach. In this I was helped greatly by Jerry's understanding and the inventiveness of his direction.

For the western scenes the old western streets on the Warners lot were varied and easily adaptable to the many requirements of the *Kung Fu* films, and we used them profusely in the subsequent three years of episodes. I am sorry to say that in 1980 when visiting the lot, I saw that in their questionable wisdom, the production department had bulldozed many of these interesting sets to make room for parking lots.

In the first *Kung Fu* film I used one of these streets, adding a painted matte shot at the end of it and creating a desert view in the back of the street. Matte shots are seldom used for TV productions because of their assumed high cost. But I found that we could achieve them economically, and in some segments I used them many times: once adding the painted matte of a seaport with moored three-masters and another time combining the street with a background, shot on location, that showed the sea and fishermen moving in and out of their boats.

With short diversions for other projects, I spent three years with *Kung Fu.* I always enjoyed finding new solutions for the various Chinese sequences, trying to invent an interesting way to present a set for each episode. I tried to achieve ambitious sets, but my guiding principle was to remain strictly within the budget.

Certainly low budgets are the scourge of TV art directors, but I had learned in France to work with little money for sets. There are many ways to create interesting approaches or unusual points of view by designing only what will actually be photographed, omitting useless ornamentation or unnecessary detail. For Chinese sets, for example, I often found intricately carved open-worked, gilded wooden partitions that gave a unique stamp to simple, plain walls; or giant, bizarre sculptured lions, which, placed in a row in the foreground of a temple or garden, gave the set an aura of grandeur. For me, these Chinese sets always had a dreamy, poetic quality.

Quite different from *Kung Fu* was the setting Norman Lloyd asked me to design for the PBS Hollywood Television Theater in 1975—a two-hour, video-taped production of *Carola,* originally a stage play by Jean Renoir.

Technical requirements for this videotaped film were different from those for theatrical film productions. *Carola* had to be shot without interruption, act by act, without the usual stops between set-ups. The drama would be rehearsed like a play in a legitimate theater, then shot with three cameras covering the action, the set-ups switching from camera to camera. Apart from the extensive rehearsals with actors, *Carola* required very exact technical rehearsals, during which movements of the three cameras were repeatedly choreographed, even more thoroughly than the actors.

For this type of nonstop production, the sets had to be easily accessible from all angles, without having that one-sided look of many live TV shows. It had to look like a well-produced feature motion picture.

Carola takes place in France on the back stage of a dramatic theater during the Nazi occupation of Paris in 1940s.

The play's underlying theme is the precariousness of life in a repertory theater, where the success of a particular play or of an individual actor determines whether the play and the theater will continue to exist. In this theater, an old one, the livelihood of actors and stage personnel depends on the success of the star actress, Carola, who feels very strongly that she is responsible for the others. This responsibility influences Carola's personal decision at the climax of the play. But Carola is not satisfied with her personal life. From the beginning of the play we feel Carola's latent dissatisfaction. However, she has found a protective shell in the everyday routine of her relations with the company; the friendship, almost devotion, of her wardrobe mistress; and even the vulgar, flamboyant presence of the director, her former lover.

The play starts with the director announcing to Carola the request of a high-ranking German general to see her. Hearing his name, Carola refuses. The situation becomes more tense as a young Free-French underground fighter, parachuted behind the Nazi lines, seeks refuge backstage. He is tracked by French police collaborating with the Germans and by the German Gestapo itself. The play, as you see, is highly melodramatic and emotional.

For the designer this production offered a challenge to evoke the special atmosphere of an old French theater and to solve certain technical problems, allowing for the smooth movements of the cameras in the complex multiple set.

From my early years I was familiar with the very special atmosphere of the back stages of old European theaters. I was always fascinated by their somehow mysterious surroundings: the special smell of painted canvas and the semidarkness of empty stages with the backdrops hanging overhead creating a world all its own.

In designing *Carola* I tried to recapture these feelings. Basically the script called for two connected sets: the backstage corridor leading to the dressing room and the interior of Carola's dressing room.

As you know, any corridor by itself is a dull setting. I remembered having seen in some old European theaters the back, brick wall of the stage, lined on each floor by a long balcony that also served as a passageway. Iron stairs led from floor to floor and down to the stage. The actors' dressing rooms opened onto these balconies. On the far side of each balcony was a wall with doors, and on the opposite side, an iron railing, often used to secure stage machinery ropes, which overlooked the stage. From the upper floors you could see down onto the stage from the balcony, and by looking upward you could see the painted backdrops or other pieces of scenery hanging from the flies. During the performance you could look down on the heads of the performing actors and hear their dialogue, the stage music, and even the applause at the end of an act.

For *Carola* I designed this sort of open-sided balcony corridor. I was after the visual effect primarily, but the open side also became technically useful. It eliminated the need to remove a wild wall when we had to place a camera for a particular shot. It also helped create the additional ambience of the far-off sound of the performance and applause. Visually this open side of the corridor also provided a convenient backing. For instance, for a shot looking outward through an open door, with the camera placed inside the dressing room, instead of having to place a wild wall on the opposite side, the shot would show set pieces hanging from the flies beyond the iron railing.

As the depth of the KCET set was insufficient for the length of corridor I considered necessary, I persuaded the studio to allow me to make an opening in the studio wall so that we would be able to build outside, the continuation of the balcony and stairways that led up above the floor and down toward the stage. In fact, this addition to the set was built above the street, on the side street on the east side of the studio. The wall texture of the set was brick. The colors, beige and brown, were two soft tones universally used in all backstage architecture in Europe.

The adjoining set and principal setting of the dramatic action was Carola's dressing room. In repertory theaters or in long runs when an actor occupies his dressing room for a long time, it becomes an odd blend of impersonal dressing room and second living room. It is sometimes decorated haphazardly but reflects the personal taste of the occupant with additions of occasional memorabilia and presents from admirers. Certain dressing rooms of star actors at La Comédie Française look like cozy overstuffed drawing rooms and bear the marks of the actors' personalities.

In designing Carola's dressing room, I tried to convey this mixed feeling of a temporary impersonal lodging, like a hotel room, and the place where the actress spends many hours daily for many months, so the place shows the imprint of her taste. I tried to show it as a cold, shabby room with cheap fittings but decorated with a cozy sofa, armchairs, personal photographs, paintings and posters, wallpaper, and a large, triple mirror. For this room I used a color scheme of soft grays and beiges, so connected in my memory with the feeling of Paris.

I had great personal pleasure in designing this old Parisian theater, and working with Norman Lloyd was a joyful experience. The well-rehearsed play was shot quickly, but in spite of the speed in shooting, I think the film fully reflected the visual impression we wanted to convey.

I found working for TV interesting and challenging. Sometimes the very urgency of the schedule stirs up creativity. The short schedules sharpen the imagination, forcing a designer to create unusual, interesting solutions. Although there are limitations in designing a TV film, the process used in designing the sets is generally similar to doing a motion picture feature. The same steps need to be followed for both, the same principles of design must be considered. TV films and motion pictures are dramatic forms and are related to each other, as in a similar manner a short story is related to a novel. Each of these forms tells a story, but in the telling, different conventions are followed.

FILM CREDITS

I: GRAND ILLUSION (1937)
French Title: *La Grande Illusion*

PRODUCTION CREDITS

Director: Jean Renoir; *Producers:* Frank Roll-mer and Albert Pinkovitch; *Screenplay:* Charles Spaak and Jean Renoir; *Dialogue:* Charles Spaak and Jean Renoir; *Art Director:* Eugène Lourié;* *Set Decorator, Locations, Props:* Maurice Barnathon; *Technical Advisor:* Karl Koch; *Director of Photography:* Christian Matras; *Camera:* Claude Renoir, Jr., Ernest Bourreaud, and Jean-Serge Bourgoin; *Music:* Joseph Kosma; music and lyrics for song "Si tu veux Marguerite" by Vincent Telly and A. Valsien; *Sound:* Joseph de Bretagne; *Assistant Director:* Jacques Becker; *Production Manager:* Raymond Blondy; *Film Editor:* Marguerite Renoir (assisted by Marthe Huguet); *Costumes:* Decrais; *Make-up:* Raphaël; *Stage Manager:* Pierre Blondy; *Production Company:* R.A.C. (Réalisation d'Art Ciné-matographique);

(Interiors filmed at Tobis and Billancourt-

---

*Eugene Lourie's name is spelled with accent marks on credits for films made in France.

Éclair studios, Epinay; locations in Alsace, in the Haut-Koenigsburg, and at the Colmar Barracks.)

CAST

von Rauffenstein: Erich von Stroheim; *Maréchal:* Jean Gabin; *de Boïeldieu:* Pierre Fresnay; *Rosenthal:* Marcel Dalio; *The Actor:* Julien Carette; *The Engineer:* Gaston Modot; *The Teacher:* Jean Dasté; *A French Soldier:* Georges Peclet; *An English Officer:* Jacques Becker; *Demolder:* Sylvain Itkine; *Elsa, the Farm Widow:* Dita Parlo; *Also appearing:* Werner Florian, Claude Sainval, and Michel Salina

2: WERTHER (1938)

PRODUCTION CREDITS

Director: Max Ophuls; *Producer:* Seymour Nebenzahl; *Screenplay:* Hans Wilhelm and Max Ophuls (based on the novel *The Sorrows of Young Werther,* by Johann Wolfgang von Goethe); *Additional Dialogue:* Fernand Crommelynck; *Art Directors:* Eugène Lourié and Max Douy; *Director of Photography:* Eugène Schufftan; *Camera:* Fedote Bourgassoff and Georges Stilly; *Music:* Paul Dessau (from music by Schubert, Haydn, Mozart, Gretry, and Beethoven); *Assistant Director:* Henri Aisner; *Film Editors:* Jean Sacha and Gérard Bensdorp; *Costumes:* Annette Sarradin; *Production Company:* Nero Films (Film also known as *Le Roman de Werther.*) (Filmed at Studio François Premier, Paris; locations in Alsace.)

CAST

Werther: Pierre-Richard Willm; *Charlotte:* Annie Vernay; *President:* Jean Périer; *Albert Hochstätter:* Jean Galland; *Aunt Emma:* Paulette Pax; *The Bailiff:* Georges Vitray; *Werther's valet:* Roger Legris; *Charlotte's brother:* Jean Buquet; *The Prostitute:* Génia Vaury; *Servant:* Denise Kerny; *Also appearing:* Léon Larive, Martial Rebe, Leonce Corne, Edmond Beauchamp, Joseph Nossent, and Henri Beaulieu

3: THE HUMAN BEAST (1938)
French Title: *La Bête humaine*

PRODUCTION CREDITS

Director: Jean Renoir; *Producers:* Robert Hakim and Roland Tual; *Screenplay:* Jean Renoir (based on the novel *La Bête humaine,* by Émile Zola); *Dialogue:* Jean Renoir; *Art Director:* Eugène Lourié; *Director of Photography:* Curt Courant; *Camera:* Claude Renoir, Jr., and Jacques Natteau; *Music:* Joseph Kosma; *Sound:* Robert Teisseire; *Assistant Directors:* Claude Renoir, Sr., and Suzanne de Troye; *Film Editor:* Marguerite Renoir (railway sequence, Suzanne de Troye); *Production Company:* Paris Film Production—Robert Hakim and Raymond Hakim (Filmed at Billancourt studios, Paris; locations in Le Havre, Evreux, and the countryside in Normandy.)

CAST

Jacques Lantier: Jean Gabin; *Séverine:* Simone

Simon; *Roubaud:* Fernand Ledoux; *Pecqueux:* Julien Carette; *Philomène (Pecqueux's friend):* Jenny Halia; *Victoire (Pecqueux's wife):* Colette Régis; *Dauvergne:* Gérard Landry; *Grand-Morin:* Jacques Berlioz; *Grand-Morin's servant:* Léon Larive; *Camy-Lamothe (Grand-Morin's secretary):* Georges Spanelly; *Cabûche, the Poacher:* Jean Renoir; *Farmhands:* Émile Genevois and Jacques B. Brunius; *The Lamp Maker:* Marcel Perez; *Flore:* Blanchette Brunoy; *The Traveler:* Claire Gérard; *The Supervisor:* Tony Corteggiani; *The Gatekeeper:* Guy Decomble; *The Railway Worker:* Georges Peclet; *Aunt Phasie:* Charlotte Clasis; *A Mechanic:* Marceau

---

4: THE RULES OF THE GAME (1939)
French Title: *La Règle du jeu*

PRODUCTION CREDITS

Director: Jean Renoir; *Producers:* Claude Renoir, Sr., and Jean Renoir; *Screenplay:* Jean Renoir, with the collaboration of Carl Koch (adapted from *Les Caprices de Marianne,* by Alfred de Musset); *Dialogue:* Jean Renoir; *Art Director:* Eugène Lourié, assisted by Max Douy; *Technical Advisor for the hunt:* Tony Corteggiani; *Director of Photography:* Jean Bachelet; *Camera:* Jacques Lemar; *Music:* Joseph Kosma and Roger Désormières (from selections by Mozart, Monsigny, Sallabert, Johann Strauss, Saint-Saëns, and Chopin); *Sound:* Joseph de Bretagne; *Assistant Directors:* Carl Koch, André Zwoboda, Henri Cartier-Bresson; *Film Editor:* Marguerite Renoir, assisted by Marthe Huguet; *Costumes:* Coco Chanel; *Make-up:* Ralph; *Stage Manager:* Raymond Pillon; *Production Company:* N.E.F. Productions (Nouvelle Édition Française)

(Working titles, *Les Caprices de Marianne, Fair Play, La Chasse en Sologne.*)

(Interiors filmed at Joinville studios, Paris-Joinville; locations in Sologne, at La Motte-Beuvron, Château de la Ferté Saint-Aubin, Aubigny, and in the coutnryside.)

CAST

Marquis de la Chesnaye: Marcel Dalio; *Christine, de la Chesnaye's wife:* Nora Grégor; *André Jurieu:* Roland Toutain; *Octave:* Jean Renoir; *Geneviève de Marrast:* Mila Parely; *Charlotte de la Plante:* Odette Talazac; *The General:* Pierre Magnier; *Monsieur de Saint-Aubin:* Pierre Nay; *Monsieur La Bruyère:* Richard Fancoeur; *Madame La Bruyère:* Claire Gérard; *Jackie, Christine's niece:* Anne Mayen; *A Guest:* Roger Forster; *The South American:* Nicolas Amato; *Berthelin:* Tony Corteggiani; *Lisette, Christine's chambermaid:* Paulette Dubost; *Schumacher, the Gamekeeper:* Gaston Modot; *Marceau, the Poacher:* Julien Carette; *Corneille, the Steward:* Eddy Debray; *The Cook:* Léon Larive; *The Servant:* Jenny Helia; *The Radio Reporter:* Lise Elina; *The Airplane Engineer:* André Zwoboda; *The Announcer:* Camille François; *The English Domestic:* Henri Cartier-Bresson

---

5: THIS LAND IS MINE (1943)

PRODUCTION CREDITS
Director: Jean Renoir; *Producers:* Jean Renoir

and Dudley Nichols; *Screenplay:* Dudley Nichols and Jean Renoir (from a story by Dudley Nichols and Jean Renoir); *Dialogue:* Dudley Nichols; *Dialogue Director:* Leo Bulgakov; *Art Directors:* Albert D'Agostino and Walter F. Keller; *Production Designer:* Eugene Lourie; *Sets:* Darrell Silvera and Al Fields; *Special Effects:* Vernon L. Walker; *Director of Photography:* Frank Redman; *Music:* Lothar Perl; *Sound:* Terry Kellum and James Stewart; *Assistant Director:* Edward Donohue; *Film Editor:* Frederic Knudtson; *Production Company:* RKO.
(Filmed in Hollywood.)

CAST

Albert Lory: Charles Laughton; *Louise Martin:* Maureen O'Hara; *Georges Lambert:* George Sanders; *Major von Keller:* Walter Slezak; *Paul Martin:* Kent Smith; *Madame Emma Lory:* Una O'Connor; *Professor Sorel:* Philip Merivale; *Mayor:* Thurston Hall; *Prosecuting Attorney:* George Coulouris; *Julie Grant:* Nancy Gates; *Edmund Lorraine:* John Donat; *Lieutenant Schwartz:* Frank Alten; *Little Fat Man:* Leo Bulgakov; *M. Lorraine:* Wheaton Chambers; *Mme. Lorraine:* Cecil Weston; *The Judge:* Ivan Simpson

---

6: SAHARA (1943)

PRODUCTION CREDITS

Director: Zoltan Korda; *Producer:* Harry Joe Brown; *Screenplay:* John Howard Lawson and Zoltan Korda (based on an incident in the Soviet film *The Thirteen.*); *Adaptation:* James O'Hanlon; *Story:* Philip MacDonald;

Art Director: Lionel Banks; *Associate Art Director:* Eugene Lourie; *Director of Photography:* Rudolph Maté; *Music:* Composed by Miklos Rozsa and directed by M. W. Stoloff; *Sound:* Lodge Cunningham; *Assistant Director:* Abby Berlin; *Production Company:* Columbia Pictures Corporation
(Working title *Somewhere in Sahara.*)
(Filmed on location in the desert near the Salton Sea in California.)

CAST

Sergeant Joe Gunn: Humphrey Bogart; *"Waco" Hoyt:* Bruce Bennett; *Fred Clarkson:* Lloyd Bridges; *Tambul:* Rex Ingram; *Giuseppe:* J. Carrol Naish; *Jimmy Doyle:* Dan Duryea; *Captain Jason Halliday:* Richard Nugent; *Ozzie Bates:* Patrick O'Moore; *Jean Leroux:* Louis T. Mercier; *Marty Williams:* Carl Harbord; *Peter Stegman:* Guy Kingsford; *Captain von Schletow:* Kurt Krueger; *Major von Falken:* John Wengraf; *Sergeant Krause:* Hans Schumm

---

7: THE IMPOSTER (1944)

PRODUCTION CREDITS

Director: Julien Duvivier; *Producer:* Julien Duvivier; *Screenplay:* Julien Duvivier; *Dialogue (adapted from French):* Stephen Longstreet; *Additional Dialogue:* Marc Connelly and Lynn Starling; *Art Directors:* John B. Goodman (head of Universal Art Department) and Eugene Lourie; *Sets:* R. A. Gausman and E. R. Robinson; *Technical Advisor:* Jean de la Roche; *Director of Photography:* Paul Ivano; *Special Photography:* John P.

Fulton; *Music:* Composed and conducted by Dmitri Tiomkin; *Film Editor:* Paul Landres; *Gowns:* Vera West; *Production Company:* Universal Pictures

(Working titles *Passport to Dakar, Strange Confession.*)

(Filmed in Hollywood.)

CAST

Clement: Jean Gabin; *Lieutenant Varenne:* Richard Whorf; *Bouteau:* Allyn Joslyn; *Yvonne:* Ellen Drew; *Hafner:* Peter Van Eyck; *Colonel de Boivin:* Ralph Morgan; *Cochery:* Eddie Quillen; *Monge:* John Qualen; *La Farge:* Dennis Moore; *Clauzel:* Milburn Stone; *Mortemart:* John Philliber; *Menessier:* Charles McGraw; *Matowa:* Otho Gaines; *Free-French Corporal:* John Forrest; *Priest:* Fritz Leiber; *Sergeant Clerk:* Ian Wolfe; *Adjutant:* William Davidson; *Prosecutor:* Frank Wilcox; *Officer:* Warren Ashe; *Soldier:* Peter Cookson; *Toba:* Leigh Whipper; *Ekoua:* Ernest Whitman; *Captain:* Grandon Rhodes; *Prosecutor:* George Irving

8: THE SOUTHERNER (1945)

PRODUCTION CREDITS

Director: Jean Renoir; *Producers:* David L. Loew and Robert Hakim; *Associate Producer:* Samuel Rheiner; *Screenplay:* Jean Renoir (based on the novel *Hold Autumn in Your Hands,* by George Sessions Perry, as adapted by Hugo Butler); *Dialogue:* Jean Renoir, with the aid of William Faulkner as script consultant; *Art Director:* Eugene Lourie; *Director of Photography:* Lucien An-

driot; *Music:* Werner Janssen; *Sound:* Frank Webster; *Assistant Director:* Robert Aldrich; *Film Editor:* Gregg Tallas; *Production Company:* United Artists

(Filmed in Hollywood; locations in the San Joaquin Valley, San Fernando Valley, and Malibu Lake; location shots made in Texas.)

CAST

Sam Tucker: Zachary Scott; *Nona Tucker:* Betty Fields; *Devers:* J. Carrol Naish; *Granny:* Beulah Bondi; *Harmie:* Percy Kilbride; *Mom:* Blanche Yurka; *Tim:* Charles Kemper; *Finley:* Norman Lloyd; *Lizzie:* Estelle Taylor; *Becky:* Noreen Nash; *The Doctor:* Jack Norworth; *Ruston:* Paul Harvey; *Bartender:* Nestor Paiva; *Jot:* Jay Gilpin; *Daisy, Sam's daughter:* Jean Vanderbilt; *Uncle Pete:* Paul Burns; *Young Girl:* Dorothy Granger; *Wedding Guest:* Early Odgkins; *Customer:* Almira Sessions; *Rex:* Zoonie

9: THE LONG NIGHT (1947)

PRODUCTION CREDITS

Director: Anatole Litvak; *Producers:* Robert and Raymond Hakim and Anatole Litvak; *Screenplay:* John Wexley, adapted from the French screenplay by Jacques Viot; *Production Designer:* Eugene Lourie; *Set Decorator:* Darrell Silvera; *Director of Photography:* Sol Polito; *Music:* Composed and conducted by Dmitri Tiomkin; *Sound:* Richard Van Hessen and Clem Portman; *Assistant Director:* Aaron Rosenberg; *Film Editor:* Robert Swink; *Production Company:* RKO

(Filmed in Hollywood; location shots made in Pennsylvania.)

CAST

Joe Adams: Henry Fonda; *Jo Ann:* Barbara Bel Geddes; *Maximilian:* Vincent Price; *Charlene:* Ann Dvorak; *Sheriff:* Howard Freeman; *Chief of Police:* Moroni Olsen; *Frank:* Elisha Cook, Jr.; *Janitor's Wife:* Queenie Smith; *Bill:* David Clarke; *Policeman:* Charles McGraw; *Peggy:* Patty King; *Freddie:* Robert Davis; *Janitor:* Will Wright; *Hudson:* Ray Teal; *Sergeant:* Pat Flaherty

10: THE RIVER (1951)

PRODUCTION CREDITS

Director: Jean Renoir; *Producers:* Kenneth McEldowney, Kalyan Gupta, and Jean Renoir; *Screenplay:* Rumer Godden and Jean Renoir (from the novel, *The River,* by Rumer Godden); *Art Director:* Eugene Lourie; *Assistant Art Director, Sets:* Bansilal Chandra Gupta; *Director of Photography:* Claude Renoir, Jr.; *Camera:* Romananda Sen Gupta; *Music Director:* M. A. Parata Sarathy (music recorded in India); *Sound:* Charles Paulton and Charles Knott; *Assistant Director:* Forrest Judd; *Film Editor:* George Gale; *Color:* Technicolor; *Production Company:* Oriental-International Films, Inc.
(Filmed in India: on the Ganges River, in Barrackapore, and in Calcutta.)

CAST

Mother: Nora Swinburne; *Father:* Esmond Knight; *Mr. John:* Arthur Shields; *Captain John:* Thomas E. Breen; *Nan:* Suprova Mukerjee; *Harriet:* Patricia Walters; *Melanie:* Radha; *Valerie:* Adrienne Corri; *Bogey:* Richard Foster; *Elisabeth:* Penelope Wilkinson; *Muffie:* Jane Harris; *Mouse:* Jennifer Harris; *Victoria:* Cecilia Wood; *Sahjn Singh:* Ram Singh; *Kanu:* Nimai Barik; *Anil:* Trilak Jetley

11: SPECIAL EFFECTS PICTURES

THE ADVENTURES OF CAPTAIN FABIAN (1951)

PRODUCTION CREDITS

Director: William Marshall; *Producer:* William Marshall; *Associate Producer:* Robert Dorfman; *Screenplay:* Errol Flynn (based on the novel *The Fabulous Ann Madlock,* by Robert Shannon); *Art Directors:* Eugene Lourie and Max Douy; *Technical Collaborator:* Guy Seitz; *Director of Photography:* Marcel Grignon; *Music:* René Cloèrec; *Sound:* Roger Cosson; *Assistant Director:* Marc Maurette; *Film Editor:* Henri Taverna; *Costumes:* Arlington Valles; *Production Supervisor:* R. E. Marshall; *Production Manager:* Sacha Kamenka; *Assistant Production Manager:* Jean Rossi; *Production Company:* Silver Films Production, released by Republic Pictures Corporation
(Working title *The Fabulous Ann Madlock*)
(Filmed in Nice, on location and at the Victorine studios; and in Paris, at the Boulogne studios.)

CAST

Captain Michael Fabian: Errol Flynn; *Lea Marriotte:* Micheline Presle; *George Brissac:* Vincent Price; *Aunt Jesebel:* Agnes Moorehead; *Henri Brissac:* Victor Francen; *Constable Gilpin:* Jim Gerald; *Madam Pirott:* Helena Manson; *Emil:* Howard Vernon; *Phillipe:* Roger Blin; *Housekeeper:* Valentine Camax; *Judge Jean Brissac:* Georges Flateau; *Cynthia Winthrop:* Zanie Campan; *Constant:* Reggie Nalder; *Defense Attorney:* Charles Fawcett; *Mate:* Aubrey Bower; *Also appearing:* Marcel Journet and Gilles Queant

A CRACK IN THE WORLD (1965)

PRODUCTION CREDITS

Director: Andrew Marton; *Producer:* Bernard Glasser and Lester A. Sansom; *Executive Producer:* Philip Yordan; *Screenplay:* Julian Halevy and Jon Manchip White (based on a story by Jon Manchip White); *Art Director:* Eugene Lourie; *Special Effects Director:* Eugene Lourie; *Director of Photography:* Manuel Berenguer; *Music:* John Douglas; *Sound:* David Hildyard and Morris Askew; *Second Unit Director:* Eugene Lourie; *Assistant Director:* José-Maria Ochoa; *Film Editor:* Derek Parsons; *Color:* Technicolor; *Costumes:* Laure de Zárate; *Production Company:* Security Pictures, released by Paramount Picutres (Filmed in Spain at the C.E.A. studios and Bronston studios in Madrid; locations in Valencia.)

CAST

Dr. Stephen Sorenson: Dana Andrews; *Mrs. Maggie Sorenson:* Janette Scott; *Ted Rampion:*

Kieron Moore; *Sir Charles Eggerston:* Alexander Knox; *Masefield:* Peter Damon; *Markov:* Gary Lasdun; *Steele:* Mike Steen; *Simpson:* Todd Marton; *Rand:* Jim Gillen

12: LIMELIGHT (1952)

PRODUCTION CREDITS

Director: Charles Chaplin; *Producer:* Charles Chaplin; *Screenplay:* Charles Chaplin; *Art Director:* Eugene Lourie; *Director of Photography:* Karl Struss; *Musical Score:* Charles Chaplin; *Orchestration:* Ray Rasch; *Music Conductor:* Keith Williams; *Assistant Director:* Robert Aldrich; *Production Company:* Released through United Artists
(Working title, *Footlights*)
(Filmed in Hollywood; special location shots made in London.)

CAST

Calvero: Charles Chaplin; *Terry:* Claire Bloom; *Neville:* Sidney Chaplin; *Postant, the Ballet Impressario:* Nigel Bruce; *Old Comedian:* Buster Keaton; *Harlequin:* André Eglevsky; *Columbine:* Melissa Hayden; *Clowns:* Charles Chaplin, Jr., and Wheeler Dryden; *Also appearing:* Marjorie Bennett, Snub Pollard, Loyal Underwood, Josephine Chaplin, Geraldine Chaplin, and Michael Chaplin

13: THE BEAST FROM 20,000 FATHOMS (1953)

PRODUCTION CREDITS

Director: Eugene Lourie; *Producers:* Hal

Chester and Jack Dietz; *Associate Producer:* Bernard W. Burton; *Screenplay:* Lou Morheim and Fred Freiberger (based on the story "The Foghorn," by Ray Bradbury); *Art Director:* Hal Waller; *Special Effects:* Ray Harryhausen and Willis Cook; *Director of Photography:* Jack Russell; *Music:* David Buttolph; *Film Editor:* Bernard W. Burton; *Production Company:* Released through Warner Brothers

(Filmed in Hollywood; locations in New York City and Long Beach, California.)

CAST

Tom Nesbit: Paul Christian; *Lee Hunter:* Paula Raymond; *Professor Elson:* Cecil Kellaway; *Colonel Evans:* Kenneth Tobey; *Captain Jackson:* Donald Woods; *Jacob:* Jack Pennick; *Corporal Stone:* Lee Van Cleef; *Sergeant Loomis:* Steve Brodie; *George Ritchie:* Ross Elliott; *Sergeant Willistead:* Ray Hyke; *Nesbitt's Secretary:* Mary Hill; *Doctor:* Michael Fox; *Radar Man:* Alvin Greenman; *Dr. Morton:* Frank Ferguson; *Dr. Ingersoll:* King Donovan

GORGO (1961)

PRODUCTION CREDITS

Director: Eugene Lourie; *Producer:* Wilfred Eades; *Executive Producers:* Frank King and Maurice King; *Associate Producer:* James Leicester; *Screenplay:* John Loring and Daniel Hyatt (from a story by Daniel Hyatt and Eugene Lourie); *Art Director:* Elliott Scott; *Director of Photography:* F. A. Young; *Special Photographic Effects:* Tom Howard; *Music:* Angelo Lavagnino; *Sound:* A. W.

Watkins; *Assistant Director:* Douglas Hermies; *Film Editor:* Eric Boyd-Perkins; *Color:* Technicolor; *Production Company:* Released by Metro-Goldwyn-Mayer

(Filmed in England, at the MGM studios, Boreham; locations in the city of London and in Ireland.)

CAST

Joe Ryan: Bill Travers; *Sam Slade:* William Sylvester; *Sean:* Vincent Winter; *Flaherty:* Bruce Seton; *Professor Hendricks:* Joseph O'Connor; *Dorkin:* Martin Benson; *First Mate:* Barry Keegan; *Bo'sun:* Dervis Ward; *McCartin:* Christopher Rhodes; *Admiral Brooks:* Basil Dignam

14: FLIGHT FROM ASHIYA (1962)

PRODUCTION CREDITS

Director: Michael Anderson; *Producer:* Harold Hecht; *Screenplay:* Elliott Arnold and Waldo Salt (based on a novel by Elliott Arnold); *Production Designer:* Eugene Lourie; *Art Director:* Tom Shimogawara; *Directors of Photography:* Joe MacDonald and Burnett Guffey; *Music:* Frank Cordell; *Film Editor:* Gordon Pilkington; *Process and Color:* Filmed in Panavision/Eastman Color; *Production Company:* Daiei—Harold Hecht, distributed by United Artists;

(Filmed in Japan, in Tokyo and at the Daiei studios in Kyoto; also at the Cinecitta studios in Rome.)

CAST

Sergeant Mike Takashima: Yul Brynner; *Colo-*

nel Glenn Stevenson: Richard Widmark; *Lieutenant John Gregg:* George Chakiris; *Caroline Gordon:* Shirley Knight; *Leila:* Daniele Gaubert; *Lucille Carroll:* Suzy Parker; *Tomiko:* Eiko Taki; *Sergeant Randy Smith:* Joe De Reda; *Japanese boy "Charlie":* Mitsuhiro Sugiyama; *Captain Walter Mound:* E. S. Ince; *Dr. Horton:* Andrew Hughes

---

15: BATTLE OF THE BULGE (1965)

PRODUCTION CREDITS

Director: Ken Annakin; *Producers:* Milton Sperling and Philip Yordan; *Screenplay:* Philip Yordan, Milton Sperling, and John Melson; *Art Director:* Eugene Lourie; *Special Effects:* Alex Weldon; *Miniatures Director:* Eugene Lourie; *Director of Photography:* Jack Hildyard; *Second-Unit Photography:* John Cabrera; *Aerial Photography:* Jack Willoughby; *Music:* Composed and conducted by Benjamin Frankel; *Sound:* Kurt Herrnfeld (editor), David Hildyard, and Gordon McCallum; *Assistant Directors:* José Lopez Rodero, Martin Sacristan, and Luis Garcia; *Film Editor:* Derek Parsons; *Process and Color:* Ultra-Panavision/Technicolor; *Costumes:* Laure de Zárate; *Production Supervisor:* Bernard Glasser; *Unit Manager:* Leon Chooluck; *Production Managers:* Tibor Reves and Gregorio Sacristan; *Production Coordinator:* Lou Brandt; *Production Company:* Sidney Harmon in association with United States Pictures, Inc., Cinerama, Inc., and Warner Brothers Pictures.

(Filmed in Spain, at the Sevilla studios in Madrid; locations in the Guadarrama Mtns.)

CAST

Lieutenant Colonel Kiley: Henry Fonda; *Colonel Hessler:* Robert Shaw; *General Grey:* Robert Ryan; *Colonel Pritchard:* Dana Andrews; *Sergeant Duquesne:* George Montgomery; *Schumacher:* Ty Hardin; *Louise:* Pier Angeli; *Elena:* Barbara Werle; *Wolenski:* Charles Bronson; *Conrad:* Hans Christian Blech; *Lieutenant Weaver:* James MacArthur; *Guffy:* Telly Savalas

---

16: KRAKATOA, EAST OF JAVA (1969)

PRODUCTION CREDITS

Director: Bernard L. Kowalski; *Producer:* William R. Forman; *Coproducer:* Lester A. Sansom; *Script:* Clifford Gould and Bernard Gordon; *Production Designer:* Eugene Lourie; *Art Directors:* Julio Molina and Luis Espinosa; *Set Decoration:* Antonio Mateos; *Special Effects:* Alex Weldon and Eugene Lourie; *Miniatures Director:* Eugene Lourie; *Director of Photography:* Manuel Berenguer; *Camera:* Edward Noe; *Second-Unit Camera:* John Cabrera; *Music:* Frank de Vol; *Lyricist and Composer:* Mack David; *Sound:* Walley Milner; *Second-Unit Director:* Frank Kowalski; *Assistant Director:* José Maria Ochoa; *Film Editor:* Maurice Rootes; *Process:* Cinerama Wide Screen Process; *Costumes:* Laure de Zárate; *Make-up:* Julian Ruiz; *Production Supervisor:* Gregorio Sacristan; *Production Manager:* José Manuel Herrero; *Production Company:* American Broadcasting Companies, Inc., and Cinerama, Inc.

(Filmed in Spain, at the Bronston and Sevilla studios in Madrid; and in Italy, at Cinecitta studios, Rome.)

CAST

Hanson: Maximilian Schell; *Laura:* Diane Baker; *Connerly:* Brian Keith; *Charley:* Barbara Werle; *Rigby:* John Leyton; *Giovanni:* Rossano Brazzi; *Leoncavallo:* Sal Mineo; *Danzig:* J. D. Cannon; *Toshi:* Jacqui Chan; *Jacobs:* Mark Lawrence; *Bazooki Man:* Geoffrey Holder; *Japanese Divers:* Sumi Hari, Victoria Young, and Midorri Arimoto; *Henley:* Neil McGuinnes; *Jan:* Alan Hoskins; *Guard:* Robert Hall

---

17: ROYAL HUNT OF THE SUN (1969)

PRODUCTION CREDITS

Director: Irving Lerner; *Producers:* Eugene Frenke and Philip Yordan; *Screenplay:* Philip Yordan (from the play *Royal Hunt of the Sun,* by Peter Shaffer); *Art Director:* Eugene Lourie; *Miniatures and Special Effects:* Eugene Lourie; *Director of Photography:* Roger Barlow; *Music:* Marc Wilkinson; *Assistant Director:* José Maria Ochoa; *Film Editor:* Peter Parasheles; *Color:* Technicolor; *Costumes:* Anthony Powell; *Make-up:* Julian Ruiz; *Production Supervisor:* Gregorio Sacristan; *Production Company:* Security Pictures, Benmar, released through Cinema Center Films (National General Pictures).
(Filmed in Spain at the Sevilla studios in Madrid; and on location in the countryside.)

CAST

Pizarro: Robert Shaw; *Atahualpa:* Christopher Plummer; *De Soto:* Nigel Davenport; *Estete:* Michael Craig; *Martin:* Leonard Whiting; *Valverde:* Andrew Keir; *Carlos V:* James Donald; *Candia:* William Marlowe; *Diego:* Percy Humbert; *De Nizza:* Alexander Davion; *Felipillo:* Sam Krauss

---

18: AN ENEMY OF THE PEOPLE (1978)

PRODUCTION CREDITS

Director: George Schaefer; *Producer:* George Schaefer; *Executive Producer:* Steve McQueen; *Screenplay:* Alexander Jacobs, based on the Arthur Miller adaptation of the play by Henrik Ibsen; *Production Designer:* Eugene Lourie; *Set Decorator:* Anthony Mondello; *Director of Photography:* Paul Lohmann; *Music:* Leonard Rosenman; *Sound:* Michael J. Kohut; *Assistant Director:* Jack Aldworth; *Film Editor:* Sheldon Kahn; *Process and Color:* Panavision/Metrocolor; *Costumes:* Noel Taylor; *Production Company:* First Artists (Solar) Productions, released by Warner Brothers;
(Filmed in Hollywood; special location research in Norway.)

CAST

Dr. Thomas Stockmann: Steve McQueen; *Peter Stockmann:* Charles Durning; *Catherine Stockmann:* Bibi Andersson; *Morten Kiil:* Eric Christmas; *Hovstad:* Michael Cristofer; *Aslaksen:* Richard A. Dysart; *Billing:* Michael

Higgins; *Captain Forster:* Richard Bradford;
Morten Stockmann: Ham Larsen; *Ejlif Stock-
mann:* John Levin; *Petra Stockmann:* Robin
Pearson Rose

19: TWO FILMS FOR TELEVISION

KUNG FU TV Series (1970–1974)

PRODUCTION CREDITS
Directors: Jerry Thorp and Various
Directors; *Producer:* Jerry Thorp; *Art
Director:* Eugene Lourie; *Production Company:*
Warner Brothers Television
(Filmed at Burbank studios, Burbank,
California.)

CAST
Kung Fu Priest: David Carradine;
(A number of actors appeared in various
roles in this series throughout its run.)

CAROLA (1975)

PRODUCTION CREDITS
Director: Norman Lloyd; *Producer:* Norman
Lloyd; *Screenplay:* James Bridges in
collaboration with Jean Renoir, based on
the play *Carola,* by Jean Renoir; *Production
Designer:* Eugene Lourie;
(Filmed at KCET-Television Studios in
Hollywood, California.)

CAST
Carola: Leslie Caron; *German General:* Mel
Ferrer; *Director:* Anthony Zerbe

FILMOGRAPHY

	L'ALIBI	Pierre Chenal
		(Serge Pimenoff, Co-Art Director)
	LE MESSAGER	Raymond Rouleau
	NUITS DE FEU	Marcel L'Herbier
		(Guy de Gastine, Co-Art Director)
1938	LA BÊTE HUMAINE	Jean Renoir
	L'AFFAIRE LAFARGE	Pierre Chenal
		(Robert de Gys, Co-Art Director)
	RAMUNTCHO	René Barberis
	LA TRAGÉDIE IMPÉRIALE	Marcel L'Herbier
		(Guy de Gastine, Co-Art Director)
	WERTHER	Max Ophuls
		(Max Douy, Co-Art Director)
	PARADIS DE SATAN	Felix de Gandera
	LA RÈGLE DU JEU	Jean Renoir
		(Max Douy, Co-Art Director)
1939	SANS LENDEMAIN	Max Ophuls
	L'OR DU CRISTOBAL	Jacques Becker
	L'AIR PUR	René Clair
	(film unfinished)	
1940	UNE FAUSSE ALERTE	Jacques de Baroncelli

FILM CREDITS AS ART DIRECTOR OR PRODUCTION DESIGNER IN HOLLYWOOD

Year	Film	Director
1943	THREE RUSSIAN GIRLS	Fedor Ozep
1943	THIS LAND IS MINE	Jean Renoir
	SAHARA	Zoltan Korda
1944	THE IMPOSTER	Julien Duvivier
	IN SOCIETY	Jean Yarborough
	THE HOUSE OF FEAR	Roy W. Neill
1945	THE STRANGE AFFAIR OF UNCLE HARRY	Robert Siodmak
	THE SOUTHERNER	Jean Renoir
1946	THE DIARY OF A CHAMBERMAID	Jean Renoir
1947	THE LONG NIGHT	Anatole Litvak
	THE SONG OF SHEHEREZADE	Walter Reisch

1948	A WOMAN'S VENGEANCE	Zoltan Korda
1951	THE RIVER	Jean Renoir
1951	THE ADVENTURES OF CAPTAIN FABIAN	William Marshall
1952	LIMELIGHT	Charles Chaplin
1953	THE DIAMOND QUEEN	John Brahm
1954	SO THIS IS PARIS	Richard Quine
1961	CONFESSIONS OF AN OPIUM EATER	Al Zugsmith
1962	SHOCK CORRIDOR	Samuel Fuller
	THE STRANGLER	Burt Topper
	FLIGHT FROM ASHIYA	Michael Anderson
1963	THE NAKED KISS	Samuel Fuller
1964	BIKINI PARADISE	Gregg Tallas
1965	A CRACK IN THE WORLD	Andrew Marton
	BATTLE OF THE BULGE	Ken Annakin
1966	CUSTER OF THE WEST	Robert Siodmak
1969	KRAKATOA, EAST OF JAVA	Bernard Kowalski
	ROYAL HUNT OF THE SUN	Irving Lerner
1971	ELIZA'S HOROSCOPE	Gordon Sheppard
	DEATH TAKES A HOLIDAY (TV)	Robert Butler
	THE DELPHI BUREAU (TV Pilot)	Paul Vendkos
1972	WHAT'S THE MATTER WITH HELEN?	Curtis Harrington
	KUNG FU (TV Pilot)	Jerry Thorp
	HAUNTS OF THE VERY RICH (TV)	Paul Ventkos
	LITTLE PEOPLE (TV)	(Various Directors)
1973	KUNG FU (TV Series)	Jerry Thorp and Various Directors
	KUNG FU (TV Series)	Jerry Thorp and Various Directors
1974	KUNG FU (TV Series)	Jerry Thorp and Various Directors
1975	CAROLA (TV)	Norman Lloyd
	KUNG FU (TV Series)	Jerry Thorp and Various Directors
	BURNT OFFERINGS	Dan Curtiss
1976	PHILEMON (TV)	Norman Lloyd
1977	CAPTAIN NEMO'S RETURN (TV, 3 Segments)	Various Directors
1978	LACY AND THE MISSISSIPPI QUEEN (TV Pilot)	Robert Butler
	LUCAN (TV, 5 segments)	Various Directors
	AN ENEMY OF THE PEOPLE	George Schaeffer
1979	SUPERTRAIN (TV)	Dan Curtiss

| 1980 | BRONCO BILLY | Clint Eastwood |
| | FREEBIE AND THE BEAN (TV Pilot) | Hy Auerback |

FILM CREDITS AS A DIRECTOR

Year	Film
1953	THE BEAST FROM 20,000 FATHOMS
1955	FOREIGN INTRIGUE (TV, 5 segments)
1956	AWAY BORDERS (TV)
1957	THE COLOSSUS OF NEW YORK
1958	THE CHEMICAL STORY (TV)
	THE GIANT BEHEMOTH
1961	GORGO

FILM CREDITS AS A SECOND-UNIT DIRECTOR

Year	Film	Director
1954	NAPOLEON	Sacha Guitry
1955	SI PARIS NOUS ÉTAIT CONTÉ	Sacha Guitry
1961	BACK STREET	David Miller
1962	THAT TOUCH OF MINK	Delbert Mann

FILM CREDITS AS A MINIATURES AND SPECIAL EFFECTS UNITS DIRECTOR

Year	Film	Director
1965	A CRACK IN THE WORLD	Andrew Marton
	BATTLE OF THE BULGE	Ken Annakin
1966	CUSTER OF THE WEST	Robert Siodmak
1969	KRAKATOA, EAST OF JAVA	Bernard Kowalski
	ROYAL HUNT OF THE SUN	Irving Lerner
1979	SUPERTRAIN (TV)	Dan Curtiss
1980	A WHALE FOR THE KILLING (TV) (Visual Effects Consultant)	Richard Heffron

CREDITS AS A STAGE DESIGNER

Year	Production	Company
1933	CHOREATRIUM	Ballet Russe de Monte Carlo
1947	MEPHISTO WALTZ	San Francisco Ballet Company
		Adolph Bolm, Choreographer
1948	PERSEPHONE	San Francisco Ballet Company
1948	HOUSE OF BERNARDA ALBA	Coronet Theater, Los Angeles

INDEX